COMMONPLACE CULTURE
IN WESTERN EUROPE IN THE
EARLY MODERN PERIOD
II

Consolidation of God–given power

COMMONPLACE CULTURE IN WESTERN EUROPE IN THE EARLY MODERN PERIOD II

Consolidation of God–given power

EDITED BY

Kathryn Banks and Philiep G. Bossier

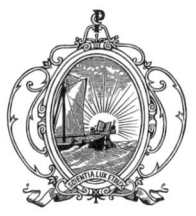

PEETERS

LEUVEN - PARIS - WALPOLE, MA

2011

Illustration on cover: *La solenniss.ma cavalcata fatta in Roma per landata di n.s. Papa Leone XI al Possesso d. S. Gio. Laterano,* etching 243 x 378 mm, ed. Giovanni Antonio de Paoli, Museo di Roma (inv. GS 48). Photo: Museo di Roma.

A catalogue record for this book is available from the Library of Congress.

D/2011/0602/16

ISBN: 978-90-429-2475-8
© Peeters, Bondgenotenlaan 153, 3000 Leuven

CONTENTS

PREFACE AND ACKNOWLEDGEMENTS

In 1999, the local Groningen Research School for the Study of the Humanities, and the Groningen members of the national Netherlands Research School for Medieval Studies succeeded in obtaining a grant for an innovative, large-scale, collective research programme entitled *Cultural Change: Dynamics and Diagnosis*. Supported by the faculties of Arts, Philosophy and Theology and financed by the Board of the University of Groningen, the *Cultural Change* programme constitutes an excellent opportunity to promote multidisciplinary approaches to phenomena characteristic of transformation processes in the fields of politics, literature and history, philosophy and theology. In order to enhance programmatic cohesion, three crucial 'moments' in European history were selected: 1) Late Antiquity to the Early Middle Ages (*c*.200–*c*.600), 2) Late Medieval to the Early Modern period (*c*.1450–*c*.1650), and 3) the 'Long Nineteenth Century' (1789–*c*.1918). In 2000 and 2002 further grants were obtained for *Cultural Change: Impact and Integration* and *Cultural Change: Perception and Representation* respectively. Several international conferences and workshops have already been organised and are planned for the coming years.

One focus of the *Cultural Change* programme has been a project entitled 'Authority and Persuasion: the Role of Commonplaces in Western Europe (*c*.1450-*c*.1800)'. This project was launched by scholars from the universities of Copenhagen, Durham and Groningen, and generously funded by the Danish National Research Foundation, the British Academy and the Netherlands Organisation for Scientific Research (NWO). The result is a series of three volumes on *Commonplace Culture*. The series aims to broaden the notion of the 'commonplace' to include means of persuasion in all kinds of texts as well as the visual arts, theatre, music and other media.

This is the second volume from the *Commonplace Culture* series. It analyses the use of commonplaces to bolster power, or sometimes to question it. The volume focuses on the seventeenth century. In the latter part of this period, the status and cognitive scope of the printed common-place book declined; yet, as the essays in this volume demonstrate, the cognitive practices evidenced in commonplace-books continued to enjoy good health. The 'commonplaces' analysed by contributors to this volume constitute cultural objects which gained persuasive potential from the exploitation of material bearing the authority of the past, yet they are not commonplaces *stricto sensu*. The essays in the volume examine not only written texts but also theatre, music, processions, ballets, and royal entries. In particular, the notion of the commonplace is taken into the visual domain, indicating that in the seventeenth century the visual was central to those diverse practices which sought to shore up God-given power through the pre-existing authority of commonplace material.

We thank the Board of the University of Groningen for the financial support given to the *Cultural Change* programmes. The editors are also particularly grateful to Heather Fenwick for helping to organise the workshop which was the inspiration for this volume, and to Gorus van Oordt for preparing the texts for publication.

Herman W. Hoen, General Editor

INTRODUCTION

Kathryn Banks and Philiep Bossier

The seventeenth century was a crucial period in the history of common-places. The status and cognitive scope of the printed commonplace-book declined in the latter part of the seventeenth century, when the mental habits which had favoured its use were undermined, as demonstrated most obviously by Descartes's radical challenge to the authority of pre-existing knowledge.[1] At the same time, the essays in this volume demonstrate that, at least where the consolidation of God-given power was concerned, cognitive practices evidenced in commonplace-books continued to enjoy good health. The 'commonplaces' explored in this volume constitute 'cultural material with both past and present currency within a given language community';[2] ar-guably they are indebted to the patterns of thought which had made com-monplace-books so central to early modern pedagogy. However, they are not commonplaces *stricto sensu*; instead, crucially, they take the notion of the commonplace into the visual domain, indicating that in the seventeenth century the visual was central to those diverse practices which sought to shore up God-given power through the pre-existing authority of common-place material.

This volume is one in a series of three books which examine the roles played by commonplaces during the early modern period. The *Common-place Culture* series analyses commonplace material in verbal, visual, musi-cal, theatrical, and kinetic forms. It brings together cultural outputs aimed only at an elite and educated audience with those which address less privi-leged groups. Some of the artefacts analysed have rarely been the focus of scholarly attention; at the same time, the series also aims to offer new per-spectives on more familiar objects of study, by juxtaposing them with less familiar ones and viewing both from the perspective of the manipulation of commonplaces. The series examines commonplaces from the perspective of Western Europe as a whole, hence contributors to this particular volume

---

[1] Ann Moss, *Printed Commonplace-Books and the Structuring of Renaissance Thought* (Oxford, 1996), pp. 255-281 (272-274).

[2] Ann Moss, 'Power and Persuasion: Commonplace Culture in Early Modern Europe', in David Cowling and Mette Bruun, eds, *Commonplace Culture in Western Europe in the Early Modern Period, vol. I: Reformation, Counter-Reformation, and Revolt* (Leuven, 2010), pp. 1-17 (1).

analyse cultural products from England, the Netherlands, France, Germany, Scandinavia, Italy, and Spain. The *Commonplace Culture* series has its roots in workshops held at the universities of Copenhagen, Durham, and Groningen over the course of 2006-2008, which were generously funded by the Netherlands Organisation for Scientific Research (NWO), the British Academy, and the Danish National Research Foundation.

Each volume of the *Commonplace Culture* series studies a particular century and a key aspect of that century's political climate. The first, subtitled *Reformation, Counter-Reformation, and Revolt*, focused on the political turmoil, theological controversies, and social change of the sixteenth century. It examined the role of commonplace-books but also the persuasive power of 'commonplaces' understood in a more general sense, asking whether such (verbal, visual, and musical) cultural outputs might arguably manifest the same patterns of thought and reasoning most readily perceptible in the printed commonplace-book. The third volume, subtitled *Legitimation of Authority* and concentrating on the eighteenth century, will examine the contestation of power and of its supposed God-given nature, as well as the responses to this by authorities who found themselves put on the defensive. While in the eighteenth century the diminished status of commonplace-books indicates the decline of cognitive strategies grounded in pre-existing authority, the essays in this volume provide other sorts of evidence for a change in persuasive techniques and in the mental habits in which they were grounded. At the same time, new media appeared and more people could participate in public debate of a verbal and textual nature. Newspapers, crucially, began to trade in 'commonplaces' of their own, which might be characterised less as accumulated past wisdom and more as recycled 'truths'.

The present volume, which has its roots in a conference held in Durham in September 2007, investigates the 'consolidation of God-given power' in the seventeenth century. All the essays examine objects of a political nature and demonstrate the importance of commonplace material in the political domain. The volume highlights both continuity and change in the use of commonplaces. It focuses for the most part on visual commonplaces, exploring theatre, processions, ballets, royal entries, and the visual depictions of these. Even where the verbal is at stake, and where commonplaces in the narrower humanist sense could be located, the focus is predominantly on similitudes, that is, on language which tends to create images and to represent even abstract ideas in visual terms; furthermore, such visual language is often inextricably bound up with the literally visual, for example with the frontispiece of *Leviathan* which gives visual form to its central similitude, or with the ballets in which Louis XIV performed the sun with which he was linguistically compared.[3]

Indeed one might speak of a 'visual turn' in the manipulation of commonplace cultural material. Certainly the visual is more prominent in this book than in its first sister volume, which examines sixteenth-century commonplaces.[4] It is as if the persuasive potential of the 'baroque' metaphor and the imagistic language central to much late sixteenth-century writing had also been harnessed in cultural outputs which are visual in the literal sense. We might recall here that users of commonplace-books had found that similitudes provided an 'abundance of opportunities to diversify';[5] in this volume, the same is shown to be true of visual commonplaces in a much wider – non-verbal – sense. At the same time, in noting the centrality of the visual in this volume, one thinks of the importance of theatre in the seventeenth century. The theatrical, though, is significant not only in the theatre but also in royal entries, rituals, and processions. Accordingly, the shared mechanisms of theatre and spectacle are discussed in essays by Bent Holm and Mårten Snickare. Thus this volume journeys outside of the enclosed 'space' of the book to analyse the persuasive apparatus employed in and through the external and literal spaces of court and city. For example, the spatial and the visual are crucial not only in the scenes displaying king and peasant in the plays examined by Rina Walthaus but also in the manipulation or re-ordering of the structures of the city analysed by Snickare.

The visual and spatial focus of the volume also means that the intended 'addressee' of the persuasion process is often a spectator rather than a reader (or rather than a pupil listening to a master within the pedagogical situation where early modern boys first encountered commonplace-books); he (or she) might also be a listener, as in Lars Berglund's discussion of music. These recipients of persuasive strategies are foregrounded in a number of essays. Thus, Jan Clarke considers the multiple audiences targeted by operas and machine plays; Rina Walthaus focuses on the communicative tools marshalled to influence the people but also points to the rather different goals which the same plays had vis-a-vis the king; Berglund considers the competing audiences of subjects, on the one hand, and competing states or rulers, on the other; Mårten Snickare interrogates the relationships – and the blurred distinctions – between participants and spectators of papal proces-

---

[3] See the contributions to this volume by Andreas Musolff and Richard Maber respectively.

[4] Cowling and Bruun, eds, *Commonplace Culture in Western Europe in the Early Modern Period*, vol. I: *Reformation, Counter-Reformation, and Revolt.*

[5] Moss, 'Power and Persuasion', in *Commonplace Culture*, p. 11. See also, in the same volume, essays by Banks, Cowling and Bussels.

sions; Vincent van Zuilen considers how the literary forms used in the Dutch pamphlet wars of 1606-1608 were designed to appeal to a diverse range of social groups, and how particular modes of argumentation were aimed at the young.

While most essays in this volume show how commonplace material played a powerful role in consolidating a power supposed to be God-given, Frans-Willem Korsten suggests that, at the same time, it was precisely God who served as the keystone to a cognitive system based in the authority of the commonplace: in other words, God might shore up commonplace knowledge as well as absolutist power. The system of commonplaces could, despite its internal dissonance, be made to cohere through even brief references to God. As a result, Korsten argues, any weakening of God's position in the seventeenth century might also undermine the power of commonplaces. Thus, Korsten suggests, the decline of commonplaces resulted from changing attitudes to God more than from a political culture centred on uniformity.[6] According to Korsten, one reason for the diminishing status of commonplaces was the reduced ability of 'God' to support a system of knowledge grounded in commonplaces.

Korsten's argument is based on the plays of Joost van den Vondel (1587-1679), one of the paramount playwrights of seventeenth-century Holland. Korsten identifies in Vondel's plays suggestions that 'God', supposed to be the driver of Christian history, is in fact a rhetorical mask for 'mere politics', for sovereign political actions by humans. Korsten's essay also sketches out a number of theoretical perspectives which, he suggests, might help us to grasp a shift from one sort of knowledge to another. First, Korsten employs Jacques Rancière's distinction between *police* and *politics* in order to think through the double potential of commonplaces to both support and undermine structures of power. For Rancière, *police* denotes the relatively rigid, solidified, and hierarchical organisation of a community or society, and politics refers to moments of change or political intervention; commonplaces, Korsten observes, played a role in both *police* and politics, so that one might question the role of political uniformity in their downfall. Secondly, Korsten suggests that a particular sort of commonplace might be termed an 'enwrapped narrative': in Vondel's plays, words, names, and short phrases can point to wider narratives which, once 'unwrapped', introduce change or contradiction into the whole; thus they function to combine unity and dissonance, the aspects of the commonplace which Korsten highlights.

---

[6] Cf Moss, *Printed Commonplace-Books*, pp. 255-281, on various reasons for this decline, esp. p. 276 (on political uniformity) and p. 275 ('In the last years of the [seventeenth] century, even the apparently least assailable and most strategically viable of all its places, authoritative quotation from Scripture, began to weaken').

While Korsten focuses our attention on the possible role of God in shoring up commonplaces, many contributors to this volume discuss God's role in shoring up political power, in particular, of course, that of the absolutist monarch. The image of Louis XIV as Sun King was undoubtedly the most spectacular representation of supreme God-given power, and two of our essays concentrate on the French king; however, following the broad Western European perspective of the *Commonplace Culture* series, the volume also draws attention to ways in which other monarchs consolidated their own God-given power, and to commonalities between the methods of Louis XIV and, for example, the Danish king, Christian IV. Indeed a number of essays show how symbols of power might be borrowed between cultures not obviously similar to one another, or indeed overtly hostile to one another (as in the case, described by Lars Berglund, of the borrowing of Roman music by Lutheran courts).

Richard Maber's essay sheds light on the depiction of Louis XIV by drawing attention to the polysemy inherent in the commonplace image of the king as sun, and by demonstrating how the notion of the Sun King evolved during the French king's exceptionally long reign. Maber traces this evolution by focusing on a range of sources including poems and the libretti of the *ballets de cour*. He highlights how, in the latter part of Louis's reign, the commonplace was employed to bolster the idea of reciprocity between monarch and people. Even where the literal coherence of the image was pushed to breaking point (since the sun does not really demand anything from the earth), this version of the commonplace proved to be an attractive one for Louis. Crucially it differed radically from the more familiar form of the metaphor so often found in the earlier years of Louis's reign, in which the sun reveals its glory, renders invisible the lesser stars, and restores political order. In the latter part of his reign, Louis had no rivals to 'eclipse', and the image mutated from that of the literal sun, which eclipses, to something closely approaching the portrayal of God, who 'illuminates' but also demands something from man in return.

Jan Clarke's essay further elucidates the use of commonplaces to represent Louis XIV. Her contribution marshals the evidence supplied by prologues to operas and machine plays from 1660-1680. As part of a general policy of employing the arts to the greater glory of the Sun King, Louis XIV and Colbert supported Jean-Baptiste Lully in his efforts to develop French opera through the *Académie royale de musique*. Unsurprisingly, then, operas often evoked contemporary political events. They did so particularly directly in the prologues which served to introduce them. Focusing on these prologues, Clarke demonstrates how, in a period where France was almost continually at war with her neighbours, Louis was repeatedly portrayed as universal peacemaker rather than warmonger. This message was underlined through visual elements as well as acoustic ones, through decors, tableaux, or machines. Commonplace figures – such as Peace – helped to create an image of Louis which effectively flew in the face of the omnipresence of war.

With Bent Holm's essay the volume moves away from France in order to study the courts of Northern Europe; nonetheless, Holm points to ways in which the staging of Danish absolutism became increasingly similar to the French model. This wide-ranging essay focuses on royal rituals and their published records from the entire seventeenth century and into the eighteenth. Holm traces both continuities and changes in strategy as Danish royalty moved towards, adopted, and then justified an absolutist model of kingship. While, as in Louis XIV's France, an enormous propaganda machine consolidated God-given power in creative ways, in the Danish and Norwegian courts Norse mythology was employed alongside biblical and classical material. Varied combinations of commonplace figures from these traditions promoted differing notions of kingship, exploring in particular its relationship with the divine, and increasingly presenting royal power as God-given.

While these essays indicate the role of commonplaces in consolidating royal power and even in presenting the king as a bringer of peace, Vincent van Zuilen's contribution shows that they were also crucial to political aims that were almost diametrically opposed: he explores their role in pamphlets arguing against peace and against any submission to aggressive power. The context is the 1607-1609 peace negotiations between the States General of the United Provinces and the ambassadors of the sovereign Archdukes of the Habsburg Netherlands, who also acted on behalf of the King of Spain. This period saw the production of a huge volume of pamphlets which attack the presumed peace policy of the States, and which mark a transition in Dutch political culture by indicating, first, a large-scale campaign of criticism of the States, and, secondly, a notion of the people as actively involved in politics. Van Zuilen provides a close reading of *The Netherlandish Bee-hive*, which gathered together and introduced the pamphlets. He shows how popular patterns of thought, images, experiences, and general knowledge were marshalled to political ends in texts designed to appeal to all groups in society. In particular, he analyses the commonplace metaphor of the bee-hive. The use of this image draws on its traditional associations with both hope and also an ideal or pure community, as well as on the commonplace identification of particular nations with particular animal species; finally, of course, the metaphor also highlights the practice of collecting – or commonplacing – itself.[7]

---

[7] On apian metaphors and commonplacing, see Moss, *Printed Commonplace-Books*, pp. 12-15 and passim.

The Netherlands – and, to some extent, persuasive tactics marshalled against Spanish kings – are also the focus for Jan Bloemendal's examination of the relationship between myth and commonplace. Concentrating upon plays and poetry, Bloemendal analyses the 'myth' of William of Orange as a *pater patriae* who united his people and liberated the Netherlands from Spanish tyranny. Bloemendal examines how commonplaces contributed to the construction of this national myth. In addition to Roman conceptions of the *pater patriae*, commonplace ideas about love, care, authority, sovereignty, fatherhood, and nation came into play. Furthermore, as Korsten suggests in his contribution, in Bloemendal's analysis of Nassau, God may be 'the ultimate commonplace'. Thus Bloemendal suggests that the narrative of William of Orange becomes, in the words of Sem Dresden's working definition of myth, a 'sacred tale (...) which also functions socially'.[8]

Rina Walthaus's essay returns us once more to peace, justice, and order presented as the results of royal rule. Walthaus turns our attention to Spanish theatre, which – while Spain was in political, economic, and social decline – reached its Golden Age; theatre, Walthaus observes, constituted an immense machine, used not only to instruct and to entertain but also for the purposes of political persuasion. Walthaus's essay focuses on public theatre for the *vulgo*, a sort of mass medium *avant la lettre* in which social and political questions could be explored. Walthaus analyses how this theatre served to bolster royal power. In particular, she highlights the ways in which public theatre manipulated commonplaces such as the figure of the shepherd and the topos of the pure and idyllic country life. In so doing, it reinforced the image of royal authority as a guarantee for peace, justice, and harmony, and persuasively presented a union or bond between king and people, encapsulated visually in the powerful scenes in which king and country people met on the stage.

The visual consolidation of God-given power is also at stake in Mårten Snickare's analysis of the Roman *possesso*, a ritual procession whereby each newly elected Pope took 'possession' of the Eternal City after his coronation. As well as the visual, though, the *possesso* also involved the bodily: the movements of its participants. Furthermore, Snickare observes that, while the procession was certainly theatrical, it differed from the theatre in that both 'participant' and 'spectator' shared the same ceremonial space, and that 'spectators' too were there to be seen. As Snickare observes, even in the case of the Pope, power could not be taken for granted: the procession dramatised unstable power relations, and served to consolidate performatively the God-given power of the Pope. Snickare analyses the histori-

---

[8] Bloemendal, p. 110 in this volume.

cal models at play behind procession commonplaces, namely the triumphal entry in ancient Rome, and the entry of Christ into Jerusalem. He also shows how our understanding of the processions can be thought through using models drawn from anthropology: Snickare borrows from Arnold van Gennep the concepts of the *rite de passage* and liminality, and from Victor Turner the idea of a tension or contradiction inherent in the processional form. Snickare suggests that, in the case of the papal *possesso* at least, Turner's thinking can help us to think about how commonplaces incorporate dissonance or difference: commonplace ideas of procession included 'the Other of pagan Rome' as well as Christian models, so that ancient ruins and remains were integrated into the *possesso* ritual.

Lars Berglund's study takes us into domains – Lutheran courts – where it was Rome itself which was 'other'. Berglund's essay also complements the visual focus of the majority of the volume by a study which focuses on music. The extensive use of Roman Catholic Church music at Protestant courts during the mid-seventeenth century provides a rather intriguing case of the exchange and dissemination of commonplace cultural material, since the cultural outputs borrowed still bore clear signs of their Catholic provenance; for example, in the case of the composition by the Roman Giacomo Carissimi borrowed by the Royal Swedish *Hofkapellmeister* Gustav Düben, it must have been obvious to any informed listener that the piece they heard (entitled *Salve rex Christe*) was actually a *Salve Regina* with some minor textual modifications. Indeed there was resistance to this borrowed music, especially in the clerical community. While musical commonplaces were given new meanings to match their new contexts, their previous associations were still close to the surface, so that the confessional source of the music was barely masked. In order to explain this, Berglund invokes Jürgen Habermas's notion of 'representative publicity' as developed in the work of Danish historian Sebastian Olden-Jørgensen: the meaning of music, Berglund indicates, was determined less by confessional implications than by value judgements about the quality of the music. It was for this reason that, regardless of confessional difference, Lutheran princes, keen to increase their 'representative prestige', deemed it necessary to acquire the music of the most esteemed composers.

The final essay of the volume might be considered a transition towards the next volume in the *Commonplace Culture* series, insofar as it treats a philosopher considered both to belong to the Enlightenment and also to contribute towards the 'Legitimation of Authority', the title of the next volume in the series. Andreas Musolff analyses the utilization by Thomas Hobbes of the metaphor of the body politic. Rejecting an approach which would place Hobbes's use of the image in a 'grand narrative' of historical progression, Musolff focuses instead on the particular ways in which Hobbes exploited it in order to put forward a new perspective on politics. Musolff shows how Hobbes brought the commonplace metaphor into play precisely to argue against meanings which it had often served to reinforce: while the image of the body politic had often been invoked to advocate co-operation and solidarity between its members, Hobbes employs it to indicate a need to combat immediately any political influences which undermine the sovereign's power. Thus Musolff highlights the processes by which a traditional meaning of a commonplace might be subverted, so that it functioned to contest established authorities while at the same time still depending upon a common frame of reference.

The seventeenth century, then, witnessed crucial changes of emphasis – as well as continuities – in systems of authoritative wisdom. While the status and cognitive value attributed to commonplace-books declined, commonplaces understood in a more general sense made a central contribution to the consolidation of God-given power. The texts, music, dramas, ballets, royal entries, and processions studied in this volume show how cultural objects gained persuasive potential from the exploitation of material bearing the authority of the past. Thus, in the face of war or otherwise unstable political situations, commonplaces served to bolster power, or sometimes to question it. Finally, commonplaces demonstrated their mastery of varied territories, often seeking visual and theatrical forms for their persuasive apparatus, and moving outside the verbal arena into the spaces of the stage, the court, and the city.

CONTRIBUTORS

Kathryn Banks is Lecturer in French at Durham University.

Lars Berglund is Associate Professor of Musicology at Uppsala University.

Jan Bloemendal is Professor of Neo-Latin Studies at the University of Amsterdam and senior researcher at the Huygens Institute KNAW.

Philiep Bossier is Professor of Historical Romance Literature and Culture at the University of Groningen.

Bent Holm is Associate Professor of Theatre Studies at the University of Copenhagen.

Jan Clarke is Professor of French at Durham University.

Frans-Willem Korsten is Professor in Literature and Society at the Erasmus University Rotterdam and at the University of Leiden.

Richard Maber is Emeritus Professor of French at Durham University.

Andreas Musolff is Professor of German at Durham University.

Mårten Snickare is Associate Professor in the Department of Art History at Stockholm University.

Rina Walthaus is Lecturer of Historical Romance Literature and Culture at the University of Groningen.

Vincent van Zuilen was a PhD student in Early Modern History at the University of Groningen.

GOD AS KEYSTONE OF THE SYSTEM OF COMMONPLACES

THE CASE OF JOOST VAN DEN VONDEL'S PLAYS

Frans-Willem Korsten

1. *The Disturbing Logic in Commonplaces*

It is very hard to understand someone else's logic if one does not get it. This may sound obvious, but it concerns a serious problem in our understanding of commonplace books. It is not hard at all to understand the logic of, say, Catweazle, who, in a famous television series, hurled himself by a feat of magic from the eleventh century into the 1960s. Luckily he carried his pet animal with him, the toad Touchwood, who helped him to cope with modern miracles such as electric lights. Catweazle regarded them as magical objects and therefore did not switch on the light but mumbled a formula while touching the switch, and hey presto: there was light! It is precisely the fact that the medieval Catweazle was turned into a funny character that illustrates our modern problem. Would we truly be able to speak with, for instance, William of Ockham (in the flesh, of course, not in his incarnation as William of Baskerville in Eco's novel *The Name of the Rose*) in such a way that we would understand each other's logic? I have strong doubts, even with this so-called arch-father of modern science.

All the major studies on commonplace books touch upon the problem. Francis Goyet addresses inconsistencies in arguments that use commonplaces. He characterizes the issue at stake more specifically as 'le conflit des lieux communs' or as a form of perturbation – one that may be caused by even the smallest of commonplaces.[1] In different words Ann Moss, at the end of her study on the commonplace book, and considering its decline in the seventeenth century, contends that it no longer fitted in new aesthetic regimes: 'its open-ended acceptance of variety and self-contradiction in its assembled quotations was a potential irritant to a political culture centred on uniformity'.[2] Ann Blair describes it in a slightly different way again: 'As a tool for composition that opened many possibilities but required none in

---

[1] *Le sublime du 'lieu commun': L'invention rhétorique dans l'Antiquité et à la Renaissance* (Paris, 1996), p. 249.
[2] *Printed Commonplace Books and the Structuring of Renaissance Thought* (Oxford, 1996), p. 276.

particular, the commonplace book was supremely tolerant of cognitive dissonance'.[3] Cognitive dissonance is something which Blair will qualify, in relation to Renaissance natural philosophy, as one of the commonplace book's 'most puzzling features'. Perhaps one should add 'puzzling to us moderns', who tend to think of logic in argumentative terms of premises and conclusions that build upon one another (whether considered strictly logical or as arguments in practice, as in pragma-dialectics)[4]. Scholastic dialectics may seem to follow the same procedure of building up arguments in a logical way, but it remains markedly different, as Erasmus and his ilk argued (although the sharp distinction between scholasticism and humanism has been reconsidered lately).[5] The reason is that scholastic dialectics had to remain within a framework that would conclude all arguments in advance: the framework of Christianity, or rather, its powerful medieval mouthpiece, the Roman Catholic Church.

To be sure, neither Goyet, nor Moss, nor Blair is talking about something that is *not* logic. Instead, they are concerned with a strange kind of logic that perturbs, irritates, or puzzles – that, in short, not so much convinces as affects its audience aesthetically and politically. For indeed politics, logic and aesthetics are all in play, indicated respectively by Goyet's 'conflict', Moss's 'political culture centred on uniformity', and by the difference between the latter's 'contradiction' and Blair's 'dissonance'. Once one contradiction is solved, for instance, others will immediately resurface that cannot easily be pulled apart in order to demonstrate a clear-cut underlying logic. It is this continuous resurfacing of other elements that is an issue less of contradiction than of dissonance. It emerges that the system of commonplaces had a double potential. It provided its users both with stable orientational poles *and* with disturbing provocations. In both cases the commonplaces played a dominant role in the combined fields of knowledge, aesthetics and politics. The aesthetic and political role of commonplaces in particular has, on the whole, perhaps been under-exposed in the study of commonplaces.

The general picture may be illustrated by the inaugural lecture of neo-Latinist Karel Enenkel in 2006.[6] In that lecture Enenkel considers Ravisius

---

[3] *The Theater of Nature: Jean Bodin and Renaissance Science* (Princeton, NJ, 1997), p. 74.

[4] On pragma-dialectics, see F. van Eemeren and R. Grootendorst, *Speech Acts in Argumentative Discussions: A Theoretical Model for the Analysis of Discussions Directed Towards Solving Conflicts of Opinion* (Dordrecht, 1984).

[5] E. Rummel, ed., *Biblical Humanism and Scholasticism in the Age of Erasmus* (Leiden, 2008).

[6] Enenkel, K. A. E., *Imagines agentes: geheugenboeken en de organisatie van kennis in de Neolatijnse literatuur* (Leiden, 2005).

Textor's *Officina Textoris* of 1520, a text that he defines as a textual museum of curiosities. Such a collection of curiosities would not have been very useful as an instrument of organisation and memory in a pedagogical sphere, he argues, but would have functioned better in the humanist sphere of the expansion of knowledge. That is why Enenkel sees the commonplace book as an instrument in the hands of humanists who wanted to collect an exhaustive quantity of items, that in turn would imply an all-encompassing body of knowledge.

This does not answer the question, however, about the use to which this expansive knowledge should be put. Was it supposed to expand knowledge just for the sake of it?[7] It is not for nothing, I think, that the questions intrinsic to Moss's work are what kind of truth is at stake, how truth is used, what knowledge is doing and – most importantly – what it renders sensible or what can be sensed through it. In this respect, my treatment of commonplaces in what follows will draw on the work of Jacques Rancière, in which a distinction is made between police and politics.[8] The first of these concerns the relatively rigid, solidified and hierarchic organisation of a community or society. The second – politics – concerns the moment of change, or of political intervention which results in change. The remarkable thing is that commonplaces played a role in both police and politics. In the context of this, I will argue that the system of commonplaces did not decline because of a political culture centred on uniformity. As can be demonstrated by the political absurdity of the Dutch Republic, Europe had political systems that were not centred at all.[9] In my view, the system of commonplaces declined

---

[7] Likewise Enenkel uses the work of Albrecht Schöne on emblems, who stated that emblems worked primarily ontologically by giving their users an immediate access to 'truth'. In the work of both Enenkel and Schöne, truth and knowledge are considered in a self-evident or instrumental way. The work that made Schöne famous was written together with A. Henkel: A. Henkel and A. Schöne, *Emblemata, Handbuch zur Sinnbildkunst des XVI.-XVII Jahrhunderts* (Stuttgart-Weimar, 1996).

[8] *The Politics of Aesthetics: The Distribution of the Sensible* (London/New York, 2004); and *Politique de la littérature* (Paris, 2007).

[9] On the complicated, if not almost incomprehensible, political construction of the Seven Provinces in practice and in thought, see M. 't Hart, *The Making of a Bourgeois State: War, Politics and Finance during the Dutch Revolt* (Manchester/New York, 1993); J. I. Israel, *The Dutch Republic: Its Rise, Greatness, and Fall, 1477-1806* (Oxford, 1995); J. L. Price, *Holland and the Dutch Republic in the Seventeenth Century: The Politics of Particularism* (Oxford, 1994); id., *The Dutch Republic in the Seventeenth Century* (London, 1998); M. van Gelderen, 'Aristotelians, Monarchomachs and Republicans: Sovereignty and Respublica mixta in Dutch and German Political Thought, 1580-1650', in: Gelderen, M. van & Skinner, Q., eds, *Republicanism: A Shared European Heritage*, Vol. I: *Republicanism and Constitution-*

because the double potential that slumbered within it could no longer be held together by one centre. Consequently, a schism occurred between two different types of knowledge and between different aesthetic and political environments. This did not happen overnight. The system of commonplaces was remarkably resilient, not only because it allowed for enormous inconsistencies but also because it was held together, in the end, by an unquestionable keystone: God. Allow me first to focus on this resilience, in relation to a play written by Joost van den Vondel in the seventeenth century.

2. *Inconsistencies and Christian Tragedy*

Vondel, Holland's most famous playwright, lived to see more than three quarters of the seventeenth century (born in 1587, he died in 1679). His time was well spent. He produced an enormous quantity of texts, including at least thirty-three plays. These are distinctive not so much because of their actions and plots but because of the complicated mixture of arguments and narratives they contain. Or, to put this differently, being predominantly argumentative, the plays are puzzling in particular because of the narrative elements they contain. It is not that narratives are being worked out in detail. This would destroy the dramatic quality of the plays. Instead narratives are used in a condensed way. In my study of other texts I called these *enwrapped narratives*.[10] Just one word, one name, or a very short phrase will function as the envelope of a narrative that is built into the argument being developed. Almost always, unwrapping the narrative will lead to contradictions and dissonances. Vondel's work is distinctly baroque, folding in and folding out, or rather whirling inward and outward.

It is the use of enwrapped narratives that reminded me of commonplaces, or perhaps more accurately, I found that Vondel's use of commonplaces often comes down to using enwrapped narratives. The result is puzzling in yet another way. Unwrapping the narratives one will find that Vondel's plays acquire a *radical* element. This is puzzling since the man himself does not appear to have been very radical. He could be defined in opposition to the systematic, abstract and rigorous Spinoza. Vondel's thoughts are often more than slightly muddled, it would seem. 'Seem', indeed, because it is possible that he is simply following a kind of logic that has become strange to us modern readers.

---

alism in Early Modern Europe (Cambridge, 2002), pp. 195-217; and E.H. Kossmann, *Political Thought in the Dutch Republic: Three Studies* (Amsterdam, 2000).
[10] Korsten, F.-W., *The Wisdom Brokers: Narrative's Interaction with Arguments in Cultural Critical Texts* (Amsterdam, 1998).

Whirling inward and outward, Vondel's work has distinct recurring and structuring themes, the most important of these being that of sovereignty. With regard to this theme Vondel's work corresponds to what has recently been described by Jonathan Israel as Radical Enlightenment: the radicalisation of European thought in the latter half of the seventeenth century by thinkers such as Benedict de Spinoza, Pierre Bayle and Fransiscus van den Enden, all of whom lived or worked in the Dutch Republic.[11] Vondel did not feel any affinity with most of these thinkers, to put it mildly, but his work nevertheless had radical characteristics. In a sense his work fitted into the tradition of radical self-reflection that Christianity had known from its beginning, partly in the shape of distinctly different forms of Christianity. The gradual establishment of an all-encompassing and powerful Roman Catholic Church did manage to suppress forms of overly radical self-reflection, but was never decisively or entirely successful in this. Thinkers such as Marsilius of Padua in the fourteenth century or Niccolò Machiavelli in the sixteenth century had criticised Christianity on an increasingly fundamental level – and in both cases this criticism was in relation to a fundamental problem that was addressed time and again by thinkers and artists alike. The problem was that, with an omniscient God and a predestined end to human history, there appears to be no space left for sovereign historical, political actions that will allow human beings to influence the outcome – either happy or disastrous – of their history.

It is a problem that vexes Vondel as well, as is evident especially in his plays. Allow me to consider one particular play, *Adonias, of Rampzalige Kroonlust* (*Adonijah, or Disastrous Desire for the Crown*), from 1661.[12] The play deals with the following story. After Absalom's death, Adonijah (Adonias in the play) has become the eldest son of King David. Yet he is not crowned king after David's death. Instead Solomon, son of David and Bathsheba (Bersaba in the play), is crowned. After David's death, his high priest Abiathar and general Joab are immediately replaced. They become the advisors, however, of Adonijah. They advise him to ask for the hand of Abishag, a beautiful young woman who warmed the limbs of David in his final days. She is, in other words, the most recent wife of King David, and it is mentioned explicitly that she did not have sexual intercourse with him.

The play begins with this Abishag. She is going to say her prayers and has to cross the square in front of Solomon's palace. There, in the middle of

---

[11] Israel, J.I., *Radical Enlightenment: Philosophy and the Making of Modernity, 1650-1750* (Oxford, 2001).

[12] I will be referring to the texts in Vondel's collected works, *De werken van Vondel: Volledige en geïllustreerde tekstuitgave in tien delen*, eds Sterck, J.F.M., Moller, H.W.E., de Vooys, C.G.N., Klerk, C.R. de (Amsterdam, 1927). These are also available online at the dbnl-website: http://www.dbnl.org/titels/titels.php?c=17&s=t.

the square, Adonijah addresses her, and bluntly proposes to marry her. Abishag responds cautiously, aware of all the political pitfalls. She advises Adonijah to quieten down and to remain silent, and then hurries away because she sees Bathsheba entering the stage. Adonijah subsequently addresses Bathsheba and asks her whether she is willing to go to Solomon and request his consent to the marriage. He knows he is playing with fire, and turns pale from fear. When Bathsheba asks him why he turns pale, he lies, replying that it must be because of his love for Abishag. This convinces Bathsheba, who likes Abishag and who thinks she will have a tempering influence on Adonijah. However, when she asks Solomon he becomes extremely angry. He senses that Adonijah is plotting against him in a bid to become the rightful king. He sends his mother away abruptly and consults his newly appointed high priest and his general, Sadock and Banaiah, and the prophet Nathan. The result of the consultation is that Solomon orders Adonijah to be killed. The latter then tries to find refuge in the home of Abishag. However, having been the object of Adonijah's scheming, and of the royal court's gossip, she refuses to give Adonijah shelter and advises him to hide in a hollow tree instead. This is where Banaiah finds and kills him. Abishag then comes running forward, regretting the fact that she did not give shelter to Adonijah. She holds him in her lap while lamenting the death of one whom she calls 'my son' (*mijn zoon*; l. 1827).

The image with which the play ends, Abishag lamenting her dead 'son' whom she holds in her lap, is remarkable. Abishag and Adonijah resemble Mary and Jesus with shocking clarity. The implications may be considerable. Solomon, chosen by David, is the one who will build the temple, which prefigures God's church. Evidently Solomon is an instrument in God's organisation of history. The strong resemblance, however, between Abishag and Adonijah on the one hand and Mary and Jesus on the other complicates the way in which we can think of this. Instead of presenting the line that runs from David to Solomon to Jesus, the line that is being presented here is one between two mothers and their sacrificed sons, the sacrifice of which is intrinsically connected to a change in history and, in relation to that, to the foundation of a church. It is this focus on the way in which Christian history is produced as the result of a *change* that makes *Adonias* such a remarkable play. By contrast, the subtitle of *Adonijah or the Disastrous Desire for the Crown* – '*treurspel*', or tragedy – is so common that one would almost ignore it. This subtitle deserves some extra attention. The play's reflection on Christian history, I would argue, turns it into a real tragedy.

Both the issue of the making of history and of tragedy lead to a considerable problem within the framework of Christianity. As W.E. Tayler has put it, Christian history has no middle.[13] It has a beginning and an end. The in-between does not really matter in a historical, or a sovereign sense. As for tragedy, several attempts have been made, so to speak, to save *Christian tragedy* through concepts such as 'necessary suffering', or the alternation of protest and acceptance.[14] All these attempts fail since the end of common and individual Christian history is that one *deserves* what one gets, be it heaven or hell. So what happens when a playwright such as Vondel, who is influenced heavily by important classical ideas on this matter, sticks to the common definition of tragedy, namely as the history of a partly undeserved misfortune of a character? The consequence within the Christian framework must be that God can – perhaps must – be held responsible for the undeserved nature of this misfortune. The subject of tragedy would not be the misfortune of this character, then, but the cruelty of a God who plays with human subjects. Yet, this would not be tragedy either. It would perhaps be satire. One could, of course, object that, especially within the Roman Catholic realm, choice plays a paramount role. Tragedy would then be the history of moral choices, in which things could turn out for better or for worse. This may be correct, but if these predominantly moral choices turned out for the worse, it would not be tragic either, for it would, again, be the deserved outcome for a sinner.

The best way to define Christian tragedy, then, has been proposed by Tayler, mentioned above. In a study of Milton's play *Samson Agonistes*, Tayler states that the tragic in Christian tragedy may reside in the sudden turn of events. We do not need a middle – that is to say, an evolving history of human actions – to develop a feeling of pity and awe, Tayler states. We can feel the same thing in a sudden turn of events as we may feel during the performance of a magician. The comparison with the act of a magician is apt. If before our very eyes a human figure is being sawn in half and restored to full order once more, we may feel a mixture of horror, awe and relief.

---

[13] W. E. Tayler, 'Milton's Samson: The Form of Christian Tragedy', *English Literary Renaissance* 3 (1973), pp. 306-321.

[14] R. H. McKinney, 'Coping with Postmodernism: Christian Comedy and Tragedy', *Philosophy Today* 41 (1997), pp. 520-529. See also (for example) R. L. Cox, *Between Earth and Heaven: Shakespeare, Dostoevsky, and the Meaning of Christian Tragedy* (New York, 1969); A. C. Yu, 'Review of Roger L. Cox 1969', *Modern Philology* 69 (1972), pp. 275-277; B. J. Hunt, *The Paradox of Christian Tragedy* (New York, 1985); M. Steele, *Christianity, tragedy, and Holocaust literature* (Westport, 1995). By far the most interesting consideration is put forward by B. Pranger who, in a chapter called 'The Artifice of Eternity', considers the tragedies of Racine as plays on which 'the shadow of God does not fall' (in: *The Artificiality of Christianity: Essays on the Poetics of Monasticism* (Stanford, Cal., 2003), p. 28). Pranger's conclusion is that it must be the condensation of 'intense sadness and intense joy' in artifice that constitutes the tragic in Christianity (ibid., p.37).

This is, of course, not tragic in the classical sense, but it is tragic in the sense in which Vondel dealt with tragedy in some of his plays. In *Jeptha*, for instance, the instant reversal of Jephtha's considerations after Act IV, cannot be explained in terms of the preceding events. Nothing in the first four acts prepares us for the remorse that Jephtha suddenly feels after having killed his daughter with his own hands. The change of events is not prepared psychologically and by the course of events; it has a sudden, magical quality.

However, whereas the possibility of Christian tragedy may have been saved in this way, the possibility of sovereign human history – hence of sovereign political action – is *not*. This becomes clear in that play by Vondel which can be characterised by its slow and painful development towards an inevitable end – the one upon which I am focusing here: *Adonias*. The pain in this play consists partly in a smothering of voices. In Act III, Abishag gets into a long discussion with Solomon. In this discussion, Abishag wants to know how justifiable, or lawfully, Solomon acts with regard to his elder brother. However, when Abishag asks 'Would you stain your first act of justice with the blood of your brother?' (l. 1047), and begins a plea that keeps returning compulsively to the issue of justice, this starts to irritate Solomon so much that he orders her to make her point and shut up; 'The law shall run its course. Cut short your plaint, and finish' (l. 1073). With this sentence, Abishag is indeed finished; she is eliminated as a character with her own voice. And she is not the only woman who has been silenced. Solomon had silenced his mother Bathsheba as well. As publicly and politically relevant speakers, the two women are eliminated in the course of the first three acts. Why?

A hint is given in the preface by means of a distinct commonplace taken from Euripides's *Phoenician Women*. Vondel, in the form of the orator of the preface, recalls how some have considered Solomon's actions to be motivated *politically*. This implies that Solomon is not the righteous player in God's scheme of things. These people, so the orator states, consider Solomon's behaviour in relation to the old saying – and here comes the commonplace: 'If one is not afraid to violate the law, use violence when crowns are at stake, and be pious elsewhere'.[15] Then there are others, the orator continues, who see Solomon's verdict as unjustified because of natural law, by which the eldest son has the right to the throne.[16] The orator then produces a fairly opaque sentence:

---

[15] 'Indien men voor geen rechtbreuck schroom, / Bedrijf gewelt / Als 't kroonen gelt: / In andre zaecken hou u vroom' (ll. 18-21). The quotation is from Vondel's own translation into Dutch of the *Phoenician Women*, *Feniciaensche*, from 1668 (in the Werken van Vondel, eds Sterck et al, vol. 10, pp. 468-544).

[16] In the 'Dedication' the orator states: 'Just as Salomon's verdict would seem to be unjust since it did not accord with natural law, or the law of peoples, according to

but they heed not how strong an emphasis this is, to sully the infallible script, since it speaks so clearly, with suspicion of falsehood, and to learn to say that which is other than the truth, far removed from lies and injustice. A careful person takes care not to oppose the Holy Ghost, who, through the mouth of King David, a man after God's own heart, speaks thus:…

(Vondel, 'Dedication' in *Adonias*)[17]

I read the odd qualification of what truth is, and the repetitive quality of the sentence, as a sign of insecurity. Most tellingly the 'man who strives against the Holy Ghost' is not qualified as being wrong, but as one who is not '*omzichtig*' (careful) enough. Note, now, that the confusion, the insecurity, the warning to be careful is expressed in relation to a commonplace, which is taken from Euripides's play, and which does not simply underpin or decorate the statement of the orator, but which presents a forceful *alternative* voice and alternative proposition. Through it the possibility is expressed that the establishment of the temple, hence of the Church, was a matter of plain politics.[18]

---

which the younger son reasonably has to make place for the elder (in particular in the case of the Hebrews, where the first born had a right to a double share of the heritage)…' ('Eveneens gelijck of Salomons oordeel onrechtvaerdigh waer, aengezien het tegens de natuurwet, en het recht der volcken street, waer by de jongste billijck den outsten broeder, (en byzonder onder de Hebreen, daer d'eerstgeboren eens zoo diep in de erfenisse taste,) behoorde te wijcken…', ll. 20-24).

[17] In the original: '…maer zy letten niet van hoe groot eenen nadruck dit zy, het onfaelbaere bladt, daer het zoo klaer spreeckt, met achterdocht van valscheit te bevlecken, en anders dan waerheit, wijt afgescheiden van logentael en onrechtvaerdigheit, te leeren spreecken. Een omzichtige wacht zich wel den Heiligen Geest te wederstreven, die uit den mont van koning David, eenen man naar Godts hart, aldus spreeckt:…' (ll. 24-30). This translation and subsequent ones have been produced for this article by Will Kelly and myself.

[18] My close reading (this much may be clear) does not focus on the explicit and conscious intentions of the seventeenth-century author. I am very much interested, however, in intentions of cultural agents as they shine through in their texts. For a discussion on these points in relation to Vondel, see F.-W. Korsten, ''Waartoe hij zijn dochter slachtte: enargeia in een modern retorische benadering van Vondels Jeptha', *Tijdschrift voor Nederlandse Taal- en Letterkunde* 115 (1999), pp. 315-333; J. Konst, 'De motivatie van het offer van Ifis: en reactie op de Jeptha-interpretatie van F.-W. Korsten', *Tijdschrift voor Nederlandse Taal- en Letterkunde* 116 (2000), pp. 153-167; and Korsten 'Een reactie op "De motivatie van het offer van Ifis" van Jan Konst', *Tijdschrift voor Nederlandse Taal- en Letterkunde* 116 (2000), pp. 168-171. For an excellent study of the complexities, ambiguities and contradictions in what people believed during the course of one lifetime, see J. Pollman, *Een andere weg naar God: De reformatie van Arnoldus Buchelius* (1565-1641) (Amsterdam, 2000). For a study of the complicated rhetorical nature of prefaces, see K. Dunn, *Pretexts of Authority: The Rhetoric of Authorship in the Renaissance Preface* (Stanford, Cal.,

If consequently we start to read the play carefully and attentively and look for the establishment of Adonijah's guilt, we are not likely to find conclusive evidence. Nor does Solomon find it. Yet Adonijah is the man whom Solomon wants to have killed, before the former is brought to justice. The murder is necessary, not because of a divine scheme but because Adonijah has to be an example for all his other brothers, as Sadock explains to Solomon when he says that it is not Adonijah but 'David's sons, your brothers' who are behind the conspiracy (l. 1352). Therefore, Sadock adds, 'all their resistance is to be smothered in this firstborn' (l. 1393). It must be said that Solomon resists the verdict. But his resistance focuses time and again not on justice, nor even on God, but on what people will say. He is only prepared to act immediately when the high priest Sadock promises him that he will acquit Solomon, 'in the name of God'. In the latter's name Adonijah is executed.

In the studies on *Adonias* scholars have emphasised how, for Vondel, tragedy concerns the sudden change, the *peripeteia*, from happiness to disaster.[19] According to all commentators, the tragic figure in this play is Adonijah, who starts off as a merry prospective bridegroom and suddenly ends up being killed. Solomon, in this reading, is the tragedy's odd man out, who simply establishes himself as the 'king of peace'. I would argue, however, that Adonijah does not start off merrily at all. He is not in love with Abishag. His love is a veil for his political machinations. He knows what may happen, so that when he meets Bathsheba to ask her permission, he is scared to death. The outcome may be a sad one for him, but it is not tragic. If there is something tragic about his history, it is Adonijah's weakness, his ability to be manipulated, his passivity.

The question therefore remains to whom the term 'tragedy' pertains. As I see it, the subject of Vondel's Christian tragedy is a woman. *Adonias* presents us with two women, qualified as mothers, at the centre of a political struggle and at the heart of religious matters. They are not to be ignored, nor to be silenced. Yet, that is precisely what churches (Catholic and Protestant) have tried to do in the course of their history. In the seventeenth century, as

---

1994). In addition, H. F. Plett argues that one should not study the rhetorical implications and effects of Renaissance texts by studying the theory of rhetoric of that period but by considering what actual impact texts may have had within a certain praxis. See Plett's 'Rhetorik der Renaissance-Renaissance der Retorik', in: Plett, H. F., ed., *Renaissance Rhetoric* (Berlin/New York, 1993a), pp. 1-20; and his 'Theatrum Rhetoricum: Schauspiel-Dichtung-Politik' in the same volume, pp. 328-368.

[19] On this point, see in particular W. A. P. Smit, *Van Pascha tot Noah: Een verkenning van Vondels drama's naar continuiteit en ontwikkeling in hun grondmotief en structuur* (Zwolle, 1962).

studies by Karen Armstrong and Hans Küng show, both the Protestant and the Roman Catholic Churches concluded a battle of ages to bar women from holding religious or political positions.[20] One of Vondel's major cultural interventions through his plays is to introduce women as publicly, politically important figures. In addition to *Adonias*, if we look at *Jeptha* or *Gebroeders*, for instance, we see how in all three plays mothers start out happy, but in the end have to experience the tragedy of learning that their innocent children have been killed. In all three cases subjects are killed for political reasons, to set an example. In all three cases the founding relation that is so crucial for Christianity, namely the one between one father and one son, is established through the elimination of alternative relationships (such as between father and daughter, mother and son, mother and daughter). Moreover, in all three cases, one essential feature of the tragedy is that the women are silenced. In this context it may be clear how Vondel's plays expose the *construction* of the foundation of the Christian Church. His plays show how politics is inherent in *doing* religion; how a particular religion is established by political means. The question consequently needing to be raised is how this all relates to the topic of commonplaces.

3. A Keystone of the Commonplace System

As we have seen, an alternative and powerful voice in the preface concerned a commonplace. Furthermore, there is something puzzling in the use of the seemingly simple phrase 'in the name of God'. To modern readers it may seem illogical that this phrase alters the meaning of the entire play, but to many seventeenth-century readers this was quite feasible. It is an enwrapped narrative if ever there was one. 'In the name of God' implies the narrative of God's intervention in human history, or the framing of that history. In light of that narrative the *Realpolitik* of certain characters can turn into divinely foreordained behaviour, or a ruthless politician can be seen as a king of peace. Obviously, the fact that 'in the name of God' is an enwrapped narrative does not turn it into a commonplace. It even seems rather absurd to consider God as a commonplace, in the sense of a *locus communis*. God is not definable as a *locus*. It is hard to consider the notion of God in the shape of a phrase or a paragraph with specific content, in the form of one amongst several headings, or as an element that would somehow be *part* of the organisation of knowledge. God exceeds knowledge or is defined by his incomprehensibility. He will be anything but common, in several senses of the word.

---

[20] Armstrong, *The End of Silence: Women and the Priesthood* (London, 1993); Küng, *Die Frau im Christentum* (Munich, 2001).

Yet with respect to knowledge there are reasons to suggest that from the very beginning God is considered to be the ultimate point of reference behind knowledge and the organisation of knowledge. God is supposed to be the ultimate source of knowledge, underpinning the entire system of knowledge with its internal relations, and framing knowledge by imposing limits upon it. Here God can be considered, in a sense, as the commonplace of all commonplaces, or the keystone of the system of commonplaces. If one considers the system of commonplaces as a collection of all kinds of phrases and fragments, caught by networks of scales and frames, indicating a method of reading, interpreting and organising knowledge, the question is how this in the end coheres – especially when the system knows many principal inconsistencies. One answer is that it can cohere by means of an ultimate point of reference, such as God, who will then act as the one that holds it all together, for instance through such a simple phrase as 'in the name of God'.

As Goyet indicated, elaborating on the etymological meaning of *commun*, commonplaces have a role to play in the establishment of a certain community. They embody what that community regards as its common knowledge. In one sense the entire system of commonplaces contributed enormously to a certain communality, in a culture that cohered because of Christianity. However, the commonplaces did not form, at any given moment, a consistent, coherent body. Rather they embodied the diffuse and incoherent nature, even the schizophrenia, if I may put it anachronistically, of European culture. With respect to the *communis* element of the commonplace, the very figure of God played an ambiguous role. Historically, culturally, the figure of God caused never-ending disruptions in the body of Christian communities for centuries. At the same time he was the only true commonplace, or the keystone of the system of commonplaces. As such it was almost impossible to say farewell to him. Yet, such a farewell is precisely what is being put forward in the seventeenth century. As a result, the system of commonplaces had to collapse.

With regard to that collapse, let me try to be as clear as possible on this notion of a system of commonplaces. In her most recent considerations on the definition of commonplaces, Moss describes them as the embodiment of:

> cultural material with both past and present currency within a given language community. Their reference is to opinions commonly accepted as valid. And they are deployed primarily as tools for argument in discourse designed to promote and reinforce culturally sanctioned modes of thought. Furthermore, commonplace propositions have a ritualised character that makes of them recognisable modes of communication coded for universal reception, be it as fa-

miliar forms of verbal expression, hackneyed metaphors, normative rules, or recurring patterns.[21]

In short, one could say that commonplaces here constitute the domain of what Barthes would have called *doxa*. However, as Moss also indicates, commonplaces in the medieval or early modern sense were linked to the institutional organisation of knowledge, to rhetoric and dialectics. This is a field closely connected to, but also principally different from, the organisation of a culture in terms of *doxa* or ideology. As for the use of commonplaces in this field Moss states that:

> the early modern concept of commonplaces was not elastic at all. It was the solid outcome of highly self-conscious theorising and critical reflection on practice. Nor was it initially designed as an instrument of non-verbal communication or as a *product* for popular consumption. The world of its genesis and evolution was the *élite* environment of the Latin grammar class in humanist schools devoted to the language arts: grammar, rhetoric, and dialectic.[22]

While I agree with the elitist domain in which the commonplaces functioned and the non-elastic use of the concept itself, the way in which the commonplaces started to work in practice was much more 'elastic'. Perhaps Moss points to this, here, through the words 'highly self-conscious' and 'critical reflection'. With regard to self-consciousness and reflection, the systematisation had a double potential since it provided its users both with stable orientational poles *and* with disturbing provocations.

This is what distinguishes the precise sense of commonplace from the looser sense one could make of the term in order to qualify a *doxa* or ideology. In the latter case, commonplaces do not have such a double potential because they are not caught in a (rhetorical, dialectical) system that requires coherence. They basically confirm and inscribe some kind of cultural organisation. The two different conceptualisations relate rather differently, then, to a culture's organisation as a whole and *principally* they relate differently to the organisation of knowledge. Consequently, if one sticks to the sharper, precise definition of commonplaces, one can analyse better how the organisation of knowledge could exert a distinct colonising force in society – not

---

[21] 'Power and Persuasion: Commonplace Culture in Early Modern Europe', in *Commonplace Culture in Western Europe in the Early Modern Period*, vol. I: *Reformation, Counter-Reformation and Revolt*, eds Mette B. Bruun and David Cowling (Leuven, 2010), pp. 1-17 (p. 1).

[22] 'Power and Persuasion', p. 1.

just a confirming force, but also a undermining one.[23] This is to say that when, in what follows, I consider how the medieval or early modern use of commonplaces changed in the seventeenth century, I do not do so in order to indicate that they simply disappeared to make way for the more general, ideological kind of commonplaces. I mean to show how the double potential that the commonplaces had, led to the rupture of a cultural body, and the formulation of a new kind of knowledge.

4. *The Political Act of Reading*

In the preface to his play *Gebroeders* (*Brothers*), performed for the first time in 1640 and published in 1641, Vondel addresses the issue of how much liberty authors have when they use biblical material. One of Vondel's closest friends, the humanist scholar Gerardus Johannes Vossius (author of the influential *Poeticae institutionis* of 1647), had already solved the matter. In private conversations and in lectures Vossius had formulated what he called 'golden rules'. These were that artists (a) may use everything mentioned explicitly in the Bible or (b) may add small things – with the utmost restraint. Whatever the case, it is (c) absolutely forbidden to make up material that is not compatible with the text and message of the Bible.

In the preface to *Jeptha*, from 1659, Vondel again mentions Vossius, who had severely criticised George Buchanan's treatment of the story. Posing as Vossius' loyal pupil, Vondel argues that he himself has stuck to the 'golden rules'. He has only changed the chronological order of events a little, in order to be able to follow the classicist rule of the unity of place, time and action. 'It is evident', says the orator, though he says it in parentheses, 'that one may not alter a single thing in the sanctuary of the Bible' (*Jeptha*, 'Berecht', ll. 23-4). Yet Vondel's posturing as Vossius's loyal pupil serves to draw the reader's attention away from the fact that Vondel has introduced two major female characters. In the Bible the daughter has no name and no history. Vondel gives her both a name, Ifis, and a prominent role. The mother is not even mentioned in the Bible.[24] Nonetheless, Vondel presents her story, and gives her a name. As Filopaie ('she who loves her child') she receives a prominent role. One could consider the introduction of these fe-

---

[23] I take the idea of colonisation from Moss, who states, for example, in relation to the Renaissance humanists: 'They colonized the cognate territories of literature, history, and philosophy' (*Renaissance Truth and the Latin Language Turn* (Oxford, 2003), p.1).

[24] For a fascinating study of the story in the Bible, see M. Bal, *Death and Dissymmetry: The Politics of Coherence in the Book of Judges* (Chicago/London, 1988). Bal, in order to counter the political implications of erasure in the text, also gives the daughter a name, which in her case is Bath – meaning daughter.

male characters to be rather inconsequential, if this were to occur in one play only. But this is not the case, as we have seen with *Adonias* (1664), or with *Noah* (1667) and as we will see with *Gebroeders*.

The play is based on Samuel 2, chapter 21, verses 1-14. It begins with a meeting between the archpriest, Abiathar, and David. The former describes how Israel is in dire circumstances because of relentless drought. People are exhausted and on the verge of collapsing, or revolting. David asks Abiathar what is to be done. Both then visit the divine oracle, which is described later as an impressive, somewhat spooky spectacle, and the meaning of which is defined by Abiathar. According to him the drought is punishment for a sin committed by David's predecessor, Saul. When conquering the city of No-be, Saul gave the order that all Gibeonites should be killed. Now reparation is called for.

Immediately David sends for representatives from the Gibeonites and asks them what they want. They want the life of seven children and grand-children of Saul, the ones called 'brothers' in the piece. David is not entirely happy with their wish. Saul's daughter, Michal, was one of his wives. The scapegoats are his brothers-in-law and nephews. But in the end David orders their death. He sends the head of the royal guard, Benaiah, to arrest the men, but two women await him: Rizpah, the wife of the deceased Saul, mother and grandmother of the seven men, and Michal, David's former wi-fe and the one who on behalf of her deceased sister has cared for the latter's children, five grandchildren of Saul. The women argue fervently with Be-naiah and, when he enters the stage, with David. Michal in particular tries to persuade David by appealing to his friendship with her brother Jonathan, whom he loved better than he loved women. It is all to no avail. The seven men are being hanged. Rizpah then insists on remaining with the corpses so that she can chase away birds of prey and scavengers. David in response decides to give the seven brothers an honourable grave, together with their father Saul.

For most scholars the play has not presented many interpretative pro-blems because to them David is without question the hero of the play. In my reading this is highly questionable. Vondel never works with one character who is the hero. He works with the forces that live and operate through and between characters. The hint that is hidden in the title may be telling here. To some scholars Vondel's *Gebroeders* is a failure since the so-called brothers play only a marginal role, in no more than two out of five acts. Ta-king the title seriously, however, one finds that there are other brothers who play a powerful role in this play: David and Saul's son Jonathan, who are brothers-in-law but who are also called brothers in a different sense. In the poem that follows the play, David laments the loss of Jonathan in these words:

Oh Jonathan, my sweet confidant,
Sweeter to me than women's love
My brother thus ended in grief;
The pain I feel defies belief.
No mother's heart was so beguiled,
So filled with love for her own child,
As mine is by your soul.
(*Gebroeders*, 'Lijckklacht' ('Lament over the deceased')).[25]

David, then, is intrinsically linked to a character who, while he may not have an explicit role in the play, is a powerful actor nevertheless. The name of Jonathan is an enwrapped narrative that plays a decisive role in all the major argumentative turning points.

Other reasons not to consider David as the unquestionable hero can be found in some commonplaces presented in the preface. In this preface the orator Vondel defends himself against those who claim that he gave a false picture of David as someone who hesitates too much and is kind and merciful. Apparently one critic had commented that, in his view, David was not particularly troubled by what happened to the house of Saul. The orator wants to argue against this, in order to save David from disgrace. In the course of his argument he presents no less than four quotations – commonplaces – from Virgil's *Aeneid*.

The longest one concerns Aeneas and Dido. The passage concerns Aeneas's departure. Dido has already begged Aeneas not to leave, but he would not listen. Now she sends her sister to make a final plea. Aeneas remains cold as ice, untouched and unmoved (*Aeneid* IV, 439). Later this is reaffirmed but also nuanced. Inside, so the text would have it, Aeneas feels pain, but that feeling remains 'rigid and stiff' (*Aeneid* IV, 448-9). Aeneas is the equivalent here of David. Both men are confronted by two female relatives who beg them not to be cruel, but to whom they do not listen. Yet in relation to the orator's argument the quotation functions awkwardly. Although trying to argue that David is kind and merciful, the orator here presents a quotation in which a character decides not to listen, with an untouched or stiff and rigid heart, in order to leave his beloved one in despair. The motive for this behaviour is pretty obvious. Aeneas has to go because there is a higher goal that awaits him: to lay the foundations for a future empire, Rome. There is another commonplace that proves this, also taken

---

[25] 'Och Jonathan, mijn zoet vertrouwen, / My zoeter dan de min der vrouwen / Mijn broeder dus verongeluckt; / Nu voel ick, hoe uw dood my druckt. / Geen moeders hart had zoo verkoren / Het eenigh pand uit haer geboren, / Als ick uw ziel' (*Gebroeders*, 'Lijckklacht', ll. 41-47; transl. Will Kelly).

from the *Aeneid*, which states that the love for nation and fatherland should stand above anything else ('Preface' l. 42). The implication is that a man may be merciful and kind, but that a higher goal may change such a man into a man who shows no mercy.

In an earlier quotation the orator refers to Aeneas visiting the underworld, where he meets the 'arrogant Phlegias, condemned to hell'.[26] The story behind this character is that Phlegyas burned down a temple of Apollo after the god had impregnated his daughter Coronis. Apollo then killed Phlegyas and threw him into the underworld. There Phlegyas warns and teaches the other souls, with a regular commonplace again: 'Learn and think of what is right, and do not deny the gods' (*Aeneid* VI, l. 620).[27] There may or may not be truth in this pagan tale, the orator then continues, but the point is that what Phlegyas warns against is exactly what Saul has done. Instead of taking the latter as a paradigm, according to the orator, one ought rather to think of David, for the latter is 'like a sun' (l. 17) and plays the 'divine harp and chords' (l. 22). However, here too the quotation complicates things considerably. Phlegyas is not speaking to just any souls in hell. He is also teaching 'those who have besmirched their lives with fratricide' (*Aeneid* VI, l. 608).[28] For a play called *Brothers* this is too much of a coincidence, the more so since David commits a kind of fratricide by killing his brothers-in-law. Furthermore, Apollo not only threw Phlegyas into hell, but also killed Coronis once he had learned that she had fallen in love with somebody else. He even tore the unborn child out of her womb. To be able to play the harp beautifully coincides well, apparently, with ruthless cruelty. Here again, instead of appearing as a straightforward kind and merciful ruler, or a skilled artist, David is by implication a far more complicated, even ambiguous character.

Vondel's text provokes the reader, then, in its use of commonplaces that are taken from a famous classical text and that imply a different, sovereign environment. As a result the commonplaces complicate reading. They not only provoke questions as to how one *should* read and they do not just prescribe how to read and interpret, but they force one to *choose* how to read in relation to radically different, sometimes mutually exclusive politico-cultural environments. It is this *choice to act in a certain way* which turns reading into something intrinsically political and aesthetic at the same time. This choice of how to read, hence how to know, plays a crucial role in the play itself as well.

---

[26] '...den verwaten en ter hell gedoemden Phlegias' (*Gebroeder*s, l. 3).
[27] 'discite iustitiam moniti et non temnere diuos...' (my translation).
[28] 'hic, quibus inuisi fratres, dum uita manebat...' (my translation).

In the discussion of the two women with Benaiah and David, Benaiah
reassures the women that they need not be afraid since David will not act
without God's consent, or Abiathar's. The women respond bitterly and ironically: 'Yes, alas, Abiathar!' When Benaiah adds that David will only allow things to happen when God allows him to allow them, Michal responds:
'Yes, well, is there anything God does not allow?' And Rizpah adds: 'Either
divine decree or biased vagary.' Evidently, God is being presented as a rhetorical vehicle that may serve to legitimise arbitrary, politically motivated,
even unjust, or cruel acts. But there is something more fundamental at stake
than simply seeing the two women argue that God is used rhetorically. They
emphasise how the high priest Abiathar used a distinct kind of *reading* –
namely a reading of the oracle. Of that reading Michal states: 'How can one
blindly judge / God's oracle? No, clarity and light are due, / Or let the
words of falsehood hold more than the true'.[29] It is not just that Abiathar is
being accused of lying here. In order to consider the agenda of Abiathar,
Michal requires light and transparency. She wants to be able to weigh up
Abiathar's reading on the basis of public scrutiny. She wants to re-read herself, on an equal level, in order to *know*, in order to be able to act politically
in a sovereign way. The result will be a different 'distribution of the sensible', as Jacques Rancière called it.

There is no mistaking the fact that, without God as a fundament or an
ultimate anchor point, as when God is turned into a rhetorical figure, knowledge does not become free in the ultimate sense of that word, nor will it be
set loose. But without God the directions that knowledge may take will differ, as becomes clear from Michal's requirements of clarity and transparency. Likewise the justification of knowledge must change and its aesthetic
embedding and embodiment will take a different shape. Allow me to turn to
my final example, Vondel's final piece too, in which all this plays an important role.

5. *The Sovereignty of the Subjected*

In 1667 when he had just turned eighty, Vondel wrote and published his
Noah with the telling subtitle '*or the ruin of the first world*'. It again addressed several issues that might have upset the orthodox, and not only Protestants. It did not upset them too much, however, because the play was not
performed. The story of Noah will be familiar. Because God is dissatisfied
with what human beings are doing, he decides to destroy the world by sen-

---

[29] 'Hoe oordeelt men zoo blind / van Gods orakel? neen, dit eischt meer licht en
klaerheid, / of laet de logentael meer gelden dan de waerheid' (*Gebroeders*, ll. 948-
950, transl. Will Kelly).

ding a flood that will end all life. He will preserve life only by giving Noah the task of building an ark in which a select number of all living beings can be preserved. As a result, life can have a fresh start after the waters of the flood have disappeared. In relation to all this, the ark is an extremely power-ful commonplace. It is read, throughout the history of Europe, as a symbol for the Church and, accordingly, the fresh start must be understood in a spi-ritual way. But in Vondel's play such a strictly spiritual reading is compli-cated.

The flood in the play has a remarkable source. In the Bible the source of the flood is first that it will rain for forty nights and days, non-stop. But once the story in the Bible is almost at its end, it says that the Lord had also opened the sources of the primeval flood. In Vondel's play this is projected backwards in time. There is no rain as yet, but the water is already coming from below. It has a source which is unknown. Whereas non-stop rains would obviously be a disaster, it would be a disaster human beings can so-mehow understand. But waters that well up from beneath have a distinctly uncanny quality, in the sense of Freud's *Unheimliche*: an uneasy, frighte-ning mixture of what is familiar and yet deeply strange. But the reason that the play presents the welling water first is precisely because it is so marked-ly a foretoken of the *strange* things that will happen, and as such a good symbol of the strange *power* that is behind all this. As opposed to the conti-nuous rainfall, the water welling up from below is *un*natural – or is counter to nature as the Dutch 'tegennatuurlijk' suggests. The natural order is, lite-rally, turned on its head. This reversal suggests that God is working not only against perverse man, whose skull he is about to crack, but also against na-ture. Is this so, and why would he do that?

In the summary that precedes the play the orator presents the history that led up to the flood. He mentions how the God-fearing sons of Seth had intercourse with the daughters of Cain. They begot giants, who were at the root of the world going astray. Because of their 'unequal mixture' these giants caused 'all kinds of impiety and evil'.[30] Later, in the play itself, the giants do not appear. Their presence is shifted into a place. All the events take place at the foot of the Caucasus, close to the *Giant's Citadel*. This shift of characters into a space that is gigantic corresponds with the way in which nature is described in the play, as something gigantic and enormously productive due to an almost unlimited sexual activity. This may explain why it is not just the society of perverse human beings that needs to be destroyed but indeed an entire world. The translation of the King James Bible tells us, in Genesis 7.21, how all the creatures *moved*: 'And all flesh

---

[30] 'ongelijke vermenginge'; 'allerhande godeloosheit en boosheit', (*Noah*, 'Inhoudt' or 'Content', transl. Will Kelly).

died that moved upon the earth, both of fowl, and of cattle, and of beast, and of every creeping thing that creepeth upon the earth, and every man.' Later on this is emphasised, in *Genesis* 7.23. The image is one of a natural world in which all life moves, creeps, mingles, or 'swarms' ('wemelt', as the latest Dutch translation renders it). This stands in sharp contrast with the discipline that God ordains: one male and one female – monogamy in the natural world.[31]

God appears, then, as the sovereign who has the right to put an existing order out or order, to call forth a state of emergency, to violate without being violated, and to produce a total reshaping of the body politic *and* of history. This is emphasised in the play by means of an extensive passage in which the incredible destruction is described. Nevertheless, as all readers familiar with the Bible will know, when life gets a fresh start after the flood, it is not that fresh. The world has not been washed clean at all, something that will become apparent, ironically, in the figure of Noah himself, who will be found drunk by his own son. It is precisely the ultimate unruliness of the ones subjected, or their potency to start life again in an unruly way that proves they have a kind of sovereignty. Something, somehow, could not be violated. As a result, life on earth, and human life within it, has the potential to make history on its own. Accordingly, God cannot be the ultimate power or signifier that rules, directs or controls this history completely.

When considering Vondel's work in the light of what the major European thinkers on sovereignty have proposed, I was struck after a while, and especially after studying *Noah*, by an issue that is addressed in almost every play by Vondel and that is not addressed in the major theories on political sovereignty. Sovereignty has by and large been defined in political theory as that ruling power which knows no power above it, and that is able to act autonomously, according to its own charter. There is another strand, however, in European thinking on sovereignty, which concerns the way in which the sovereignty of the individual subject – the one subjected to a ruler or a certain power – is respected or is made possible. Subjects do have, and often recognise, a power above them, yet they still claim to have some sort of sovereignty. The question therefore is how these two conceptualisations of sovereignty relate to one another. That question, I think, is pivotal in Vondel's work, and is explored in relation to the question of how God intervenes in human history.

The relation between God and human history has two major embodiments. God can be a figure who intervenes in human history – as he did

---

[31] 'And every living substance was destroyed which was upon the face of the ground, both man, and cattle, and the creeping things, and the fowl of the heaven; and they were destroyed from the earth' (Genesis 7.23).

when he sent the flood, for instance, or when he sent his Son – or God can be a figure underpinning an earthly institution: the church, for instance, or royal sovereignty. In relation to the first embodiment, Vondel's plays portray a type of sovereignty in which God as *the* supreme power may act arbitrarily and violate at will. Yet Vondel's plays also show that somehow, in some way, the sovereignty of the subjected is able to remain inviolate, even if only in part, residing in peculiar potencies that can lead to new starting points, or can be put to use, historically, to open up history. Subsequently, when Vondel's plays investigate the political nature of religious organisations, such as the Church or the priesthood, or the religious underpinning of kingship, or of a judicial order, God starts to function as a figure that can be used rhetorically. This use opens up the planes of aesthetics, politics *and* of knowledge. Sensibility, scrutiny, investigation, questioning, and reading can all be used as a weapon against the powers of rhetoric. And, as the word 'weapon' suggests, this is not an easy battle, nor is it an apolitical quest for truth. It is a battle for another kind of politics in a field full of contradictions and dissonances.

When reproached for the choice of the name Urania for one of his protagonists by Joachim Oudaen, the smart Vondel wrote back that the name went back to biblical '*ur*', which means 'fire'. However, since Dirck Pieterszoon Pers had published his well known *Urania, of hemelsangh* (*Urania, or Song of the Heavens*) in 1640 this is hard to believe. To all readers Urania must have meant Muse of the cosmos. Moreover, if it was truly the case that Vondel went back to '*ur*' he might have been in more trouble. Oudaen should have responded that this meant *divine* fire or light, symbol of God, as Ruusbroec had argued in Dutch literary and religious history. This would have placed Urania on a divine plane, in biblical terms. However, she obviously represents an alternative. In the classical world *kosmos* means a total system in a state of harmonious order, as opposed to *kaos*. Moreover, the connotations of ornamentation in *kosmos* indicate that this is a pleasurable, beautiful system. And indeed, the world that queen Urania rules, at the beginning of the play, *is* such a system: full of love, beauty and a certain peace. If one were to describe what history consists of in this world it would be existence *in time*, not through time, in a state of well-being. Here, God not only intervenes but also violates the entire living world in order to reorganise the polity and start a distinct history. The lustful, swarming, baroque and intrinsically *unruly* or abundant world has to be violated in order to be replaced by what Foucault calls a biopolitically organised world, a classicist world of oppositions, in which life is contained in the artificial ark and in which human beings are the rulers of life.[32]

In the above I hinted at a split that occurred in the seventeenth century between two radically different aesthetic regimes. One was classical, and tended towards uniformity, towards closed and well-structured systems, defined by mathematical logic and clear-cut hierarchies. The other was baroque and tended towards ambiguity, towards limitless and folded systems, defined by the logic of affects and entwined hierarchies. With regard to the latter it would be worthwhile considering in more detail the metamorphosis from the commonplace system into the baroque. Moss, for instance, mentions the commonplace book's 'primary qualities of abundance and display'. This 'abundance' (a term that will return in Moss's work on the use of the Latin language as well) or 'copiousness' of the system does not just imply the absence of an overall restricting or unifying force but implies that there is no – and can be no – limit to the system.[33] Or, remaining within the system, the abundance may exist in the fact that the constituting elements preserve their own sovereign, somehow inviolable quality and force, as a result of which we find ourselves in a world of productively entwined hierarchies.

Of course, the system of commonplaces had this other potential as well: of organising the elements in a well-structured whole, of systematising things, in order to be able to find and use them better, instrumentally. This potential, however, was developed increasingly *separately* in the seventeenth century, either in classicism, or in scientific empiricism, or in the desire of radical philosophers such as Spinoza to think logically, on the basis of axioms, in a mathematical sense.

When in the course of the seventeenth century God ceased to be able to serve as the keystone of all commonplaces, holding the system together, this was perhaps not only a result of the radical nature of that century. God had, already, always been a figure that could only just about keep the system of commonplaces together 'in the name of God'. Memorising enormous quantities of fragments of texts, medieval and early modern subjects did not just 'take in' pieces of language with which they could act at will. These pieces

---

[32] According to Michel Foucault, in European societies politics changes into biopolitics from the eighteenth century onwards, when it becomes more and more important that life as a whole is organised or disciplined. On this, see *The Order of Things: An Archaeology of the Human Sciences* (New York, 1973) and *The History of Sexuality*, Volume 1 (New York, 1980). My argument is that the construction of this new kind of politics could already be sensed in the seventeenth century, or perhaps more fundamentally, that policies associated with biopolitics were virtually embodied in Christianity.

[33] Moss, *Printed Commonplace Books*, p. 275, and *Renaissance Truth*, p. 79.

of language lived through, and shaped their users, whilst keeping – in however fragmented, tempered or distorted a manner – their own sovereign force.[34] When this became more and more evident, not only the concept of God but also the nature of knowledge changed. Knowledge was split apart into, on the one hand, a practical and systematised kind of knowledge, an instrumental one, that would lead in a rather straight line to modernity, and on the other hand a more sensuous, perhaps even capricious (but in that sense deeply humane), kind of knowledge, one that would somehow make human beings feel lost, or alienated, in the modern world.

I dare say the split still troubles us. When we are puzzled by the logic of the system of commonplaces, this need not be due to that system. Talking about Lipsius's *Politica*, Moss concludes that the book 'appears to be an attempt to perform fragmentation, to explicate division, and at the same time to write fragmentation and division into a nexus which its readers would immediately recognise as that which structured their universe of thought and culture'.[35] Trained to have well-defined goals in mind, and used to instrumental forms of knowledge, we moderns tend to have difficulty with understanding systems that have no clear-cut goal and that basically present fragments of different ages and cultures on an equal level, without forcing them into one unified system of production, distribution and consumption. In a distinctly disturbing sense one could argue that the system of commonplaces was somehow more open, even with God securing it, than our current 'system'.

---

[34] I am thinking here of the thesis put forward by Burcht Pranger (*The Artificiality of Christianity*) of an artificiality caused by the required passage through the classical *artes liberales*.

[35] A. Moss, 'The *Politica* of Justus Lipsius and the Commonplace-Book', *Journal of the History of Ideas* 59 (1998), pp. 421-436 (p. 430).

THE SUN KING AND HIS SUBJECTS

RECIPROCITY IN A COMMONPLACE OF POWER

Richard Maber

No commonplace about the nature of power has ever undergone so glorious an apotheosis as that which likens or assimilates the monarch to the sun. The image of Louis XIV as the Sun King – *le Roi-Soleil* – was the ultimate expression, and justification, of supreme, 'top-down', God-given authority and power. The iconography of the *Roi-Soleil* has of course been extensively studied, and by far the greatest emphasis has always been on the ubiquitous use of solar imagery – Louis as Apollo – to convey the king's glory, splendour, regularity, and unchallengeable universal dominance.[1] In its literary expression, Louis's panegyrists use this commonplace to suggest simultaneously the dazzling opulence, moral superiority, and absolute supremacy of the French king as he dominates the firmament of Europe and spreads the power of his radiance in every land and every corner of life.

However, when analysed in detail, the image can be seen to be more polysemic than it might at first appear. I propose in this essay to study two different aspects of the commonplace of the king-as-sun which have received comparatively little attention. Firstly, I wish to consider the evolution of this image, and the pre-existing associations that it carried with it when first applied to Louis in the early years of his reign; and, secondly, the idea of reciprocity between monarch and subject, which was built into the image from a very early stage, and the forms that this took both in theory and in practice.

1. *The evolution of an image*

The metaphorical identification of the monarch with the sun is of course an extremely old and universally familiar commonplace, which long antedates

---

[1] The all-encompassing scope of this imagery is admirably summed up in the very title of J.-P. Néraudau's study, *L'Olympe du Roi-Soleil, ou comment la mythologie et l'Antiquité furent mises au service de l'idéologie monarchique sous Louis XIV à travers la littérature, la peinture, la musique, les fêtes, la sculpture, l'architecture et les jardins, à Vaux-le-Vicomte, Meudon, St Cloud, Sceaux, Marly, St Germain et Versailles* (Paris, 1986).

its spectacular adoption by Louis XIV.[2] It is particularly interesting to note how it tends to be invoked with especial insistence in contexts where its purpose is to emphasise the restoration of order and the re-establishment of firm, stable government: just as the sun eclipses envious lesser stars and dissipates obscuring mists, so the strong monarch eliminates feuding factions, and rectifies the disorders of the state. These are the associations that lie behind Prince Hal's famous speech in Shakespeare's *1 Henry IV*, I, 2:

> Yet herein will I imitate the sun,
> Who doth permit the base contagious clouds
> To smother up his beauty from the world,
> That when he please again to be himself,
> Being wanted, he may be more wonder'd at,
> By breaking through the foul and ugly mists
> Of vapours that did seem to strangle him.[3]

Although ostensibly speaking about his relationship with Falstaff, the Prince is symbolically anticipating his crushing of rebellion in this play, and his future transmutation into an ideal king. The familiarity of these connotations of the king-as-sun commonplace is shown in the diversity of ways in which they can be evoked. To remain with Shakespeare, the same image is used in consecutive scenes in Act III of *Richard II*, in exactly opposite contexts – the first time to anticipate easy success:

> So when this thief, this traitor, Bolingbroke,
> Who all this while hath revell'd in the night
> Whilst we were wandering with the antipodes,
> Shall see us rising in our throne, the east,
> His treasons will sit blushing in his face,
> Not able to endure the sight of day... [4]

and in the second instance, ironically anticipating failure:

> See, see, King Richard doth himself appear,
> As doth the blushing discontented sun
> From out the fiery portal of the east,

---

[2] See for example the brief survey in Néraudau, *L'Olympe du Roi-Soleil*, pp. 27-35.

[3] In: W. Shakespeare, *The Complete Works*, eds Wells, S., Taylor, G., Jowett, J., and Montgomery, W. (Oxford, 1986), p. 513, lines 194-200. All quotations from Shakespeare will be from this edition.

[4] III. 2. 47-52 (p. 429); the image is developed in full in lines 36-52.

When he perceives the envious clouds are bent
To dim his glory and to stain the track
Of his bright passage to the occident.[5]

In each case, though, what is being emphasised is the expectation, so commonly associated with the image, of restorative power in the sun in its splendour: the same association as is found in the *devise* of Victor Amadeus I of Savoy (1587-1637, ruled 1630-1637), of a sun with the motto 'soluit dum uidit' ('he disperses (darkness, mists etc) as he looks on them').[6] In just the same way, when a monarch is likened to Apollo it is characteristically to the heroically active Ovidian Apollo of the early creation, who slew the monstrous Python and restored order to the world.[7] Recent French history had been such that it was possible for the allusion to be applied, in gratitude or in hope, to most kings during the previous century; it proved particularly useful in the encomiastic verse written for Louis XIII after the defeat of the Protestants at La Rochelle in 1628.[8]

The same associations underlie the early applications of solar imagery to the young Louis XIV in the first twenty years of his reign, 1643-1663. This is particularly striking in the 1650s, with the chaotic and genuinely threatening civil wars of the Frondes a very recent memory, and Cromwellian Britain across the Channel as an awful warning of where such disorders could lead.

An exceptionally valuable medium for following the evolution of the king-as-sun imagery in France is provided by the libretti of the *ballets de cour* in the 1650s and 1660s. These texts are particularly revealing in that they give the possibility of studying a sequence of different representations of the same role – Le Soleil – danced by the King in different *ballets* which were all written by a single hand. Just such a sequence can be found in the work of the king's favourite ballet librettist, Isaac de Benserade.

Benserade wrote twenty-four *ballets de cour* from 1651 to 1681; the texts were published separately after the performances, each with a preface and generally some explanatory material. At the end of the century, these

---

[5] III. 3. 62-67 (p. 432).

[6] Néraudau, *L'Olympe du Roi-Soleil*, p. 33.

[7] Ovid, *Metamorphoses*, ed. F. J. Miller, 2 vols (repr. London/Cambridge, Mass., 1968-1971), I, p. 32 (Book I, lines 438-444).

[8] Thus the first such volume to be published after the fall of La Rochelle, Pierre Le Moyne's *Les Triomphes de Louys le Juste en la reduction des Rochelois et des autres rebelles de son royaume* (Reims, 1629), is permeated with images of Louis as the restorative sun, melting the snows of winter, causing flowers to bloom, and so on. This is notably different from Le Moyne's use of solar imagery in the middle decades of the century, discussed below (Section 2).

verse texts were all collected together and published as the second volume of Benserade's *Œuvres* (1698). It thus became possible for a contemporary reader to follow the complete evolution of the genre in Benserade's hands, and the portrayal of king and court within it.[9]

As Marie-Claude Canova-Green notes, the king danced a total of no less than sixty-seven different roles in Benserade's ballets, never dancing the same role more than three times. He took the part of Le Soleil in three ballets, and also that of Apollo once, each time at particularly important moments in his reign. On each occasion there is a significant change in the implications of the king-as-sun image.[10]

In the sumptuous *Ballet Royal de la Nuit* of 1653, the climax of the fourth and final part is the dawn and the rising of the sun, danced of course by the 15-year-old Louis. There is, strikingly, a double emphasis in the symbolism. The familiar topos of the anticipation of future glories, and a new Crusade, is stated but postponed: 'Quand i'auray dissipé les Ombres de la France...' ('After I have dissipated the darkness of France...') (I, p. 159; *Œuvres*, p. 64). Instead, the emphasis is on the sun's power to re-establish firm authority, an emphasis that is paralleled in the lines from Shakespeare quoted above. The Sun's first priority is to sort out the obscurity that has enveloped France. Lesser stars that triumphed in the absence of a clear focus of light are now forced to acknowledge the new sun's supremacy. At the start of this concluding tenth 'Entrée', the 'Recit de l'Aurore', L'Aurore sings:

---

[9] The texts are quoted from the modern edition of the *livrets*: I. de Benserade, *Ballets pour Louis XIV*, ed. Marie-Claude Canova-Green, 2 vols (Paris, 1997). The editor comments that 'les livrets des ballets de cour louis-quatorziens ne furent jamais – ou presque – réédités' (the texts of the *ballets de cour* written for Louis XIV were never – or almost never – reprinted), noting just one ballet that was reprinted in the seventeenth century (I, p. 36); yet she strangely makes no mention of the fact that the verse texts were all reprinted together in *Les Oeuvres de Monsieur de Bensserade*, 2 vols (Paris, 1698), which also had a Dutch edition in the same year ([Amsterdam?], Suivant la Copie à Paris, 1698). Vol. 2 of the *Oeuvres* consists of the 'Seconde Partie, Contenant les Vers des Balets dansez par Sa Majesté'. It is significant for the argument of this paper that late seventeenth-century readers could follow the consecutive development of the image in this way. For this reason, page references to the second volume of the *Œuvres*, 1698, have also been given for the quotations. On the development of the *ballet de cour* in general, see M.-F. Christout, *Le Ballet de cour de Louis XIV (1643-1672)* (Paris, 1967). The place of the *ballets de cour* among the other *fêtes de cour* (among them *entrée royale, carrousel, fête galante*, and other kinds of *fête*) is discussed in M.-C. Moine, *Les Fêtes à la Cour du Roi Soleil* (Paris, 1984).

[10] *Ballets pour Louis XIV*, I, p. 33 and n. 51.

La trouppe des Astres s'enfuit
Dés que ce grand Astre s'auance,
Les foibles clartez de la Nuict
Qui triomphoient en son absence
N'osent soûtenir sa presence;
     Tous ces volages feux s'en vont éuanoüys,
Le Soleil qui me suit c'est le jeune LOVIS.

                            (I, p. 157; *Œuvres*, p. 63)

The crowd of stars flee away as soon as this great star appears, the feeble lights of Night, which triumphed in his absence, do not dare to suffer his presence: all these inconstant flames fade and go, the Sun which follows me [the speaker is the Dawn] is young Louis.

Then, in the glorious conclusion, 'Le Roy, representant le Soleil leuant' ('The King, as the rising sun') makes it clear that there will be no more dissent:

Et qui ne voudroit pas auoüer ma lumiere
Sentira ma chaleur.

                            (I, p. 158; *Œuvres*, p. 63)

And whosoever will not admit my light shall feel my heat

– and that ambitious upstarts seeking power for themselves – like Phaëton – will be destroyed:

En montant sur mon Char i'ay pris soin d'écarter
Beaucoup de Phaëtons qui vouloient y monter,
Dans ce hardy dessein leur ambition tremble,
Chacun d'eux recognoist qu'il en faut trébucher,
Et qu'on verse toûjours si l'on n'est tout ensemble
Le Maistre, et le Cocher.

                            (I, p. 158; *Œuvres*, p. 64)

When I mounted my chariot I took care to sweep aside numerous Phaëtons who were attempting to mount it themselves; their ambition trembles in their bold design: they all recognise that they will inevitably stumble, and that one always crashes if one is not both master and driver.

Similarly the next year, in the *Ballet Royal des Nopces de Pelée et de Thetis* of 1654, the King comes in as Apollo at the start of the 'Premiere En-

trée' – the Apollo who slew the Python of revolt – and announces unambi-
guously:

> J'ay vaincu ce Python qui desoloit le monde,
> Ce terrible Serpent que l'Enfer, et la Fronde
> D'vn venin dangereux auoient assaisonné:
> La Reuolte en un mot ne me sçauroit plus nuire…

(I, p. 181; Œuvres, p. 66)

I have vanquished the Python that was laying waste the world, that terrible ser-
pent whose dangerous venom had been brewed by Hell and the Fronde: in a
word, Revolt can no longer harm me…

In the *Ballet Royal d'Hercule Amoureux* of 1662, just after the fall of
the over-ambitious *Surintendant des Finances* Foucquet and the definitive
inauguration of Louis's personal rule, the same points are made as in the
Ballet Royal de la Nuit, using the same imagery, but now with much more
of the sense, not of urgency, but of the presentation of a *fait accompli*. It is
worth noting that this was also the year in which Louis formally adopted the
emblem of the sun as his own. At the end of the *ballet*, the seventeenth 'Entrée' begins with six stanzas of verses 'Pour LE ROY, representant le Soleil', where both Phaëton and the 'petits feux' are dealt with briskly:

> Des secrets Phaëtons les grands et vastes soins
> Pouroient bien s'atirer la foudre et le nauffrage (…)

> Voyant plus par ses yeux que par les yeux d'Autruy,
> Il empeschera bien ces petits feux de luire…

(II, p. 594; Œuvres, p. 247)

The great ambitious schemes of secret Phaëtons may well draw on them thun-
derbolt and ruin (. . .) He [i.e. the Sun / the King] can see more with his own
eyes than through the eyes of anyone else, and he will stop these little lights
from shining…

Finally, when it comes to the *Ballet Royal de Flore* in 1669, and the
king's appearance as the Sun at the start of the first 'Entrée', the verses
'Pour SA MAJESTÉ, representant LE SOLEIL' make it clear that Louis's
glory is not only unchallenged but in every way irresistible: unlike Apollo,
no Phaëton can trouble him, and no Daphne elude his pursuit:

Ie doute qu'on le prenne auec vous sur le ton
  De Daphné, ny de Phaëton,
Luy trop ambitieux, Elle trop inhumaine,
Il n'est point là de piége où vous puissiez donner.
  Le moyen de s'imaginer,
Qu'vne Femme vous fuïe, et qu'vn Homme vous meine?

            (II, p. 834; *Œuvres*, p. 333)

No-one will behave to you like Daphne or Phaëton – he too ambitious, she too unkind; you cannot fall into either of those traps. It is impossible to imagine that any woman could resist your advances, or any man direct you.

By 1670, then, internal troubles in the state have been eliminated, and over-mighty subjects crushed. These traditional associations of solar imagery when applied to the monarch have become irrelevant, and the commonplace has evolved to its definitive form.

2. *Reciprocity*

The second aspect of the king-as-sun commonplace that I wish to consider is the idea of reciprocity between monarch and people that is often implicit within it, but again in complex and evolving forms. It was itself a common-place of monarchy that, along with absolute temporal supremacy, the king also had moral obligations to his people to reward them for their loyalty; this is, for example, strongly emphasized in the magnificent volume *De l'art de regner* that was published in 1665 by the famous Jesuit writer Pierre Le Moyne, as a huge and splendid folio dedicated to the king.[11] In terms of solar imagery, as the sun draws up water vapour from the rivers and lakes, so it also dispenses it back again in kindly fructifying rain. This image had in fact already been used by Le Moyne himself twenty years earlier, but ad-dressed to the current *Surintendant des Finances*, Nicolas de Bailleul. In his poem *Le Ministre sans reproche* of 1645, Le Moyne develops a lengthy parallel between the wise finance minister and the sun: everything the fi-nance minister extracts from the population through taxes, he returns in the form of national prosperity, security, and military success:

Il est comme un Soleil, pompeux distributeur
De fruits et de beaux jours, de calme et de bonheur (…)
Comme il leve à regret, ce qu'il leve il le rend;
Et par divers canaux sur l'Estat le répand (…)

---

[11] *De l'art de regner* (Paris, 1665).

Et les Imposts qui vont en ses coffres par grains,
Changez par la vertu de ses fidelles mains,
Sur le peuple et le Roy, quand la matiere est preste,
Retournent en richesse, en victoire, en conqueste.
        Ainsi l'Astre Intendant des Ans et des Saisons,
Dispense les vapeurs et les exhalaisons,
Ces humides tributs que pour le bien du monde,
Il leve également sur la terre et sur l'onde (…)
Il en dore les champs de fertiles moissons;
Et sans rien reserver pour ses propres usages,
Répand le tout en grains, en vins, en pasturages.[12]

He is like a sun, which nobly dispenses fruits and fine days, peace and happiness (…) He takes unwillingly, and what he takes he returns, and spreads
through the state by a variety of channels (…) and the taxes which come into
his coffers like seeds, changed by the skill of his faithful hands, return to the
people and the king, when the time is ripe, as riches, victories, and conquests.
So the great star which governs the seasons and the years gives back the mists
and vapours, those liquid tributes which, for the benefit of the whole world, it
raises equally from land and sea (…) With them, it gilds the fields with fertile
harvests; and without saving anything back for its own use, it dispenses it all in
grain, in wine, in pastures.

After the fall of Foucquet in 1661 it had become highly inappropriate to
give any such credit to a finance minister, and in any case the king by now
effectively had a monopoly on the application of solar imagery. So in a long
solar poem, *Le Soleil politique*, that accompanied *De l'art de regner* in
1665, Le Moyne transferred the same ideal to the king. The sun speaks, in
terms which must have struck many contemporary readers as implausibly
optimistic when related to their taxes:

Et le tribut leger, qui me vient de la plaine,
Sans contrainte exigé, comme payé sans peine,
N'est pas si-tost levé, qu'à ruisseaux je le rends,
En raisins aux costaux, en javelles aux champs.[13]

---

[12] Quoted from *Les Œuvres poetiques du P. Le Moyne* (Paris, 1671), p. 254 (=264);
first published separately as *Le Ministre sans reproche* (Paris, 1645).
[13] *Œuvres poetiques*, p. 239.

And the light tribute which comes to me from the plain, demanded without compulsion, and paid without difficulty, is no sooner raised that I give it back in streams, in grapes on the hills, and swathes in the fields.

If there was reflected in the solar imagery, at least in the early decades of Louis's reign, an underlying expectation of reciprocity from the king in return for the offerings of his people, that reciprocity also worked in the other direction: in return for the favours of the king, the subject was ex-pected to display appropriate practical gratitude. Although in theory the King, like the sun, was serenely transcendent in his universal benefaction, in practice there was a clear expectation of some kind of repayment for any benefits received. This attitude soon came to dominate the consideration of the mutual relationship between monarch and subject; but it was much less easy to express through the poetic repertoire of solar imagery. Poets tried hard to maintain the king-as-sun imagery, but there is a lack of adequate parallels in the natural world for the sun being rewarded by the earth, and the figurative language tends often to become incoherent, as we shall see.

When in 1673 Louis declared himself to be the protector of the Académie Française and moved it to the Louvre, the Académie of course responded with great enthusiasm, and announced that the subject of its annual poetry prize for that year was to be: 'Sur l'honneur que le Roy a fait à l'Académie Françoise, en acceptant la qualité de son Protecteur et la logeant au Louvre' ('On the honour which the King has bestowed on the Académie Française, in agreeing to be its Protector and housing it in the Louvre'). The entries were, as usual, later collected together and printed.[14]
Some of the poets do their best with solar imagery, turning the Louvre into the Temple of the Sun:

Venez voir aujourd'huy dans un grave appareil
Les Muses prendre place au temple du Soleil (…)
Ainsi de vos faveurs l'influence feconde,
Grand Roy, de beaux Esprits repeuplera le monde.

(pp. 238-239)

Come today and see the Muses, soberly clad, taking their place in the Temple of the Sun (…) Thus the fertile influence of your favour, great King, will re-populate the world with *beaux esprits.*

---

[14] *Recueil de plusieurs pieces d'eloquence et de poësie, presentées à l'Academie Françoise pour les prix de l'année 1673* (Paris, 1694). Page references are to this edition: the poems are on pp. 219-259.

Without exception, though, all are absolutely explicit that what the King requires (and will get) in return for his favour is an unceasing outpouring of praise and thanksgiving. As one of the anonymous authors puts it, giving up any attempt at literal coherence, the Academicians are:

> Quarante Astres rangez autour de leur Soleil,
> Qui, sans aucun déchet de leur clarté premiere,
> Versent de toutes parts des torrents de lumiere.
>
> (p. 244)

> Forty stars ranged around their Sun, who, without diminishing in any way their original brightness, pour forth floods of light from all directions.

This is a complete reversal of the familiar metaphorical commonplace so often found in the early years of Louis's reign, of the sun revealing its glory and making invisible the lesser stars. The conception of the dynamic role of the king-as-sun has by this point been transformed. Louis has no rivals to eclipse; instead, his universal *rayonnement* inspires a reciprocal flow of light (i.e. praise) back towards him.

This poem makes it clear in its conclusion that, in return for the King's favour, the celebration of his glory is not a voluntary expression of gratitude, but on the contrary an absolute imposed obligation:

> il faut que (…)
> Tu peignes ce Soleil au poinct de son midy:
> Car c'est à ta main seule, ô docte ACADEMIE,
> D'achever les tableaux d'une si belle vie;
> Et si les autres Arts n'en ont pas le pouvoir,
> Ton Roy par ses faveurs *t'impose ce devoir*.
>
> (p. 247, my emphasis)

> You are obliged to paint this Sun at the point of its meridian: for, O learned Academy, your hand alone can complete the depictions of so wonderful a life; and if the other arts are incapable of doing this, your King, through his favours, *imposes this duty upon you*.

The most high-profile of all the demonstrations of Louis's literary benevolence was the system of royal *pensions*, or 'gratifications', inaugurated by Colbert in 1662-63 and continued sporadically in subsequent decades. The largesse was extended to include foreign scholars, particularly those with a high international prestige such as Nicolaas Heinsius, Gronovius, and Huyghens. This was intended to convey the message of Louis's continental supremacy through the spectacle of his altruistic munificence to scholars and men of letters on a European scale. There is no doubt about its success, particularly as regards the king's reputation in France, and his impartial rewarding of intellectual virtue became established as an essential component of the royal image. Thus the Jesuit Dominique Bouhours's highly influential end-of-century anthology *Recueil de vers choisis* (first edition 1693) contains, among several similar works, a 'Portrait de Louis le Grand. Vers libres', by one M. Bosquillon. In neatly-turned verses, the author catalogues the unparalleled achievements of Louis, and it is revealing to see how the king's enlightened patronage of learning has its place along with his military glory, commercial expansion, and financial prosperity:

> D'un monde d'ennemis vainqueur de toutes parts,
> Tout chargé de lauriers, et tout couvert de gloire
> Faire monter la Paix sur son char de victoire;
>   Faire fleurir le commerce, les arts;
> *Enrichir les Sçavans*, étendre les sciences;
> Rétablir, conserver l'ordre dans ses Finances...[15]

(p. 188, my emphasis)

Everywhere victorious against a world of enemies, crowned with laurels and decked in glory, making Peace ride with him on his victory-chariot; causing trade and the arts to flourish; *enriching the learned*, expanding the sciences, re-establishing and maintaining order in his finances...

Just as the sun's rays shine over all, so Louis will 'enrichir les Sçavans' wherever they deserve it.

However, the reality was slightly different. There was an unspoken but brutally enforced *quid pro quo*: the recipients of the royal bounty were expected to show due gratitude, through substantial panegyrics in verse and prose, dedications of major works, or other suitable obsequience, or else the sun ceased to shine on them. The practical effects of these expectations can be seen in two brief case-studies, separated by twenty years, one involving a famous French figure and the other a celebrated scholar in the Low Countries.

Gilles Ménage (1613-1692) was one of the most outstanding scholars and men of letters of his time, an immensely learned and well-connected polymath and, simultaneously, a noted wit and successful poet in four languages (French, Italian, Latin, and Greek). It came as no surprise when, in the first round of royal *pensions* in 1663, he was awarded one of the largest

---

[15] Quoted here from the expanded edition of 1701: *Recueil de vers choisis, nouvelle edition* (Paris, 1701), ed. D. Bouhours, pp. 187-190.

sums of all (an annual 2,000 livres, the same as Pierre Corneille, and far more than almost all other writers). Yet Ménage was a complex personality, deeply sensitive about his personal independence, and often independent-spirited to the point of imprudence. While being very active in helping his many friends to gain *pensions* and, particularly, to respond appropriately, he flatly refused to make any public demonstration of flattery and humble gratitude himself; as he put it, that would be to diminish both the recipient and the giver. Instead, he provocatively dedicated his next two major works not to the king but to his two oldest friends, the scholar Emery Bigot and the lawyer Louis Nublé.[16] Such an attitude, however enlightened, was not at all well received by those in power: the real point of the *pensions* was not to reward excellence, but to purchase influence. Colbert was displeased; and Ménage's *pension* was withdrawn after 1665.[17]

Ménage was, typically, glad on a personal level to have made his point, but he remained highly active in helping others. In 1685 he was instrumental in gaining a generous *gratification* for a friend in the Low Countries, Johann-Georg Grævius (1632-1703), the most distinguished classical scholar and orator of his generation. It was clearly felt that, through his talents and his international fame, Grævius could prove extremely useful to France at this particularly delicate moment in European relations. However, in this case for once the underlying intentions failed, and the reactions in Paris show the reality behind the pretence of impartial generosity.

On receipt of his *gratification* Grævius did the expected thing and expressed his gratitude appropriately, but the gift failed to buy his political allegiance. Four years later he caused severe dismay in Paris by publicly celebrating the Glorious Revolution and the achievements of William III, with whom he had excellent relations.[18] The reaction of those in power, and the assumptions underlying the royal benevolence, are conveyed in a letter from Ménage to Pierre-Daniel Huet, the *précepteur du Dauphin*, dated 3 August 1689: 'Notre Ami Mr. Graevius a publié depuis peu un Panégyrique pour le Prince d'Orange: ce que je souhaitterois qu'il n'ait point fait: car outre que la Piéce n'est que médiocre, vous savez les obligations qu'il a au Roy'

---

[16] Respectively, his folio edition of Diogenes Laertius with his own immense scholarly commentary, *Laertii Diogenis de vitis, dogmatis et apophthegmatis eorum qui in philosophia claverunt libri X* (London, 1664), dedicated to Bigot, and his influential legal work *Juris Civilis amœnitates* (Paris, 1664), dedicated to Nublé.

[17] On this whole episode see R. Maber, 'Colbert and the scholars: Ménage, Huet, and the royal pensions of 1663', *Seventeenth-Century French Studies* 7 (1985), pp. 106-114.

[18] In his *Oratio de auspicatissima Expeditione Britannica: cum Guilielmus, Arausionensis Princeps, Angliæ, Galliæ et Hiberniæ Rex inauguraretur* (London, 1689), published also in the same year in English and Dutch.

('Our friend Mr Grævius has recently published a panegyric of the Prince of Orange, which I wish he had not done; for, apart from the fact that it is only a mediocre piece, you know the obligations that he has towards the king').[19]

Huet replied on 8 August, agreeing with Ménage but expressing sympathy for Grævius's difficult position in a way which is very revealing of the problems that Louis's international pretensions could cause: 'Je suis bien de votre avis, que notre amy Mr. Graevius, aprés les graces qu'il a receues du Roy ne devoit pas faire le Panégyrique du Prince d'Orange / mais peut estre y a t il esté obligé pour effacer l'opinion que ces graces mêmes avoient donnée de luy' ('I do agree with you, that our friend Mr Grævius, after the favours which he has received from the king, should not have written the panegyric of the Prince of Orange / but perhaps he was forced to do so, to counter the bad impression that these very favours had given of him').[20]

Nevertheless, the matter was not taken lightly by those in power, and Ménage was still concerned for his friend. He is recorded as returning to the subject in conversation: 'Je suis faché de ce que mon ami M. Grævius à qui M. le Duc de Montausier a fait donner une grosse pension de la Cour, a fait un Panégyrique du Prince d'Orange. On dit que ses Maîtres l'y ont obligé: mais il devoit s'en exempter. Cela lui fait tort' ('I am upset that my friend M. Grævius, for whom the Duc de Montausier obtained a large *pension* from the Court, has written a panegyric of the Prince of Orange. I am told that his masters forced him to do it: but he should have got out of it. It damages him').[21] As the experiences of Ménage and Grævius show, there was a hard-edged realism that underlay the spectacular public image of the Sun King.

The image of the *Roi-Soleil* was arguably the most successful of all commonplaces of power in the seventeenth century; and yet, as Frans-Willem Korsten has brought out in his essay in this volume, it was a period in which

---

[19] Biblioteca Medicea Laurenziana, Florence, MS Ashburnham 1866. 1277. These letters from Ménage (but not the replies) are reprinted, not always entirely accurately, in G. Ménage, *Lettres inédites à Pierre-Daniel Huet (1659-1692), publiées d'après le dossier Ashburnham 1866 de la Bibliothèque Laurentienne de Florence*, ed. L. Caminiti Pennarola (Naples, 1993); here no. 222, p. 258. The '/' sign is a typical mark of Huet's idiosyncratic punctuation.
[20] BNF, Paris, MS n.a.f. 1341, fol. 288r.
[21] *Ménagiana*, 4 vols (Paris, 1729), II, p. 128. In the event, Grævius took no notice of the official French disapproval and maintained his public support of William and Mary. When Queen Mary died on 28 December 1694, he responded with a laudatory funeral oration, *A Funeral Oration (. . .) upon the Death of Mary II* (London, 1695; editions of the original Latin *Oratio* were published in Utrecht and Helmstedt in 1695); and then he followed it up with another on the death of William: *In obitum Guilielmi III (. . .) oratio* (Utrecht, 1702).

even the most familiar of commonplaces could contain within them unexpected complexities. The process of evolution of the Roi-Soleil image in the first decade of that sun's rising was not forgotten forty years later; on the contrary, with the publication in 1698 of all Benserade's ballet verses in chronological order in the second volume of his *Œuvres*, its development could be followed more clearly than ever before.[22]

As we have seen, however, in an important later development, when the solar imagery is adapted to illustrate the obligations of those that receive the benefits of royal munificence, its literal coherence breaks down. When, echoing the reality of royal largesse, poets strive to emphasise the subject's duty of praise and thanksgiving, there is no parallel to be found in the real world: in nature, we may admire the sun but it demands nothing of us, and no human response makes the slightest difference to it. Despite the persistence of solar iconography, the image presented of the king has mutated from the sun to something very closely approaching the portrayal of God. After all, as the psalmist had sung, 'For the Lord God is a sun and shield: the Lord will give grace and glory…'.[23] One is reminded of La Bruyère's extraordinary description of the courtiers in the chapel at Versailles, turning their backs on the altar of God to face and adore the King:

> Les grands de la nation s'assemblent tous les jours, à une certaine heure, dans un temple qu'ils nomment église; il y a au fond de ce temple un autel consacré à leur Dieu, où un prêtre célèbre des mystères qu'ils appellent saints, sacrés et redoutables; les grands forment un vaste cercle au pied de cet autel, et paraissent debout, le dos tourné directement aux prêtres et aux saints mystères, et les faces élevées vers leur roi, que l'on voit à genoux sur une tribune, et à qui ils semblent avoir tout l'esprit et tout le cœur appliqué (…) ce peuple paraît adorer le prince, et le prince adorer Dieu.[24]

> The Grandees go every day at a certain hour to a Temple they call a Church, at the upper end of the Temple there stands an Altar consecrated to their God, where the Preacher celebrates the Mysteries which they call holy, sacred and dreadful. The Great men make a vast circle at the foot of the Altar, standing with their backs turn'd to the Preacher and the Holy Mysteries, and their faces erected towards their King, who is seen on his Knees upon a Throne, to whom

---

[22] See note 8 above.

[23] Authorised Version, Psalm 84. 11.

[24] *Les Caractères*, 'De la Cour', no. 74; J. de La Bruyère, *Œuvres complètes*, ed. J. Benda (Paris, 1951), pp. 239-240.

they seem to apply all their hearts and all their devotion (…) the people appear adoring their Prince, and their Prince adoring God.[25]

The implications latent in the image of the Roi-Soleil are powerful indeed. Through this analysis of the evolution of the image's application, and also of the concept of reciprocity contained within it, I hope to have contributed to an understanding of how it came to gain such extraordinary force, both as a statement of authority, and a means of persuasion.

---

[25] *The Characters, or the Manners of the Age. By Monsieur De La Bruyere, of the French Academy. Made English by several hands* (London, 1699).

THE REPRESENTATION OF PEACE IN OPERA
AND MACHINE PLAY PROLOGUES (1660-1680)

Jan Clarke

This article will examine representations of peace in the prologues to a number of seventeenth-century theatrical works performed during the majority of Louis XIV. This choice of topic might seem surprising, since the commonplace view of Louis amongst subsequent critics at least is that he was a warmonger, and France was, indeed, only at peace for some twenty years of his seventy-two year reign. However, in the works we will be considering, the emphasis is not so much on Louis as a wager of war but as a bringer of peace, in what is an ingenious and almost perverse inversion of truth for political purposes.

The works in which this type of propaganda is most evident belong to the spectacular genres of opera and machine play. The first operas to be produced in France were Italian, brought to his adopted land by Mazarin in the 1640s. These triggered a nationalist reaction in the form of the machine play, in which scenes, usually of tragedy, were interspersed with spectacular episodes involving the use of stage machinery, most often to facilitate the appearance of divinities in *gloires*,[1] clouds or other flying machines. Changes of decor were fundamental, causing such works to stand in marked contrast to the 'classical' plays that were increasingly the norm. Music was also of vital importance, being used to cover the noise of scene changes as well as to provide a source of entertainment in its own right.[2]

The step from machine play to French opera was a short one, and the first French opera to be performed in public was *Pomone*, given by Pierre Perrin's *Académie de musique* in 1671. The popularity of music and spectacle did not go unnoticed, and the ambitious court composer Jean-Baptiste Lully soon gained control of Perrin's Academy, thereafter known as the

---

[1] 'In plays and other spectacles, the raised and illuminated area where the open sky is represented with mythological divinities' (*Dictionnaire de l'Académie-Française* (1694), my translation.
[2] See C. Delmas, *Mythologie et mythe dans le théâtre français (1650-1676)* (Geneva, 1985) pp. 55, 77; J. Clarke, *The Guénégaud Theatre in Paris (1673-1680). Volume Three: the Demise of the Machine Play* (Lewiston-Queenston-Lampeter, 2007), pp. 65-88.

Académie royale de musique, and set about developing French opera.[3] The King and Colbert supported Lully in this undertaking, which can be seen as part of a general policy of employing the arts to the greater glory of the Sun King.[4] It is not surprising, therefore, that we find in opera the greatest number of references to the political events of the day. For the most part, such direct political comment is contained within the prologues that serve as introductions to the operas or machine plays, and which frequently have only a peripheral connection with them; the texts or libretti themselves tend to make their points more allusively. Occasionally, though, explicit political content is included elsewhere, in *intermèdes*, epilogues or dedications, and these will also be considered where relevant. Machine plays and operas were spectacular works where the visual elements were just as important as the acoustic (whether spoken or sung). One of my concerns, therefore, will be to demonstrate how the spectacle itself served to underline the message to be disseminated, by means of decors, tableaux or machines.

Operas and, to a lesser extent machine plays, had multiple audiences, since they were frequently created at court before being given for the general public in town. At court, they would have been directed primarily at the King himself, their most privileged spectator, who sat in the centre of any assembly, surrounded by his courtiers, as much if not more of an attraction than the play itself. It is hardly remarkable, then, that works produced in such circumstances, and which benefited from direct financial subsidy from the King,[5] should have sought to reinforce the self-conscious construction of his identity, whether as Mars or Apollo, exculpating him where necessary, and placing a positive spin on even the most unfortunate turns of events. Nowhere is this more evident than in the presentation of conflict as stemming from a desire for peace. The courtiers would have colluded in this flattery, since their position depended directly on the beneficence of their monarch, and (in the case of the men at least) their *gloire* was similarly dependent on military success.[6]

---

[3] See J. Clarke, *The Guénégaud Theatre in Paris (1673-1680). Volume One: Founding, Design and Production* (Lewiston-Queenston-Lampeter, 1998), pp. 13-16; Clarke, *The Guénégaud Theatre in Paris (1673-1680). Volume Three*, pp. 228-234.

[4] For a full discussion of this topic, see R. M. Isherwood, *Music in the Service of the King: France in the Seventeenth Century* (Ithaca, 1973).

[5] From 1675 onwards, all Lully's operas were created at court so that Louis could attend rehearsals as well as premieres and subsequent performances, with the King paying for all rehearsal and preparation expenses (J. de La Gorce, *L'Opéra à Paris au temps de Louis XIV: histoire d'un théâtre* (Paris, 1992), p. 54); J. de La Gorce, *Carlo Vigarani* (Paris, 2005), pp. 171-172.

[6] Members of the *noblesse d'épée* were expected to provide military service for the King. *Gloire* in this period was defined as the 'honour, praise, esteem, reputation

The situation was rather different when the works were performed in Paris. Here audiences were more mixed, including aristocrats, bourgeois, soldiers, women, and even valets and servants,[7] all of whom would have been involved in some way in the war effort, and who would each have received the messages transmitted in subtly different ways. Moreover, war and theatre were both seasonal occupations, and interconnected ones at that, with the theatrical season proper only beginning once the campaigns were over for the winter and the military had returned to town.[8] This is reflected in the works, which contain frequent references to the inclement weather and the need to enjoy love and pleasures, both as temporary respites from conflict and as pauses in which to plan future campaigns. In such circumstances, the works may also have provided audience members with a degree of comfort along with the glorification of their King, since they seek to demonstrate that the causes for which they or their relatives are fighting and dying or, more prosaically, are paying, are all worthwhile. Hence the emphasis is on peace rather than war; if French expansionism is, in some cases, presented as justified, it is as proof of the greater glory not only of the King but also of the entire French nation for which he stands and of which the audience members are also a part.

Louis XIV's reign was a long one, spanning seven decades, and the list of spectacular works produced during it is equally as long. As is well known, the King was an enthusiastic supporter of theatre and ballet in his youth. However, in the latter part of his reign he came to spurn the art forms he once had championed, and did not even attend those plays given at court for the benefit of the younger generation.[9] The present study is limited, therefore, to those works performed following the end of the War with Spain in 1659, and during the course of what have been described as Louis's 'wars of *gloire*': the War of Devolution and the Dutch War, which ended almost twenty years later.[10]

---

proceeding from a person's merit, the excellence of his actions or works' (*Dictionnaire de l'Académie Française*, 1694, my translation).

[7] See J. Lough, *Paris Theatre Audiences in the Seventeenth and Eighteenth Centuries* (London, 1957).

[8] S. Chappuzeau, *Le Théâtre français* (Lyon, 1674) (repr. Plan de la Tour (Var), 1985), p. 59.

[9] For an analysis of the King's declining theatre attendance, see J. Clarke, 'The Expulsion of the Italians from the Hôtel de Bourgogne in 1697', *Seventeenth-Century French Studies* 14 (1992), pp. 97-117 (pp. 103-104).

[10] This term is taken from J. A. Lynn, *The Wars of Louis XIV 1667-1714* (Harlow, 1999), chapter 4.

The War with Spain is not generally included among Louis's wars of glory since he did not start it himself.[11] He did, though, contribute to its ending by virtue of his marriage to the Infanta Maria Theresa. Indeed, Mazarin reputedly declared to Louis's mother, Anne of Austria, herself a Spanish princess: 'I bring you peace and the Infanta'. Accordingly, the war came to an end with the Treaty of the Pyrenees in November 1659, and Louis and Maria Theresa were married by proxy on 3 June 1660 and in person six days later.[12] Later that same year, the marquis de Sourdéac decided to give a performance at his Normandy home in honour of the royal couple. He commissioned a machine play from no lesser a dramatist than Pierre Corneille, had it prepared by the Troupe du Marais, and the resulting work, *La Conquête de la Toison d'or* was premiered before the King and his bride at Neufbourg in November 1660, then given in Paris in February 1661.[13]

The introduction to the Prologue of *La Toison d'or* states explicitly that, since the play was produced to celebrate the peace and the marriage, it would have been impossible for the author to select anything else as its subject.[14] Thus, the decor for the Prologue shows a 'Païs ruïné par les guerres' '([C]ountryside ruined by wars'),[15] with a similarly damaged town in the distance, intended to symbolise 'le pitoyable estat où la France estoit réduîte avant cette faveur du Ciel, qu'elle a si long temps souhaitée, et dont la bonté de son illustre Monarque la fait jouir à present' ('the pitiful state to which France had been reduced before that favour of the Heavens she had so long desired, and which the goodness of her illustrious monarch causes her to enjoy at present' (pp. 114-115)). The action opens with a conversation between France and Victory. France complains that, although Victory is considered fickle, she has followed France faithfully. Thanks to her, France is now esteemed and feared to the ends of the earth, but still she longs for peace and grieves at the price she has had to pay, which sentiment is expressed in surprisingly strong terms:

---

[11] The War with Spain was embarked upon by the King's father, Louis XIII, in 1635.

[12] A. Fraser, *Love and Louis XIV: the Women in the Life of the Sun King* (London, 2006), pp. 53-57.

[13] For information on the production of *La Conquête de la Toison d'or*, see P. Corneille, *La Conquête de la Toison d'or*, ed. M.-F. Wagner (Paris, 1998), Introduction.

[14] Ibid., p. 114.

[15] All translations are my own.

L'Estat est florissant, mais les Peuples gemissent,
Leurs membres décharnez courbent sous mes haus faits
Et la gloire du Trône accable les Sujets (p. 116).

The State is flourishing but the people are moaning, / Their fleshless limbs
bend under my great deeds / And the glory of the Throne crushes its subjects.

The consequences of war are also chillingly evoked: 'Je me lasse de voir
mes villes désolées, / Mes habitants pillez, mes campagnes brûlées' ('I am
tired of seeing my towns desolate, / My inhabitants pillaged, my countryside burned' (ibid.)).[16] Such complaints might be seen as criticism of royal
policy; Louis is, however, in fact being praised for having responded to the
people's wishes by bringing the war to an end. As France tells Victory:

Mon Roy que vous rendez le plus puissant des Rois,
(...)
De ce glorieux Trône où brille sa vertu
Il tend sa main auguste à son Peuple abatu;
Et comme à tous momens la commune misere
Rappelle en son grand coeur les tendresses de pere,
Ce cœur se laisse vaincre aux vœux que j'ay formez
(pp. 116-117)[.]

My King whom you have made the most powerful of Kings, / […] / From that
glorious throne where his virtue shines / Holds out his hand towards his down-
cast people; / And as at all times the common misery / Awakens in his great
heart a father-like tenderness, / His heart allows itself to be vanquished by the
wishes I have formed[.]

The 'Ciel' then opened (the shutters masking the upper stage were
drawn aside) to reveal Mars 'en posture menaçante, un pied en l'air, et
l'autre porté sur son Estoille' ('in a menacing posture, with one foot in the
air and the other born on his star' (i.e. his machine)), who flies down to rep-
rimand France. He calls her ungrateful and maintains that with just five or
ten years' more effort she would have had all of Europe in her power and
been able to define her own borders. An intriguing point made in support of
this assertion is that the whole of Europe is learning France's language as a
preliminary to adopting her laws. Mars then reveals a tableau in which

---

[16] France was repeatedly invaded by enemy forces during the war with Spain, with
Spanish troops even coming within fifty miles of Paris in 1636.

Peace is shown, 'prisonnière dans son Palais, entre les mains de la Discorde et de l'Envie' ('prisoner in her palace in the hands of Discord and Envy' (p. 118)). This palace, which was no doubt also revealed on the upper stage, has columns made of canons with mortars for bases and bullets for capitals. It is decorated with trumpets and drums (the musical instruments associated with war), and has panels with military trophies.

Peace, languishing in her chains, is confident that she will soon be helped by a god even more powerful than Mars, namely Hymen, the god of marriage. This happy state of affairs is credited to Anne of Austria, who was a sister of the bride's father, Philip IV of Spain: 'Ses tendresses de sœur, ses tendresses de mere, / Peuvent tout sur un fils, peuvent tout sur un frère' ('Her tenderness as a sister and a mother, / can have every influence on a son and a brother' (p. 119)). Peace is also fulsome in her praise of the negotiators who have effected the reconciliation between the two countries, whom she describes as: 'Les sublimes intelligences / Qui de leurs grands Estats meuvent les vastes corps' ('The sublime intelligences / Who move the vast bodies of their great States' (pp. 119-120)). Hymen has been waiting for their agreement to liberate her, since without it, his authority would not be recognised, but Peace now concludes with the triumphant cry: 'France, ouvre ton coeur à la joye, / Et vous, Monstres, fuyez, ce grand jour est venu' ('France open your heart to joy / And you, Monsters [Envy and Discord] flee, this great day has come' (p. 120)).

At this signal, Hymen appears holding a shield decorated with a portrait of the Queen. He shows this to Discord and Envy, 'qui trébuchent aussi-tost aux Enfers' ('who immediately fall down into hell'), presumably through a trap in the upper stage floor. He then waves it at the chains with which Peace is bound and they break and fall. The newly-liberated Peace tells Hymen they must go down to satisfy the wishes of people on earth. Immediately, 'Quatre Amours descendent du Ciel' ('Four cherubs descend from the heavens'), and carry Peace and Hymen down from the upper stage to the main stage. The cherubs then return 'dans les nuës' ('into the clouds') by means of a complicated crossing flight (pp. 121-122).[17] On the lower stage, a grateful France welcomes Peace as:

Adorable souhait des Peuples gemissans,
Feconde seureté des travaux innocens,
Infatigable appuy du pouvoir legitime,

---

[17] Crossing flights were particularly difficult to effect and are invariably signalled in the *livres de sujet* or explanatory booklets that were sold to accompany spectacular productions.

Qui dissipez le trouble, et détruisez le crime,
Protrectrice des Arts, mere des beaux loisirs (p. 122)[.]

Adorable desire of a groaning people, / Fertile security of innocent labours, / Tireless supporter of legitimate power, / Who dissipates care and destroys crime, / Protector of the Arts and mother of leisure pursuits[.]

Peace replies that France should 'Fais éclater [s]a joye en de pompeux spectacles' ('Cause [her] joy to burst forth in sumptuous spectacles'),[18] but the latter protests that theatrical production is somewhat difficult in the circumstances: 'Est-il effort humain qui jamais ait tiré / Des spectacles pompeux d'un sein si déchiré?' ('Has human effort ever succeeded in drawing / Sumptuous spectacles from so torn a breast?'). Hymen, however, promises to help:

Nous serons à l'envy nous-mesmes ton soutien.
Porte sur ton Theatre une chaleur si belle,
Que des plus heureux temps l'éclat s'y renouvelle[.]

We will give you our entire support. / Bring to your theatre so beautiful a warmth, / That the brilliance of happier times will be renewed there[.]

Victory now recognises that she is superfluous to requirements and offers to disappear, but Peace replies consolingly that France can always send her to her friends, and that in any case war will inevitably give way to other forms of combat:

D'ailleurs, mon plus grand calme aime l'inquietude
Des combats de prudence, et des combats d'estude,
Il ouvre un champ plus large à des guerres d'esprit [.]

Besides, my greater calm likes the agitation
Of combats of prudence and combats of learning,
It opens the way to wars of the mind' (p. 123).

---

[18] Interestingly, Peace additionally advises France that she has no need to imitate foreign art forms: 'Ton Theatre a souvent d'assez riches couleurs / Pour n'avoir pas besoin d'emprunter rien ailleurs' ('Your theatre has rich enough colours / Not to need to borrow from elsewhere'). This has been seen as a rejection of the Italian-style spectacle that had been popular under both Mazarin and Richelieu (Corneille, *La Conquête*, p. 122, n. 154).

Victory agrees, therefore, to continue to serve France and the King's brother, Philippe d'Orléans, in particular, but only outside France, in what may be a first hint in these works of French expansionism: 'Et sous d'autres climats couronner ses hauts faits / Des lauriers qu'en ceux-cy luy dérobe la Paix' ('And to crown his high deeds in other climes / With the laurels that in these he is robbed of by Peace' (p. 124)).

Hymen, for his part, intends to give Philippe 'un prix de toute autre valeur, / Que ceux que tu promets avec tant de chaleur' ('a prize of far greater value / Than those you promise with such warmth' (p. 124)). This refers to the prince's engagement in August 1660 to Henrietta, sister of Charles II of England (the couple would be married in March 1661).[19] Thus, Hymen is able to tell France that, thanks to Peace, at the end of the war, Spain and England 'Te livre[nt] par ma main leurs plus rares tresors' ('Give up to you, by my hand, their richest treasures'), namely Maria Theresa and Henrietta (p. 124). Finally, Peace asks Hymen to keep his word and 'par de nouveaux miracles' ('by new miracles') use 'ce chef-d'œuvre des Cieux' ('this masterpiece of the heavens'; the portrait of Maria Theresa) to change 'la face de ces lieux' ('the appearance of this place') so that the play can begin (p. 124). Hymen obediently proffers his shield once more and the stage picture changes from a scene of desolation to a magnificent garden. Such visible scene changes, known as *changements à vue*, were a defining feature of both machine play and opera and were particularly appreciated by the public, no doubt for their absolute contrast with the neo-classical conventions that were increasingly the norm.

The Treaty of the Pyrenees that brought an end to the war with Spain and concluded in the King's marriage was followed by eight years of peace, which the aspirations of the young Louis – defined by John Lynn as consisting of a desire to prove himself in a great war, expand his domains and add brilliance to his *gloire* – rendered increasingly fragile. According to Lynn, Louis hoped to pick up territory that had once belonged to Spain (in particular the Spanish Netherlands), in which ambition he was encouraged by the young noblemen who surrounded him at court, as well as by his general Turenne, who had never agreed with Mazarin's decision to end the Spanish war in 1659, and who, like Mars in *La Toison d'or*, believed that France could have conquered the Spanish Netherlands with one more campaign.[20]

The death of Philip IV of Spain in 1665 provided Louis with the pretext he needed. As part of the Treaty of the Pyrenees, Maria Theresa had forfeited her claim to any Spanish inheritance contingent on the payment of her

---

[19] P. Erlanger, *Monsieur, frère de Louis XIV* (Paris, 1981), pp. 59-60
[20] Lynn, *The Wars of Louis XIV*, p. 33.

dowry. However, this had never been received, allowing Louis to assert that her renunciation was null and void and that several provinces in the Spanish Netherlands should 'devolve' upon his wife.[21] To prove his point, he led an army into the Spanish Netherlands in May 1667, thereby embarking on what would become known as the War of Devolution. In January 1668, he concluded a treaty with the Holy Roman Emperor, Leopold I, concerning the inheritance of the new King Carlos II of Spain, and in February, his general Condé successfully invaded the Franche-Comté. The Dutch patched together a Triple Alliance with England and Sweden to resist him, and Louis grudgingly accepted peace, with the Treaty of Aix-la-Chapelle being signed in May. However, this was only ever a temporary cessation in hostilities, and, as Lynn so memorably puts it: 'He would be back'.[22]

Some nine months after the Treaty of Aix-la-Chapelle, another machine play featuring Peace was performed in Paris: *La Fête de Vénus* by Claude Boyer, which, when published, was dedicated to the King's sister-in-law, Henriette d'Angleterre.[23] *La Fête de Vénus* and *La Toison d'or* were both performed during times of peace. *La Fête de Vénus* differs, though, from the earlier machine play in its expression of an awareness of the precariousness of the current peace and a concomitant desire to prepare its spectators for war. A question that might be asked is why the play should have propounded such a message when it was first performed in a public theatre that was seemingly independent of court control. However, the fact of its dedication to the King's much-loved sister-in-law suggests that its author shared the prevalent desire to ingratiate himself at court, which may go some way to explaining the Prologue, unless it were quite simply commissioned.

As the curtain goes up, Peace is revealed lying on a couch of grass and flowers, shaded by palm, olive and laurel trees, and enjoying the music of flutes and bagpipes. Victory and Renown fly down to interrupt this pastoral idyll, the latter blowing her proverbial trumpet, causing Peace to exclaim with justifiable irritation: 'Quel est ce bruit affreux, quel Dieu mal à propos / Ose troubler la Paix dans le sein du repos?' ('What is that terrible noise, what inconvenient god / Dares trouble Peace while she is resting?' (p. 1)). Victory sings as she descends:

---

[21] These were provinces where the law held that a daughter from a first marriage could claim a share of her father's possessions even though there was a son from a second marriage.

[22] See Lynn, *The Wars of Louis XIV*, pp. 33-34.

[23] C. Boyer, *La Fête de Vénus* (Paris, 1669) This was shortly before Henriette was to play a major part in negotiations leading up to the signing of the secret Treaty of Dover between Louis and Charles II of England in May 1670.

Croissez Palmes, croissez Lauriers,
Louïs porte si loin sa gloire et son empire,
Que s'il faut couronner tous ses exploits guerriers,
A peine pourrez-vous suffire. (p. 2)

Grow palms, grow laurels, / Louis carries so far his glory and his empire, / That
if we must crown his warlike exploits, / You will scarcely be sufficient.

These two terms of *gloire* and *empire* will reappear frequently in the prologues under discussion. The prevalence of the first lends support to the
categorisation of these early conflicts as the wars of Louis's *gloire*, while
the use of the second is, I would contend, indicative of the expansionist nature of the King's foreign policy.
Peace accuses Victory of tempting Louis to abandon her:

Vous croyez donc qu'un jeune Roy
Cherche à vous rendre vostre employ,
Et que n'aymant que vous dans le fonds de son ame
N'écoutant rien que sa valeur,
Il ne faut que s'offrir encore à ce Vainqueur,
Pour réveiller toute sa flâme. (p. 2)

You think, then, that a young King / Seeks to give you back your employment,
/ And that loving nothing but you in the depths of his soul, / Listening to nothing but his valour, / You only have to offer yourself to this Conqueror, / To re-
awaken his whole flame.

Victory retorts that any such change in policy is rational rather than emotional, since Louis would rather be considered a conqueror than a peacemaker (p. 2). Peace defines the 'affreuses beautez' ('terrible beauties') of
Victory's appeal as consisting of 'la gloire qui suit la fureur des combats: /
Ce mélange de sang, de poussiere, et de larmes', which can only be otained
by 'mille morts' ('the glory that follows the fury of combats: / That mixture
of blood, dust and tears'; 'a thousand deaths' (p. 3)). She, on the other hand,
offers 'cette gloire tranquille / Que la Vertu produit au milieu du repos'
('[T]hat tranquil glory / Produced by Virtue in the midst of repose' (p. 3)),
which may not be heroic or glorious, but which:

Fait fleurir les Loix, les Arts, et l'Innocence,
Faire regner par tout l'honneur et la vertu,
Et tenir sous le joug d'une juste puissance
L'injustice étonnée, et le vice abattu[.] (p. 3)

Causes Laws, Arts and Innocence to flourish, / Causes honour and virtue to reign everywhere, / And holds beneath the yolk of a just power / Injustice confounded and vice overthrown[.]

Under such a system, valour would be employed only to 'calmer les tempestes' ('calm the tempests'), and the Hero would be restrained by the duties of the King, coming eventually to prefer 'Une grandeur paisible, un glorieux repos' ('a peaceful grandeur and a glorious repose') to the delights of conquest. This Peace presents as being the true nature of glory: the valour of kings lies in keeping themselves under control, rather than in acquiring 'tout l'Empire du monde' ('all the Empire of the world' (p. 3)).

Inevitably, Victory is not convinced, maintaining that war is part of the French way of life:

Croyez-en son courage, et ne pretendez pas
De desarmer ainsi tant de braves Soldats
Qu'enfante à son grand Roy la belliqueuse France;
Et de corrompre leur vaillance
Par vos infidelles appas. (p. 4)

Believe in his courage, and do not aspire / To disarm the many brave Soldiers / Whom bellicose France breeds for her great King; / And corrupt their valour / By your faithless attractions.

With increasing desperation, Peace finally maintains that she represents 'cette gloire suprême' for which many heroes are willing to die, and accuses Victory of presenting the means of achieving it (war) as being better than the glory (peace) itself. She further adds that Louis will not trust Victory because she is inconstant, causing the latter to cite Louis's achievements in winter as well as in summer as signs of her fidelity — perhaps a reference to Condé's February invasion of the Franche-Comté.[24]

The two goddesses having arrived at an impasse, Mercury descends to settle their dispute, but refuses to decide between them: 'Chacune a ses honneurs, son temps, et son employ, / Chacune sert LOÜIS, sa gloire, et son Empire' ('Each has her honours, her time and her employment, / Each serves Louis, his glory and his Empire' (p. 6)). He tells them to work together, instructing Victory to serve Peace:

---

[24] Lynn, *The Wars of Louis XIV*, p. 108.

Mais aussi c'est à la Victoire
A fonder pour jamais avec ses propres mains
Et vostre Empire et vostre gloire. (p. 6)

But it is up to Victory / To found for ever with her own hands / Your Empire
and your glory.

In other words, the new war looming on the horizon is presented as being
justified since its ostensible aim is peace — a commonplace if ever there
was one. Finally, he transmits a message from Cupid to the King: there is
more than one way of acquiring glory and the King should take advantage
of peace to conquer hearts, thereby combining glory with pleasure (p. 6).
This association of peace with love and leisure activities is another trope
that will regularly reappear.

    In January 1672, a second opera was performed by Perrin's Academy
of Music: Gilbert's *Peines et plaisirs de l'amour*. This work was similarly
given during the brief peace between the end of the War of Devolution and
the start of the Dutch War, and its Prologue reiterates many of the themes
found in Boyer's machine play, together with an expression of France's
right to expand her empire. Thus, Venus describes Louis as a 'un nouvel
Apollon' ('a new Apollo') and 'le Soleil des François' ('the Sun of the
French'), who eventually 'de tout cet Univers ne fera qu'une Cour' ('will
make a single Court out of the entire Universe'), and Renown claims to
have spread his name eastwards so that 'Inde' will one day form part of his
domain.[25] This is probably a reference to the Indian Ocean Strategy of the
Minister of Finance, Colbert, to whom the work was dedicated, since, as
Glenn Joseph Ames puts it, the decade 1664-74 was crucial 'as regards the
attempt of the French Crown to establish itself as a viable power in the rich
Indian Ocean trade'.[26] A French fleet had, in fact, set sail in March 1670
with the aim of founding fortified establishments on Ceylon and in Indone-
sia so as to ensure France's commercial and military position in the region.
It reached Surat in October 1671, where its commander took the title of
viceroy, and succeeded in expelling a Dutch garrison and reclaiming the
Malabar coastal town of Alicot (ibid., pp. 548-551).

    In *Les Peines et les plaisirs*, this commercial and military project is
equated with what we might call a 'hearts and minds' campaign. Thus, Venus instructs her cherubs to go 'sur la Terre et sur l'Onde / Dire qu'il a con-

---

[25] G. Gilbert, *Les Peines et les plaisirs de l'amour* (Amsterdam, 1705).
[26] G. J. Ames, 'Colbert's Indian Ocean Strategy of 1664-1674: a Reappraisal',
French Historical Studies 16 (1990), pp. 536-559 (p. 537).

quis les coeurs de tout le Monde' ('over Land and Sea / to say that he [Louis] has conquered the hearts of the whole World' (p. 6)), and Renown refers to the King's victories both past and present:

Déja les habitans et du Nil et du Tage,[27]
Et les plus éloignez de l'Empire François;
Les Sauvages sans Loix
Viennent lui rendre hommage. (p. 6)

Already the people of the Nile and the Tagus / And the furthest reaches of the French Empire, / The Lawless Savages, / Come to pay him homage.

To demonstrate this point, representatives of 'les Nations', professing themselves 'Charmez de sa valeur' ('[C]harmed by his valour'), come 'Pour divertir en paix ce Roi victorieux' ('To entertain in peace this victorious King'), and the Prologue concludes with a ballet featuring Spaniards, Indians, Moors and Egyptians.

The references to Egypt and Egyptians are particularly topical. By 1671, it was clear that Louis was preparing to go to war against the Dutch in Europe. Alarmed, the philosopher Leibniz came up with an ingenious scheme to distract the King by inviting him to take Egypt as a stepping stone towards the conquest of the Dutch East Indies. His plan was submitted to the King in the winter of 1671 by means of a *placet*, and Leibniz himself arrived in Paris in February 1672.[28] Sadly for Europe, if not for Egypt, his proposal was ignored, but some members of the audience would surely have recognised the significance of these allusions to Egypt, even if the references to its inhabitants' 'hommage' are with hindsight a little premature.

The much predicted war was not long in coming: March 1672 saw the outbreak of hostilities between the English and the Dutch, which Louis

---

[27] The Tagus flows through Spain and Portugal.

[28] Leibniz's plan is most clearly outlined in a second *placet* addressed to the King, whom he did not actually succeed in meeting: 'La conquête de l'Egypte, cette *Hollande de l'Orient*, est infiniment plus aisée que celle des Provinces-Unies. Il faut à la France la paix en Occident, la guerre au loin. [...] C'est en Egypte qu'on vaincra la Hollande; c'est là qu'on lui enlèvera ce qui seul la rend florissante: les trésors de l'Orient (H. Martin, *Histoire de France depuis les temps les plus reculés jusqu'en 1789*, 17 vols (Paris, 1855-60), vol. XIII (1858), p. 369), his italics. ('The conquest of Egypt, that *Holland of the Orient*, will be infinitely easier than that of the United Provinces. France needs peace in the West and war at a distance. [...] It is in Egypt that Holland will be defeated; that is where she will be relieved of that alone which makes her great: the treasures of the Orient.')

joined on side of the English the following month.[29] The next work to be
examined, therefore, *Cadmus et Hermione*, the first of the celebrated operas
on which Lully collaborated with the librettist Philippe Quinault, is different
from those previously considered in that it was premiered at a time of war,
in February 1673. This is reflected in its dedication, where the newly-
founded Royal Academy of Music complains to the King: 'Mais je viens
vainement Vous en offrir les charmes; / Vous ne tournez les yeux que du
côté des armes' ('But I come vainly to offer you charms, / Your gaze turns
only to arms').[30] Louis had, though, taken Leibniz's advice in one respect at
least, for the latter had opined that 'Il faut à la France la paix en Occident, la
guerre au loin' (see n. 58). Thus, whereas France in *La Toison d'or* had
complained of the devastation of her countryside, the dedication to *Cadmus*
expresses French satisfaction at being able to enjoy peace at home, 'lorsque
Vous allez jusqu'au bout de la Terre / Combler vos ennemis des malheurs
de la guerre' ('while You go to the ends of the earth / To burden your enemies with the miseries of war' (p. 2)).

However, the attitude to expansionism expressed in this dedication is
interesting, since the King is told in no uncertain terms that his country pre-
fers peace to that type of glory:

> L'Empire où Vous régnez, sans chercher à s'accroître,
> Trouve assez de grandeur à Vous avoir pour Maître,
> Votre règne suffit à sa félicité,
> Souffrez qu'il en jouisse avec tranquillité.
> Soyez content de voir, au seul bruit de vos armes,
> Tant d'états agités de mortelles alarmes,
> Vos plus fiers ennemis abattus pour jamais,
> Et l'Univers tremblant Vous demander la paix. (p. 2)

> The Empire over which You reign, without seeking to get bigger, / Finds
> enough grandeur in having You for its Master, / Your reign is enough for its
> happiness, / Allow it to enjoy this in tranquillity, / Be content to see, at the mere
> sound of your weapons, / So many states agitated by mortal fears, / Your
> proudest enemies for ever crushed, / And the trembling Universe asking You
> for peace.

---

[29] Lynn, *The Wars of Louis XIV*, p. 113.
[30] P. Quinault, *Cadmus et Hermione* (Paris, 1673), in: *Livrets d'opéra*, ed. B. Norman (Toulouse, 1999), pp. 1-51 (p. 2).

It is, though, acknowledged that peace can only be achieved once the uppity Dutch have been taught a lesson:

> Qu'un peuple, dont l'orgueil attira la tempête,
> Par son abaissement l'écarte de sa tête,
> Et quand il n'est plus rien qui puisse résister,
> Que la foudre de vos mains dédaigne d'éclater.
> D'un regard adouci calmez la Terre et l'Onde,
> Ne Vous contentez plus d'être l'effroi du Monde,
> Et songez que le Ciel Vous donne à nos désirs
> Pour être des humains l'Amour et les Plaisirs. (p. 3)

Let a people whose pride attracted the storm, / Turn it aside by their humiliation. / And when there is no longer anything that can resist, / Let the thunder bolt in your hand disdain to burst forth. / By a newly-soft look calm the Earth and the Seas, / Be content no longer to be the terror of the World, / And think that the Heavens have given you to fulfill our desires / And to be the Love and Delight of all Humankind.

Having discussed the Dutch War so thoroughly in his dedication, Quinault alludes to it only obliquely in the Prologue, where Apollo is shown destroying the monstrous Python by a rain of fire, noting that 'Le sens allégorique de ce sujet est si clair, qu'il est inutile de l'expliquer' ('The allegorical nature of this subject is so clear that it is unnecessary to explain it' (p. 7)).

A number of machine plays and operas produced between 1673 and 1676 contain references to the progress of the war rather than reflections on the desirability or otherwise of peace, and so will only be considered briefly here. They include a set of *intermèdes* composed in 1673 to entertain the King upon his return from the Dutch campaign, in the Epilogue to which representatives of different nations 's'empressent pour se ranger sous la domination d'un si digne Vainqueur' ('rush to place themselves under the domination of so great a Conqueror').[31] Quinault's *Alceste* (1674) alludes to Condé's crossing of the Rhine and the Dutch flooding of their countryside to protect Amsterdam (both in June 1672).[32] In the Prologue to the same author's *Thésée* (1675), the emphasis is on the contrast between external war and internal peace. Thus, Mars orders that nothing should trouble Venus and her cherubs and that pastoral music should prevail over military drums

---

[31] Anon., *Intermèdes pour une comédie* (Paris, 1673), p. 31.
[32] Lynn, *The Wars of Louis XIV*, pp. 113-117; P. Quinault, *Alceste* (Paris, 1674), in: *Livrets d'opéra*, ed. B. Norman (Toulouse, 1999), pp. 53-106 (pp. 54, 60)

and trumpets. However, he also tells Bellona to fly off and 'Portez aux em-
menis de cet Empire heureux / Tout ce que la guerre a d'affreux' ('Take to
the enemies of this happy Empire / All that war has that is frightful').[33] As
she does so, Venus asks Mars why the King has so many jealous enemies,
and wonders whether they will ever be happy again in the absence of peace.
Mars tells her not to worry: he has only increased the number of the King's
enemies to enhance his glory. France will inevitably triumph and those who
have forced the 'Great Hero' to take up arms will come to grief (p. 112).
And the Prologue concludes with the instruction that, in the midst of war,
the gods and their followers should enjoy the delights of peace (p. 113).

A machine play given in the same period, Thomas Corneille's *Circé*
(March 1675), has as the decor of its Prologue a temple built by Glory in
honour of the King. This is decorated with military trophies and depictions
of Louis's conquests, as well as a statue of Louis himself, accompanied by
Victory and Glory.[34] In the text, there are allusions to a league of jealous
princes and to the fact that the King's troops have twice invaded the
Franche-Comté, as well as to his many successful battles and sieges (pp. 8-
9).[35] Above all, Louis's military undertakings are represented as being to
'maintenir de légitimes Droits' and to confound tyrants ('To uphold legitimate rights' (p. 12)).

In 1676, the Lully-Quinault offering was *Atys*, the Prologue to which
includes a reference to the seasonality of war, when Flora explains her appearance in winter by saying that if she had waited until spring her Hero
would already have departed.[36] Assorted classical heroes fight until Iris descends to restore harmony, asserting that 'l'Empire puissant, où règne un
nouveau Mars' ('The powerful Empire where a New Mars reigns') is the
only sanctuary of pleasures. And the Prologue concludes with all agreeing
that this 'temps de Jeux et du repos' ('time of Games and rest') will allow
Louis time to plan new conquests (pp. 175-176). *Atys* was followed in 1677
by *Isis*, where the decor of the Prologue is the palace of Renown. Again the
theme is one of jealous conspiracy against the King:

---

[33] P. Quinault, *Thésée* (Paris, 1675), in: *Livrets d'opéra*, ed. B. Norman (Toulouse,
1999), pp. 107-169 (p. 109).
[34] T. Corneille, *Circé*, ed. J. Clarke (Exeter, 1989), p. 5.
[35] The Franche-Comté was seized by French troops for a second time after a campaign of only six weeks in Spring 1674. Louis himself was present at the sieges of
Besançon and Dole (Lynn, *The Wars of Louis XIV*, p. 124).
[36] P. Quinault, *Atys* (Paris, 1676), in: *Livrets d'opéra*, ed. by B. Norman (Toulouse,
1999), pp. 171-227 (pp. 173-174).

C'est lui dont les Dieux ont fait choix
Pour combler le bonheur de l'Empire Français;
En vain, pour le troubler, tout s'unit, tout conspire,
C'est en vain que l'Envie a ligué tant de Rois.
Heureux l'Empire
Qui suit ses lois![37]

It is he whom the Gods have chosen / To complete the happiness of the French Empire; / In vain, to trouble him, everything unites and conspires, / In vain Envy has leagued together so many Kings. / Happy is the Empire / That follows his laws!

Neptune emerges from the sea to underline Louis's naval victories during the Sicilian campaign the previous year:

Mon Empire a servi de théâtre à la guerre;
Publiez des exploits nouveaux:
C'est le même Vainqueur, si fameux sur la Terre,
Qui triomphe encor sur les eaux (pp. 232-233).[38]

My Empire has served as a theatre of war; / Publish his new exploits: / He is the same Conqueror, so famous on Land, / Who triumphs again on the seas.

Following such successes, it now seemed possible to contemplate an end to the war. Thus, Calliope orders the 'bruit terrible des armes, / Qui troublez le repos de cent climats divers' ('terrible noise of arms / that trouble the peace of a hundred different climates') to cease temporarily so that the songs of the Muses might be heard 'dans une auguste cour' ('in an august court'), as Melpomène puts it. However, Calliope and Thalia are forced to remind her that the time is not yet quite right: 'La Paix, la douce Paix n'ose encore descendre / Du céleste séjour' ('Peace, sweet Peace, does not yet dare descend / From her celestial dwelling' (p. 234)). Nonetheless, the Muses all pledge to 'attendre Son bienheureux retour [...] près du Vainqueur' ('await Her most happy return near to the Conqueror'), and Apollo expresses the Arts' delight at the prospect of peace associated with artistic activity (p. 234). Renown, on the other hand, combines caution with continuing bellicosity:

---

[37] P. Quinault, *Isis* (Paris, 1677), in: *Livrets d'opéra*, ed. B. Norman (Toulouse, 1999), pp. 229-280 (p. 231).
[38] Lynn, *The Wars of Louis XIV*, p. 148.

Il n'est pas encor temps de croire
Que les paisibles jeux ne seront plus troublés;
(...)
Ennemis de la paix, tremblez;
Vous le verrez [le Héros] bientôt courir à la victoire,
Vos efforts redoublés
Ne serviront qu'à redoubler sa gloire. (p. 234)

It is not yet time to think / That these peaceful games will no longer be troubled; / […] / Tremble, enemies of peace; / You will soon see [the Hero] run to
victory, / Your increased efforts, / Will serve only to increase his glory.

When called upon to prepare his opera for 1678, Lully was unable to
work with Quinault, who had fallen into disfavour, and so turned to the machine play expert, Thomas Corneille. The published text of their first col-
laborative offering, *Psyché*, is again accompanied by a Preface in which
French expansionism, the satisfactory progress of the war and recent successful sieges are all commented upon, and astonishment is expressed that
France has been able to expand her territory and 'dompter l'Univers' ('tame
the Universe') while continuing to enjoy the 'mille plaisirs offerts' ('thousand pleasures on offer') at home.[39] Indeed, war and culture are presented as
being curiously interlinked, so that for Louis, 'vaincre, où tu fais voler tes
Etendards, / C'est la suite des soins que tu prends des beaux Arts'
('[C]onquering, where you cause your Flags to fly, / Is the consequence of
your concern for the Arts'). Again, the peaceful situation inside France is
compared to that of people elsewhere, and the end of the war is predicted:

Quel trouble pour l'Europe, et combien d'épouvante
Jette dans tous les coeurs ta valeur triomphante!
Ces peuples contre nous ardents à se liguer
Attendent le moment qui les va subjuguer.
Nous seuls goûtons la paix que tes exploits nous donnent,
Et tandis qu'en tous lieux les Trompettes résonnent,
Que leur bruit menaçant fait retentir les airs,
Paris ne les entend que dans nos seuls Concerts.

---

[39] T. Corneille, *Psyché* (Paris, 1678) (n. p.). Louis himself had been present at the
siege of Ghent just a month before *Psyché* was performed, and which is described in
the Preface in hyperbolic detail, before moving on equally successfully to Ypres. In
addition, during the Roussillon campaign, he had seen the successful siege of the
mountain fortress of Puigcerda, which fell in May 1678 (Lynn, *The Wars of Louis
XIV*, pp. 153-156).

What trouble for Europe, and how much terror / Does your triumphant valour cast into all hearts! / Those people who were so eager to unite against us / Await the moment of their subjugation. / We alone enjoy the peace your exploits provide, / And while everywhere else the Trumpets sound, / And their threatening noise causes the air to resound, / Paris hears nothing but our Music.

In the Prologue itself, Flora invites Venus to descend with the following invocation:

Ce n'est plus le temps de la Guerre;
Le plus puissant des Rois
Interrompt ses Exploits
Pour donner la Paix à la Terre[.]

It is no longer a time of War; / The most powerful of Kings / Is interrupting his Exploits / To bring Peace to the Earth[.]

And a chorus of divinities echoes her sentiments:

Nous goûtons une paix profonde;
Les plus doux Jeux sont icy bas;
On doit ce repos plein d'appas
Au plus grand ROY du Monde.

We enjoy a profound peace / The sweetest Games are here below; / We owe this calm full of charms / To the greatest King in the World.

In June 1678, just two months after the premiere of *Psyché*, the Dutch States General voted in favour of peace with France, and the Treaty of Nijmegen was signed on 10 August. A Franco-Spanish treaty followed on 17 September, and one with the Emperor on 6 February 1679.[40] Consequently, the second Lully-Corneille collaboration, *Bellérophon*, premiered in January 1679 and published some months later, emerged into a Brave New World of European peace. This new state of affairs is referred to in the dedication to the published text:

Le Roy ayant donné la Paix à l'Europe, l'Académie Royale de Musique a creu devoir marquer la part qu'elle prend à la joye publique par un Spectacle, où elle pust faire entrer les témoignages de son zele pour la gloire de cet Auguste Mo-

---

[40] Lynn, *The Wars of Louis XIV*, p. 156.

narque. Elle s'y est creuë d'autant plus obligée que la protection qu'il donne aux beaux Arts les a toûjours fait joüir, pendant le cours méme de la Guerre, de l'heureuse tranquillité qui leur est si nécessaire.[41]

The King having given Peace to Europe, the Royal Academy of Music thought it should mark its share in the public rejoicing by a Spectacle in which it could include demonstrations of its zeal for the glory of this August Monarch. It felt itself all the more obliged to do so on account of the fact that the protection he gives the Arts has caused them to enjoy, even during the course of the War, the happy tranquillity that is so necessary to them.

The Prologue itself opens with a representation of 'le Parnasse Fran-çois' ('the French Parnassus'): 'une agreable Vallée, en forme de Costeaux delicieux, au fond desquels paroist le Mont Parnasse' ('an agreeable Valley formed of delicious Hills, to the rear of which appears Mount Parnassus'), where Apollo and the Muses have come to celebrate 'le retour d'une paix si glorieuse à la France' ('the return of a peace that is so glorious for France'). The sun god imagines a spectacle based on Bellerophon's destruction of the Chimera — the single monster snake of *Cadmus* having metamorphosed into this new triple-headed creature, clearly intended to represent the Triple Alliance, and he instructs the Muses as follows:

Le plus grand Roy de l'Univers
Vient d'asseurer le repos de la Terre;
Sur cet heureux Vallon il répand ses bien-faits.
Apres avoir chanté les fureurs de la Guerre,
Chantons les douceurs de la Paix.

The greatest King in the Universe / Has just ensured the calm of the Earth; / On this fortunate Valley he spreads his bounty. / After having sung the furies of War, / Let us sing the sweetness of Peace.

Bellérophon is unusual in that the close identification of the action of its plot with the current political situation allows for a further expression of delight at the return of peace in the work's conclusion, which is certainly more to do with the recent treaties than it is with the defeat of the Chimera. Thus, a Chorus of People rejoices that:

---

[41] T. Corneille, *Bellérophon* (Paris, 1679) (n. p.)

Le plus grand des Heros rend le calme à la Terre,
Il fait cesser les horreurs de la Guerre.
Joüissons à jamais
Des douceurs de la Paix.
(...)
Que la paix qui succede à la peine
Fait aisément oublier les soûpirs !
Si le Ciel nous soûmit à la haîne,
Un heureux sort satisfait nos desirs.
Dans les beaux jours qu'un Heros nous raméne,
Cherchons les Ris, les Jeux, et les Plaisirs.

The greatest of Heroes has made the Earth calm, / He has caused the horrors of
War to cease. / Let us forever enjoy / The delights of Peace. / (...) / Let the
peace that follows trouble / Make us quickly forget our sighs! / If the Heavens
brought us hate / A happy destiny satisfies our desires. / In the happy days a
Hero brings back to us / Let us seek Games, Laughter and Pleasure.

After two collaborations with Thomas Corneille, Lully was reunited with
Quinault, and the final work to be considered here is their *Proserpine*, premiered in February 1680, a year after the signing of the peace treaty with
the Emperor. Here, as in *La Toison d'or*, which had been written in similar
circumstances, we find Peace represented as an allegorical character. Thus,
the decor of the Prologue is the grotto of Discord, who is holding Peace,
Happiness, Abundance, Games and Pleasures in chains. Peace sings the following lament:

Héros, dont la valeur étonne l'Univers,
Ah! quand briserez-vous nos fers?
La Discorde nous tient ici sous sa puissance;
La barbare se plaît à voir couler nos pleurs!
Soyez touché de nos malheurs,
Vous êtes dans nos maux notre unique espérance;
Héros, dont la valeur étonne l'Univers,
Ah! quand briserez-vous nos fers?[42]

Hero, whose valour has astonished the Universe, / When will you break our
chains? / Discord keeps us here in her power; / The barbarian takes pleasure in

---

[42] P. Quinault, *Proserpine* (Paris, 1680), in: *Livrets d'opéra*, ed. B. Norman (Toulouse, 1999), pp. 1-54 (p. 3).

seeing our tears flow! / Be moved by our miseries, / In our suffering you are
our only hope; / Hero, whose valour has astonished the Universe, / When will
you break our chains?

Hate, Rage, Grief, Jealousy, Spite and Despair demonstrate their delight at
Peace's subjugation, and Discord taunts her captive with the idea that Victory is preparing to lead the King towards new combats, in an echo of earlier debates:

> Soupirez, triste Paix, malheureuse captive,
> Gémissez, et n'espérez pas
> Qu'un héros que j'engage en de nouveaux combats
> Écoute votre voix plaintive.
> Plus il moissonne de lauriers,
> Plus j'offre de matière à ses travaux guerriers.
> (...)
> La Victoire, empressée à conduire ses pas,
> Se prépare à voler aux plus lointains climats;
> Plus il la suit, plus il la trouve belle.
> Il oublie aisément pour elle
> La Paix et ses plus doux appas. (p. 3)

> Sigh, sad Peace, unfortunate captive, / Groan, and do not hope / That a hero I
> am engaging in new combats / Will hear your plaintive voice. / The more he
> harvests laurels, / The more I offer subjects for his warlike labours. / [...] / Vic-
> tory, eager to lead his steps, / Is preparing to fly to the most distant lands; / The
> more he follows her, the more he finds her beautiful. / For her, he easily forgets
> / Peace and her more gentle attractions.

Indeed, a reference to the defeated being imbued with 'une nouvelle audace'
hints that the recent conflicts might not yet be entirely over.
      However, Discord is contradicted when drums and trumpets are heard
and Victory descends to summon Peace to join her:

> Venez, aimable Paix, le Vainqueur vous appelle,
> La Victoire devient votre guide fidèle;
> Venez dans un heureux séjour (p. 4).

> Come, gentle Peace, the Conqueror calls you, / Victory has become your faith-
> ful guide; / Come to a happy realm.

Victory's followers release Peace and her companions and chain up Discord and her suite in their place, while the goddess expresses her jubilation: 'Ah! qu'il est beau de rendre / La Paix à l'Univers!' ('Oh! how beautiful it is / To restore Peace to the Universe!'). In vain, Discord tempts Victory and her Hero master with the promise of laurels and glory 'au bout du monde' ('at the ends of the earth'), since Victory merely modifies her song:

> Après avoir vaincu mille peuples divers,
> Quand on ne voit plus rien qui puisse se défendre,
> Ah! qu'il est beau de rendre
> La Paix à l'Univers! (p. 5)

> After having defeated a thousand different peoples, / When there is nothing left to see that can defend itself, / Oh! how beautiful it is / To restore Peace to the Universe!

Mercury's instruction in *La Fête de Vénus* has been fulfilled and Victory has served to establish peace on earth (or so we are told). This is demonstrated theatrically when Discord is cast down into a 'gouffre plein d'horreur' ('gulf full of horror') — presumably via traps in the stage floor, being given barely time to bewail the fact that the Conqueror has 'triomphé de son courage' ('triumphed over his courage') so that she will see no more 'sang et (...) carnage' ('blood and carnage'). Victory then orders the 'triste séjour' ('sad place') to change so that everyone might enjoy the power of 'la Paix triomphante' ('Peace triumphant'), and Discord's 'affreuse retraite' ('frightful retreat') is immediately transformed into an agreeable palace, as Victory and Peace sing together in praise of the conquering hero:

> Le Vainqueur est comblé de gloire;
> On doit l'admirer à jamais.
> Il est servi de la Victoire
> Pour faire triompher la Paix (p. 6).

> The Conqueror is crowned with glory; / He must be forever admired. / He has used Victory / To cause Peace to triumph.

And the Prologue concludes with the usual assertion that in place of war and tears there will be happiness, games and love.

In *La Toison d'or*, Peace was released from her chains by Hymen in celebration of the King's marriage. In *Proserpine*, it is Victory who performs the same service. The King's military exploits are thereby justified as being for the greater good not only of the French nation but also of the 'universe' as a whole (conceived of in the widest of terms), if only its inhabitants would see sense and consent to submit to his rule. The right-minded obviously rush to do so, with the only possible explanation for continued resistance being jealousy of French superiority. The message promulgated by Louis and his ministers and echoed back to him is clear: how wonderful it is that by military conquest this 'new Mars' has been able to increase his *gloire* and *empire*, while simultaneously bringing peace to the world; and how still more wonderful that he is able to do so with comparatively little hardship at home. The result is the construction of a contemporary commonplace that stands in stark contrast to the current one born with the benefit of hindsight. Moreover, these spectacular works not only propound this view but are also an illustration of it, since they constitute examples of the very arts and pleasures of which they speak and that Louis is credited with having caused to flourish. Rarely can theatrical productions have been so loaded with meanings, serving at the same time as entertainment, political propaganda and illustrations of at least one facet of the message that is being propagated, and with different things to say to each of their many categories of spectator, from the King himself on down.

STAGINGS OF DIVINE POWER

Bent Holm

General remarks

My focus will be on stagings of Danish royalty in the time of transition to formalized absolutism. Real absolutism was introduced in 1660. The material will be performances of royal ceremonies and of theatrical events. The distinctions between these two are frequently fluid. My intention is to observe their allegorical imagery in a historical-political context. Continuity will deliberately be stressed more than ruptures. Three types of imagery will be especially observed: the Christian, the Classical, and the Norse. The combinations of these are considered more significant than the distinctions. A 'Roman' procession may imply Norse references and Christian themes. On the other hand each theme colours in particular one of the following phases: 1. the time before 1660, 2. the time after 1660 and 3. the echoes of the Baroque in the eighteenth century. Throughout these periods the notion of 'the king' is in itself a commonplace, a figure that represents strength and power beyond discussion or need for explanation. Now the question is how and on which levels this continually present figure nevertheless undergoes transpositions, and in which ways and to what degree the notion of 'the king' varies.

The overall movement goes from a conception of the royal post as divine, to a conception of the royal person as divine. The period's intensified focus on monarchy and monarch was a consequence of the wars of religion and the social disorder that was seen in Europe after the weakening of institutions like the Catholic Church and the universal Empire. The princely dynasties increasingly assumed the role of guarantor of peace and security. In order to do so they needed unquestionable authority. Artists, poets and historians contributed to the process by praising the prince and the dynasty.

It is in that specific connection that the European Renaissance was introduced into Denmark, through, among other things, powerful representations of princes as classical gods and heroes. The princes took a leading position in the Lutheran church organisation which had been introduced in 1536. In this re-definition of power even the national legendary past was gradually involved. The image of the prince depicted him not only as a strong ruler, but also as a focus of religious and ontological concerns. Architecture, imagery, and literature were to contextualize the deeds of the king; and ephemeral phenomena like triumphal arches, processions, and performances staged his glory and fame in complex allegories. The feasts were published using a variety of literary and visual strategies.

Divine Monarchy

The Coronation

In the early seventeenth century the realm of Denmark included parts of Northern Germany, all of Norway, parts of primarily southern Sweden, Greenland, Iceland, and the Faroe Islands. Besides Poland, Denmark was the most powerful nation in the Baltic area. After the Thirty Years War its wealth and strength were dramatically reduced.

The ruler was an elective king. Theoretically he received his power from the Rigsråd, the council of twelve members of the high nobility. In practice each new king was almost automatically the former king's son. In 1588 Frederik II died, and his eleven-year-old son Christian became the ruler under the regency of four members of the Rigsråd, before, on August 29 1596 at the age of eighteen, being crowned as King Christian IV. The coronation was an extraordinary political and propagandistic display of magnificent proportions, including the participation of a number of European princes and their entourage, hundreds of people in all. The king's brother-in-law, King James VI of Scotland, was prevented from coming, and sent a delegation of sixty people. Christian's future father-in-law, the prince-bishop of Magdeburg and future prince-elector Joachim Friedrich of Brandenburg from the house of Hohenzollern, showed up with an entourage of over two hundred people and five hundred horses. The festivities went on for several days. On their way to the city of Copenhagen the guests were welcomed with allegorical fireworks. However, the real starting point was obviously the religious ceremony, the anointment and the coronation in the cathedral of Copenhagen. It was followed by a series of celebratory activities.

The following year the whole corpus of festivities was published for an international audience both in German, with illustrations, and also in Latin; in 1598 they were published in Danish for the national audience, so that even the common man might be informed about the obligations concerning king and people, which were expressed during the ecclesiastical ceremonies, as the translator, the Court chaplain Anders Bentsen Dallin, clearly explained. The various texts are not identical, and nor do the texts correspond perfectly to the images. The Danish text contains more details than the others. The author of the text, the theologian August Erich, was an eye-witness. The engravings, produced in Frankfurt and based on sketches from the events, combine various moments in one picture, thus making simultaneous what was successive.

In his sermon of coronation the bishop of Sealand, Peder Vinstrup, explained the ideological basis of the ceremony; he spoke first in Latin, about the divinity of monarchy, then in Danish about the meaning of the coronation, that is, the obligations that it entailed for the king. Royalty was instituted by God, he explained; the king had his power from God; and, it was the subjects' duty to honour and obey God's earthly representative, in order to guarantee peace, justice and the true worship of God. The Latin part of this sermon was left out of the official account. In it, Vinstrup declared that:

> Because of their divine mission God makes the princes share His name, calling them in various places in the Holy Scripture gods and the sons of the sublime one, and decorates and honours them with other sublime titles, for with the name gods He demonstrates that they are His helpers, who as His living and animated picture on earth take His place and practise divine tasks and duties.[1]

By virtue of God's direct intervention, the anointment implied a proper transformation of the king's person, according to Vinstrup.

This implied an emphasis on the theocratic aspects of monarchy. However, although royal power was thus given by God, at the same time the members of the Rigsråd put their hands on the crown when it was conveyed to Christian, symbolically demonstrating that it was given to him by them. They had elected him. This contradiction and conflict between divine and secular roles led to continual complications throughout Christian's reign. In general, statements about the figure of the ruler or the notion of royalty are often ambiguous or contradictory. So the image of the ruler was not necessarily stable or coherent, and depended upon the given context. In any case, the theocratic radicalization was not formalized until 63 years later, under full absolutism.

Lutheran theology emphasized the narrow relationship between terrestrial authority and celestial supremacy. Through his oath, Christian promised to be the imitator and Vicar of Christ. He became the *summus episcopus* of the church and the armed defender of the true faith. Various performative reflections of those circumstances are found in the following festivities.

---

[1] Quoted from Heiberg, S., *Christian IV – en europæisk statsmand* (Copenhagen 2006) p. 57; on theocratic royalty see Johannsen, H., 'Den ydmyge konge' in Johannsen, H., ed., *Kirkens bygning og brug* (Copenhagen 1983), p. 134; cf. Skovgaard-Petersen, K., 'Danske konger og romersk herskersymbolik' in Due, O.S. and Isager, J., ed.s, *Imperium Romanum* II (Aarhus 1993) p. 410; a survey of the period's festivities is in Andrup, O., 'Hoffet og dets Fester' in Clausen, J., and Krogh, ed.s, *Danmark i Fest og Glæde* I (Copenhagen 1935), p. 273ff.

Christian had ordered a new and splendid crown for the coronation, weighing three kilos. At the ceremony Bishop Vinstrup explained that the crown's gold meant that Christian's reign should be pure; the precious stones symbolized particularly the Danish noblemen who, like the stones, would remain close to the king.[2] Three personifications of cardinal royal virtues: *Fortitudo*, *Justitia* and *Caritas* (Strength, Justice and Love) were placed over, respectively, his right arm, his left arm and the back of his head, the latter signifying Christian's love for God and for his subjects, his mercy and his role as the head of the church. The main symbol of Christian's royal and Christian power was, however, the pelican that feeds its young with blood from its own breast. This image appeared three times: placed over each ear and over his forehead. The pelican is a well known symbol of Christ's self-sacrifice which, in this instance, pointed not only to that sacrifice but also to the king's role and duties, as well as to the interaction of these concepts of Christ and king.

The authorized interpretation of these symbols was given by the secretary of the German Chancellery – the 'ministry of foreign affairs' – August Erich, who was the author of the aforementioned official description of the coronation celebrations. Erich explains the meaning of the crown's twelve peaks like this: twelve angels on the crown indicate that the king's virtues 'which make him shine and glitter more than common people' are bestowed on him from Heaven. He continues:

> On the highest peak, the one in the position of his face, stood a pelican over its chicks, which was pecking blood from its breast with its beak, made out of gold and decorated with precious diamonds. As is well known, that bird indicates not only our Lord Jesus Christ, but also every Christian authority who is ready to offer his blood to his faithful subjects.[3]

Erich emphasizes the double meaning of the symbol, namely its reference to both Christ and the Christian ruler. The other personifications – Strength, Justice, and Love – are described in non-complex ways. They simply mean what they mean. By contrast, the pelican entails an obligation on the crown's bearer which refers to his oath at the end of the ceremony, and thus to his role as Christ's Vicar on earth. As already mentioned, this official interpretation was aimed at the 'ordinary man'.

In the year of the coronation it was said in the king's mirror *Alithia* by Johannes Damgaard that 'because a Christian Lord and King is the instru-

---

[2] See Boesen, G., Danmarks Riges Regalier / The Danish Coronarion Regalia (Copenhagen 1986) p. 78ff
[3] Quoted from Boesen, *Regalier*, p. 64, cf. Heiberg, *Christian 4.* pp. 58 and 61

ment and toil of Christ, he definitely ought to imitate his Lord, who is Christ, and sometimes take off his crown of gold and put on a crown of thorns (...) He should sometimes follow his Lord over the brook and into the Garden of Gethsemane'.

The king gets his power, his realm 'from the King of the Kings and the Lord of the Lords Jesus Christ as if from hand to hand.'[4] Christian attached great importance to the 'text'. Later on such conceptions of the royal function as grounded in suffering came to play a literal role in Christian's professional and personal career and in the imagery that accompanied it.

Although theocratic notions had been present in Denmark since the Middle Ages, presentations of the ruler like those which followed the coronation had never been seen before. Jean Bodin's *République* of 1576 referred to Denmark as a kingdom without a sovereign majesty. That was now changing. It happened at the same time as Christian's brother-in-law King James VI of Scotland was elaborating his thoughts about royal power. In other words, if observed in a larger European context, Christian's redefinition of the royal role is just one example of a wider phenomenon.

After the coronation Christian made his ritual entry into the capital Copenhagen like a Roman emperor. On the route from the cathedral to the royal palace, he passed a particularly magnificent triumphal arch decorated with the blue lions of the national coat of arms, and equipped with four martial giants who bowed their heads to hail the king: Alexander, Scipio, Hannibal and Hector. While passing through the arch he was symbolically crowned with a golden garland by a mechanical angel of victory (fig. 2). This implied that the coronation had divine or superhuman origins.

The following evening a pyrotechnical drama was performed, presenting Roman virtues of self-sacrifice, represented by the heroic Marcus Curtius from the fourth century BC. The story, taken from Titus Livius, recounts that, when an abyss opened up at the Forum Romanum, it became clear that it could only be closed, and the Roman realm remain there, if people recognized what constituted the greatness of Rome and sacrifice it to the place. Curtius declared that Rome's greatness was made up of arms and courage, and then immediately threw himself into the chasm. To the character of Curtius were added three figures: a woman with donkey's ears, personifying diabolical lying and hypocritical and fraudulent Heresy; an Indian with feathers; and a Turk, representing paganism. Curtius was followed by the three figures when he plunged into the fire during the pyrotechnical performance. This patriotic performance was a signal of the young king's firm decisiveness to act as a new Curtius in fighting infidelity; there are certain

---

[4] Quoted from Johannsen, 'Den ydmyge' pp. 139 and 135, cf Heiberg, *Christian 4.* p. 322f

overtones of a self-sacrificing Christ. Roman heroism was interwoven with the king's role as the defender of faith, with his promise to defeat heresy and paganism.

On September 3 and 4 the so-called 'inventions' were performed in the city, as a prelude to tournaments in the form of riding at the ring.[5] 'Invention' was the term for a particular kind of symbolic staged entry, consisting of processions and pageants, and referring to religious, ideological or political issues, with roots in antique triumphal processions and Renaissance *trionfi*. They were richly decorated with allegorical and emblematic personifications and representations; the participants were dressed with reference to the theme. The context and pomp suggested the overall signification: the demonstration of the new ruler's virtues and intentions, and the overwhelming display of his strength and magnificence. On the other hand, the decoding of sophisticated details was more problematic.[6] The presentation of the inventions was a competition. On this occasion the winning invention was the *Mountain of Virtue*, which comprised a number of classical Roman heroes, including, once again, Marcus Curtius.

The king had sent out the invitations to the tournament in the name of Pope Sergius VI. The inviting prince was called the *mantenador*, whereas his challengers or opponents were named *aventurines*. In the papal name of Sergius the call had even been proclaimed around the city by heralds. During the festivities, the fictitious Pope Sergius VI was carried in a sedan chair by 'clergymen' in a triumphal procession through the town, and a pageant with painted views of Rome was rolled in, equipped with musicians dressed as monks and hermits. The Pope was performed by the king himself wearing a triple crown on his head and surrounded by monks with thuribles and aspersoriums, bishops with tiaras and crosiers, and cardinals on mules. Even the Swiss guards took part in the procession (fig. 3). After the Pope followed an allegorical mountain, sometimes described as the mountain of Venus, and then, immediately afterwards, there were groups of Magdeburg participants representing exotic barbarian pagans. The papal procession was obviously the Lutheran prince's grotesque depiction of the adversary, a dis-

---

[5] The riders tried to catch a ring hanging from a gallows with a spear. He who took most rings was declared the tournament's winner. The king's performance was impressive.

[6] To what extent are various kinds of significations readable, and by whom, and what kind of pre-existing knowledge is required? Such questions are relevant in many respects in relation to topics like this one. Reports from the events differ in a small number of cases concerning what the observer has seen. We know from, for example, analogous Swedish events that, even for educated people, allusions were not necessarily immediately readable. cf. Heed, Sv.Aa and Forser, T., ed.s, *Ny svensk teaterhistoria* I (Hedemora 2007), p. 117.

play of heresy. In a sense, this continued the fraudulent impersonation sacrificed in the pyrotechnical show the day after the coronation: in both cases, heresy was accompanied by paganism.

The man in charge of the exotic 'invention' that was performed by the delegation from Magdeburg was the king's future father-in-law, the prince-bishop Joachim Friedrich, who appeared as the Turkish prince 'Mehemet of the royal tribe of Fessa'. In the tournament, prince Joachim Friedrich was the Pope's (the king's) leading *aventurine*. In other words, the 'Turk' was challenging the 'Pope'. Two figures central to contemporary political and religious tensions were thus in play. Both were performed by religious leaders, the Danish *summus episcopus*, and the Magdeburg prince-bishop.

The image of the 'Turk' played a significant role in the public mind of early modern Europe. Both the Pope and the Turk had previously been objects of symbolic destruction in ways which may be described as ritualistic. On the occasion of the baptism of Christian in 1577, four decades after the introduction of the Reformation in Denmark, the Pope as Antichrist had been blown up together with four monks on a castle of fireworks during a pyrotechnical show in the Copenhagen palace yard. Eleven years earlier the inauguration of the castle of Kronborg had been celebrated with a pyrotechnical destruction of the infidel Turks. Events like baptism and coronation were initiatory and transformative: the subject moved from one state to another. The defeat of the Turk opened and closed the coronation festivities. Upon the arrival of the guests in Copenhagen, the festivities began with the burning of a 'Turkish fortress' thirteen metres high and displaying a crescent moon on the steeple. Likewise, they ended, at the castle of Kronborg, Elsinore, with a pyrotechnical depiction of a war against the Turk.

The display of the Pope and the Turk in the 1596 linear procession is in itself significant. In the ideological context of the era the constellation of those two figures refers to a pre-existing combination of enemy images, an actual conspiracy or axis of evil in the Lutheran mind. The motif had been introduced by Martin Luther in his dissertations about the 'Turk', written on the occasion of Suleiman I's siege of Vienna in 1529. The author takes as his point of departure Daniel's apocalyptic prophecies in The Old Testament, and the identification of the four monsters that Daniel sees in his vision of four Empires. The prophecy thus corresponds to the historiographical doctrine about the Assyrian-Babylonian, the Persian-Median, the Greek and the Roman empires. In Luther's reading of Daniel, the last of the hideous animals, the Roman Empire, has iron teeth and copper claws and ten horns, after which an eleventh horn shall emerge, with eyes and a big mouth. The last protuberance, the eleventh horn, that shall push aside three other horns, is the Ottoman Empire. The argument applies, or is applied, to actual, contemporary historical events. As the Turk has already conquered

the three 'horns' Asia, Egypt and Greece, he shall not succeed in defeating
the German Empire, although he fiercely rips apart its borderlands. Daniel,
as interpreted by Luther, tells us that, in a cosmic drama with diabolical and
divine implications, there are two key players on the side of the diabolical:
'In the same way as the Pope is Antichrist, the Turk is the Devil incarnate.'[7]
He states as fact that the Devil has first sent the Pope to kill us spiritually,
and then the Turk to kill us physically. In other words, the threat of the Turk
signifies the End Times, Doomsday, and the return of the Saviour. He who
fights the Turk, fights the Devil. And he who falls because of the Turk's
bloodthirsty cruelty will immediately become a martyr, proceeding directly
to Paradise. The Devil thus deceives himself; for the earlier Paradise is
filled up, the sooner the Saviour will return.

Luther's texts had an enormous impact on the conception of, first, the
Catholic Church, represented by the Pope as Antichrist, and, secondly, the
Islamic world, the Ottoman Empire, personified by the image of the Turk as
the devil. Luther's hymn about the Pope and the Turk, asking God to protect
us from those two menaces, 'des Bapsts [sic] und Türkens Mord', was translated for the Danish hymn book in 1556 and stayed there for three centuries.
Echoes are found in pamphlets and in popular beliefs.[8] The conspiracy
between Pope and Turk was commonly perceived as fact, and therefore the
performance was readable to a Lutheran public: Antichrist and the Devil in
interaction.

So, when in the linear progress of the 'inventions', the Pope was followed by the Turk, the two figures thus performed the advance of the diabolical shock troops described in Luther's theological interpretation of contemporary history. As the main characters in the drama of the Devil's
mission, they represented the forces of both spiritual corruption and also
physical destruction. The Danish king and the German prince embodied
figures from Luther's interpretation of Daniel's apocalyptic prophecies.
They appeared as the incarnations of heresy and paganism respectively.

Christian IV displayed his sovereignty by performing as the adversary,
and, in doing so, gained status rather than losing it. He presented himself as
the real Lutheran prince, the defender of true faith against heresy and paganism. As in real life, the two figures, Pope and Turk, fought each other.
However, basically they were allied. In the symbolic perspective of the entire display they belonged to the dimension of anti-virtue that threw the
royal virtues into relief. From a ritualistic perspective they were mastered or
overcome by being performed by their superiors. The king demonstrated his

---

[7] Luther, M., 'Heerpredigt wider den Türken 1529' in *Martin Luthers Werke* XXX.
(Weimar: Metzler 1883-1929), p. 160ff. My translation.
[8] Holm, B., 'Tyrken og tæven' in *Kritik* 179 (Copenhagen 2006) p. 31ff.

own strength by showing the courage to appear as a fool, and at the same time he exposed the adversary's impotence as a target of desecrating ridicule. The enemy's power was thus broken in a performative act. That the king was the performer conveyed the act with more than merely symbolic significance. As has already been suggested, this strategy of employing official events for political display was well known. The wedding feast of Christian's niece, James I's daughter, in 1613, included strongly anti-Catholic pageants and tableaux.

On September 4 the show of 'inventions' continued. The king emerged dressed as a woman – a Roman courtesan according to some viewers – accompanied by an entourage also dressed as women; after this there appeared a mountain equipped with musicians and allegorical figures, followed by a camel with four singing virgins and in addition a long row of symbolic, allegorical and grotesque figures and figurations, angels, monks, Death, musicians appearing as ostriches, symbolic carriages drawn by deer or by the sun and the moon, ships, Turks, wild men, hunters and so forth.

For the following day's tournament invitations were sent out in the names of the *mantenadors* Alexander, Scipio, Hannibal and Hector, the heroic figures from the triumphal arch. The letter of invitation claimed that those excellent heroes were attracted by the reports of Christian's coronation. Christian appeared as Alexander, whose martial skills were displayed and even proved during the tournament. His role-playing had thus shifted from present political to general and moral to historical and legendary connotations. He was at once Alexander who had heard about Christian, and also Christian himself, the equal of Alexander; this multiple identity is typical of the complex display of realities employed in this mode of expression. Christian IV was no exception from the Renaissance love for playing with signification in words and in images. Semantic co-existence and ambiguity – rather than exclusion or contradiction – are characteristic of the era's mode of generating signification.

Triumph and Suffering

Frederiksborg Castle, situated about thirty-five kilometres north of Copenhagen, was intended to be a demonstration of royal splendour and magnificence at the highest European level, a fitting stage for one of the mightiest Lutheran princes. The construction began some years after the coronation, in 1602, and went on for several years, during which the king's military, economic, and artistic initiatives and projects were successful. In the castle his qualities and reputation were displayed in complex codes.

Roman arches and portals are recurrent in the architecture of the castle. They are characteristic even of the church. The magnificent chapel's entry portal presents the baptism of Jesus in the river Jordan, and the resurrection.

It has the shape of a Roman triumphal arch, and furthermore is decorated with the figures of two of the king's legendary ancestors, the first Christian king and his successor, father and son. The realm's ancient religious, symbolic and historical foundation is demonstrated in a composition drawing upon Christian, Roman, and Norse traditions. Inside the church the royal regalia are passed down from the heavens, the ceiling. The symbol of the pelican figures a couple of times.[9]

In the private oratory the king had placed a series of paintings showing the life of Christ, together with a painting of the king kneeling wrapped in a shroud in front of a vision of the heavenly saviour. He is at once a humble devotee and an imitator of the sacrificed lord. The picture has been modified. To begin with, Christian appeared in his royal splendour. At some point, he had this changed into a humble shroud. This change is connected to significant changes in the king's self-understanding due to developments in a variety of domains. A range of evidence bears witness to that process. Christian had involved himself militarily in the religious wars, and his ambitions were great. In 1625, when the military situation began to look disastrous, Christian had a vision while he was praying for the beleaguered evangelical church; in a short handwritten text he describes how the humiliated and suffering Christ appeared to him. Christian had his vision painted in order to express his obligation to shed his blood for the church and for his people as a true Christian prince, in other words to express his status as Christ's vicar and living image.

Years later, on the evening before the battle of Lister in 1644, where the king faced the risk of defeat and death, he had a dream of his death and glorious resurrection. He had that dream, too, painted, depicting the king's assumption into heaven. The painting is based on an engraving of the baptism of Christ in the river Jordan, which was understood as the symbolic basis of the royal anointment. In the painting the king takes the position of Christ in the engraving.[10] Once again, this was in accordance with the theology of the time, as well as with its image of the ruler. And it was part of the staging of royalty. The church took part in communicating the notion of the ruler and his authority that had been expressed in the coronation sermon (fig. 4).

---

[9] The period's panegyric poetry included allusions to an affinity which existed between Christ and the king simply by virtue of Christian's name. Johannsen, 'Den ydmyge' p. 138 mentions examples from 1589, 1605 and 1611. On the pelican as a reference to the coronation and the crown, see Boesen, *Regalier* p. 78. The king was later praised in prayers and sermons as a saviour who risks his life for the sake of the realm and the gospel, for instance in connection with his fatal involvement in the Thirty Years war. Cf. Johannsen p. 139f.

[10] Johannsen, 'Den ydmyge' p. 142.

Parallels can be found in the depiction of other rulers. Queen Elizabeth was compared to the holy Virgin in the funeral sermon for her:

> So there are two excellent women, one that bare Christ and an other that blessed Christ; to these we may joyne a third, that bare and blessed him both. Shee bear him in hir heart as a wombe, she conceived him in faith, shee brought him forth in abundance and good workes'.

She is a counterpart to the holy Virgin, 'In earth the first, in heaven the second virgin.[11] Similarly, her successor James I wrote in 1617 *A Meditation upon the 26, 27, 29 Verses of the XXVIIth Chapter of Saint Matthew or a Paterne for a Kings Inauguration*, for Christian's nephew, the future Charles I, saying for instance that 'the Croune of thornes went never out of my mind, remembering the thorny cares, which a King (if he have a care of his office) must be subject unto, as (God knows) I daily and nightly feel in my own person'. In addition, the birth of Louis XIV in 1638 was called miraculous ('la naissance miraculeuse'), and he was called a 'Messie' (Messiah) upon his anointment in 1654. The coronation sermon to him used exactly the same biblical quotations about the divinity of royal power and its agent as those used at the coronation of Christian IV. And when, in 1686, King Louis underwent an operation for haemorrhoids, the official journal with the description of the surgical intervention was based on the model of the passion of Christ. Undoubtedly these circumstances appear exotic in later times but this does not mean that the ruler or the era did not act rationally and pragmatically. Their reality was different from that of today.

The Great Wedding Feast

His failing military fortune did not prevent Christian from investing enormous efforts in demonstrations of pomp and power. Prestige (*reputatio*) depended on the staging of splendour. Although in 1631 antique pagan gods had been removed from school books due to the increasing Lutheran orthodoxy, they did not disappear from artistic or ritualistic imagery. Great importance was still attached to rich mythological and allegorical expressivity.

The most extravagant demonstration of this was *The Great Wedding Feast*, the wedding in 1634 of the prince-elect Christian, the cousin of Charles I, and princess Magdelena Sibylla, daughter of the prominent Lu-

---

[11] On Elizabeth, see Heiberg, S., ed., *Danske dronninger i tusind år* (Copenhagen 2000) p. 195, cf. Roy Strong, *The Cult of Elizabeth* (London 1977); on James, see Johannsen, 'Den ydmyge' p. 140 and Bøgh Rasmussen, M., 'Portrætter af Christian 4.' in Heiberg, S., ed., *Christian 4. og Frederiksborg* (Copenhagen 2006)p. 249; on Louis, see Holm, B., *Solkonge og månekejser. Ikonografiske studier i Francois Fossards Cabinet* (Copenhagen 1991) pp. 65 and 75.

theran Electoral prince Johann Georg I of Saxony. The political goal was to demonstrate that Denmark had recovered after the disasters of war and that Christian was a prince of the highest European status and furthermore a prince of peace. Sweden, the strong rival, was momentarily weakened. It was a matter of seizing the moment. The preparations went on for one year, and the king took a lively interest in the planning and the design. He insisted for instance on the nobility's dance training as a preparation for the Court ballets and dances that were part of the staging of the ruler and his realm. The actual power of the nobility was gradually diminishing, while at the same time its representative functions were increasing.

The festivities went on for almost two weeks. Artists like Simon de Pas and Karel van Mander, a pupil of Rembrandt's, were responsible for the visual design, and Heinrich Schütz for the musical dimension. Envoys arrived from the Emperor, from Spain, France, Sweden and Poland and from a number of German states. The delegation from Saxony arrived with an entourage of 532 persons and 479 horses. The entire celebration was described in an official publication by the bookseller Jørgen Holst in German in 1635 under the Latin title *Triumphus nuptialis Danicus* and later on in Danish in 1637 as *Regiae Nuptiae*, and once again in 1648 in German, supplied with engravings by Crispin de Pas, under the original title. The author emphasizes the importance of the communication of knowledge about the event to 'High mighty Potentates, as well as those of the more humble classes', and he remarks that the 'inventions' 'contained hidden and clandestine interpretations and remarks'.[12] Another source is the description by the French representative count Claude de Mesmes' secretary Charles Ogier.

The celebration included immensely expensive plays, ballets, fireworks, tournaments, and riding at the ring combined with inventions, in all eighteen, with the participation of royal and noble persons. Peace was the overall theme. The invitations were sent out in the names of the two Scipios, Publius Scipio Africanus and Lucius Scipio Asiaticus, who announced that they had come to Denmark because they had heard rumours of this great 'festivity of joy'; although Europe is disturbed by the ongoing war, the Scipios invite guests to a celebration of the bliss of peace.[13] The king's own magnificent invention presented the ages in terms of classical mythology and history, nature and human life, focused especially on four carriages symbolizing four seasons and four ages of man. The first part of

---

[12] Skovgaard-Petersen, 'Danske konger' p. 414ff.

[13] These texts contained keys to interpretation of the performance. Ogier found that the king and the prince were dressed in a Roman way like Marcus Aurelius on old coins. And he admired and enjoyed the musical and visual abundance and splendour. The sensuous experience of colours, music, noises, movements, and rhythms was overwhelming, which in itself communicated a message of strength.

the very detailed and sophisticated royal invention was a development of the motif of chaos, and it concluded with the depiction of peace and prosperity as a result of the good ruler's virtuous and wise government, related to a long row of Roman personifications of virtues and to the ship of Mercury, Neptune and Fortuna. In the procession the victorious Scipios were impersonated by the king and his son, the prince-elect (fig. 5). In front of them rode their armour bearers, displaying their standards with the sun and the moon respectively painted on them (fig. 1). The sun was shown on the king's standard, and supplied with the inscription *Instantia nubile solvet* ('It shall dissolve threatening clouds'), implying a promise that the menace of chaos would be transformed into prosperous order. On the prince's standard was written *Speranti aspirabitur* ('It will be breathed upon, as it is hoping for'), meaning that as the moon shall receive the sun's beams, so the son will obtain the paternal grace and wisdom.

Other inventions presented the four rulers of the world according to the aforementioned conventional interpretation of Daniel's prophecy in the Old Testament, namely the Assyrian, the Persian, the Greek, and the Roman founders of empires, Ninus, Cyrus the Great, Alexander the Great, and Julius Caesar. These heroes wanted to attend this magnificent wedding feast, evidently considering the Danish monarch their equal. Even the Norse past was involved: invitations were sent out in the *mantenadors'* names of Gotrik, Frode, Halvdan and Siger, legendary heroic kings and predecessors known from the medieval historian Saxo Grammaticus. Ancient Danish history was thus equalized with classical antiquity.[14] Plays and ballets where a Nordic aspect was inserted into classical mythology paid homage to the majesty and the prince amid a multiplicity of cultural references. Even a group of Pantaloons participated, the first physical appearance of *commedia dell'arte* masks in northern Europe. The crucial point in the total staging of the feast was, however, the depiction of the progress from chaos to order, suggested by the figure of the sun.

The sun is one of the strongest expressions of power's superhuman implications. In the image of the sun, divinity and royalty are connected in numerous ways, from primitive magic to sublime symbolism. When Christian was elected crown prince in 1580, a play was performed called *The swearing of the oath of allegiance to King Solomon* and depicting the old king David who had his son Solomon anointed as his successor in order to secure peace and prosperity. At the swearing of the oath, the young prince,

---

[14] In 1637 the king ordered a series of eighty-four paintings of his (partly legendary) predecessors' heroic deeds executed by Dutch artists. The pictures were meant to be distributed in the shape of engravings in order to display the glory of his realm on the European stage: from the Cimbri defeating the Romans onwards.

symbolically representing Christian, performed as the centre of circles of
planets and angels who surrounded and protected him: he was the sun. In
other words, he was the focal point of a solar system closed in upon itself.
(The role of prince Solomon was played by an actor). In 1603 Christian had
made his ritual entry into the city of Hamburg, appearing in a pageant as
'Herr Sol', Sir Sun, as part of a procession, an open, linear structure very
different from the closed structure of the solar system evoked in the 1580
play. The ceremonial procession was a linear practice, with a direct appeal
to the public. That, too, was the case in *The Great Wedding Feast*, where
Christian, apart from being the equal of classical heroes, was symbolized by
the sun that manages to ban chaos.

Normally Danish court culture of the first part of the seventeenth century is compared to analogous German practice, evidently due to the strong
connections between Denmark and the German sphere, in addition to the
English and the Dutch links. However, a tentative examination of, for example, French court culture shows significant similarities to that of Denmark, indicating a certain homogeneity of European royal culture in spite of
great cultural differences. Cosmological notions of the prince's figure and
function are found in French court ballets and in symbolic choreographic
shows on horseback, the so-called carrousels, where they are communicated
through the metaphor of the sun as the centre of the planetary system, as the
expeller of chaos, and as the source of prosperity. In 1653, a few months
after his solemn *entrée* into Paris, Louis XIV as a young prince performed
the part of the *Roy Soleil*, the Sun King, in the court ballet *La Nuit* (*The
Night*), where he drives away the forces of night, darkness and chaos, thus
implying that the sombre time was disappearing, the sun was rising. Ten
years later, in 1663, when Louis performed in *Le Grand Carrousel*, His
Majesty appeared as the centre of the planetary system and of power, performing as the Sun, and at the same time as Caesar; his brother Monsieur
appeared as the moon, and others represented bodies further out in the universe, according to their positions in the state hierarchy.[15] The closed solar
system around the central figure did not imply an immediate interaction
with the public, unlike entries, 'inventions', and pageants that moved
through the city. Two different aspects and conceptions of court and power
are reflected by, respectively, the closed, circular system and the open, linear performance. The circular formation demonstrates and confirms the system of power. The progressive movement has to do, literally, with ritualistic
transition, which gained intense power from the public's applause. Gener-

---

[15] On the representation of Louis XIV as sun-king, see Richard Maber's essay in this
volume.

ally speaking, during the 17th century the ruler tended to become an increasingly distant figure.

The Divine Monarch

Stagings of Formalized Absolutism

In the staging of the pageants, Christian IV had performed as various characters, which merged in dialectical ways with his own royal identity. The king did not attempt to create the theatrical illusion that he was the Pope. The point was that it was precisely the king who performed as the Pope. The signification was found in the complexity of roles. It was an act of grotesque exorcism which, given the coronation context, had ritualistic overtones. In many ways this was also true of *The Great Wedding Feast*. Through the flickering multiplicity of connotations, the king embodied determination and wisdom.

After *The Great Wedding Feast* the genre of the 'invention' disappeared. The genre implied the king playing a role; he appeared as a symbolic and/or mythological figure which conveyed a complex of meanings about him. After the disappearance of the genre, the king performed as himself in the ceremonial processions. He was simply the king, a figure which on the other hand in itself implied metaphysical significance.

The king might for instance 'take part' in the pompous funeral processions in the form of a dead body. Christian died in 1648. The prince-elect had died even earlier, so Christian's successor was his younger brother Frederik (III). Magnificent ceremonial display was limited, partly due to the financial state of the realm. The allegorical stagings, formerly known from the 'inventions', took the shape more of mostly closed panegyric court ballets, in the beginning including noble performers, but later on as professional performances.

Hereditary monarchy and formal absolutism was introduced in Denmark by Frederik III with a *coup d'état* in 1660, that is one year before Louis XIV took over personal government in France. This implied the abolition of the coronation charter, meaning that the king was now explicitly responsible to God alone. The contradictions and conflicts which had complicated the governing situation of Christian IV were dissolved. Now the prince, the king, was unquestionably a divine being, an earthly god. In the six volumes, 1143 pages in all, of his *De Jure Regio*, published between 1663 and 1672, professor and Bishop Hans Wandal explained the theological and theoretical basis of absolutism. Thus the church participated in communicating the message about the subjects' obligation to absolute obedience.

The king became king the moment his father died. The binding relation to God occurred immediately when the king inherited royal power. When he was anointed and crowned at the castle of Frederiksborg in 1671 as the first hereditary king, Christian V himself, rather than a bishop, placed the crown on his head. Nor were the other royal regalia, placed on the altar, conveyed to him by others. Christian V's alliance was directly with God. A number of details were removed from the ceremony: it was not for any man to point out to the absolute monarch his duties. The *Royal Law* had substituted the coronation charter as the constitution of the realm. Its rather radical content had been kept secret until the coronation, when it was read aloud, but still not published. According to this law the king does not need to be crowned. It is only out of consideration for the public, that 'it is Our will that the King publicly is anointed in the church with the due ceremonies'.[16] Christian IV became king when he was crowned, whereas Christian V was crowned to show he was king. From now on, the ceremonies, with the exception of the anointment of Christian VII, took place in the chapel of Frederiksborg created by Christian IV, and not in Copenhagen, which gave the event a closed, distant character. The crown was new, and so was the interpretation of its symbolism. Bishop Hans Wandal, whose anointment account and sermon was published in 1671, explained for example that the jewels stood for the king's virtues. The symbolic message of Christian IV's crown was that the king's strength depended on his noblemen. Now it was interiorised to concern his own exceptional qualities.[17] The royal circle was closing around itself.

In his sermon Wandal declared, that Christian V was a successor of Solomon, indeed he was like Solomon himself. He was God's son. He was man and god at the same time, as the ceremony suggested. The words spoken at the anointment are completely identical to the words used at the anointment of Louis XIV in 1654. Wandal used the same arguments and the same Scripture texts, the same biblical references, especially Psalm 82 about the kings' divinity, and the same conclusions. As has been observed above, they had even featured in the coronation of Christian IV, but then formally concerning the post, not the person. Even the reference to the Sun occurs at the anointment of Christian V: 'God reveals himself in the Kings, like the Sun in its beams'. Christian should be an emergent sun, said Wandal. His offspring should be like the moon.

On the occasion of Christian V's anointment, the important hymn writer Thomas Kingo wrote a panegyric poem, *Hosiannah*, where the king, the queen and the peers of the realm are compared to the sun, the moon and

---

[16] Eller, Poul, *Salvingerne på Frederiksborg* (Copenhagen 1976) p. 10.
[17] Boesen, *Regalier* p. 114.

the stars. Again, the planetary metaphor corresponds with, for example, the *Grand Carrousel* with Louis XIV as the centre of the universe with the minor planets circling around him. And Kingo goes on to describe his Majesty's manly chest as 'circular, loaded with power'. This image of the royal chest as the disc of the sun reminds us immediately of the image of *Le Roy Soleil*. Louis's costume included the image of the sun on his chest. This is not a question of influence, but rather of shared ideas of the prince as a life-giving power.[18]

However, the model for the marketing of Danish absolutism became to a high degree French, in its conception as well as its stagings in rituals and the arts. As a crown prince Christian had visited the court of Louis XIV, and as king he adopted various customs and strategies from Louis's court. Generally speaking, the absolute ruler did not impersonate or imitate: he embodied.[19] The ruler took the shape of a metaphysical being in his own right, not a performer of complex identities. His symbolic image was that of a Roman emperor. At the same time a systematic hierarchization and ritualization of society and social life was introduced. The social roles were strictly defined.

In the audience hall at Frederiksborg Castle, Christian had four allegorical women depicted, representing the four continents, as a message of the universal kingdom, together with paintings of his dynastic predecessors, and celestial angels or *putti* floating around the crown over the king's monogram and portrait as a Roman emperor, in an easily readable symbolism. The royal house of Oldenburg, the dynasty, was displayed, together with the inherited nature of royal power.[20]

The Nordic perspective appeared in some connections, unlike the practically absent Christian aspect. In 1683 Thomas Kingo's opera-ballet *King*

---

[18] Kingo is quoted from Akhøj-Nielsen, M., ed., *Thomas Kingo. Digtning i udvalg* (Copenhagen 1995) p. 29ff; in the same year the Court poet Anders Bording called the new king 'your people's sun' in a homage poem, cf. Sønderholm, E., ed., *Anders Bording* (Copenhagen 1986), p. 168ff. The metaphor lived on. In 1737 a panegyric poem to Christian VI proclaims: 'Long live! Our Glory, Sun, and joy / next to the invisible God our visible God and jewel'.

[19] Cf. the introductory phase of Louis XIV's regime, when his symbolic identity was as Apollo, *le Roy Soleil*, Alexander, Caesar and so on. Later he tended to be a divine figure in his own right, *Louis Le Grand*.

[20] The 'Roman' costume, combined with the full-bottomed wig, is known as a model in the depictions of Louis XIV, in monuments, reliefs, paintings and carousels. It was imitated even in the carousels organized by Christian V. The most interesting point is that it is also the heroic costume in elevated drama and opera, in France as well as in Germany. The 'Roman' costume is found on the Danish stage until the last part of the eighteenth century, when it began to seem outdated and pathetic. As knowledge about dress in Nordic antiquity was minimal, Norse heroes on the stage appeared as modified Greeks and Romans.

Dan was performed on the occasion of the king's birthday, of his allegedly victorious Scanian war and of the promulgation of the body of laws, the *Danish Law*. It was performed at the mansion of Charlottenborg, in the centre of the capital, and was communicated to the public via a newspaper. The performance takes place in Elysium, equipped with green trees, a big fountain and the throne of Jove. King Dan, the legendary founder of the dynasty, surrounded by a variety of famous historical figures, praises the present king's great merits and virtues and asks Jove permission to visit Denmark and his descendant brave King Christian whom Jove has bestowed with his lightening and thunder. With great joy Jove has learnt the fame of Christian's gallantry and deeds, and he explains to Dan that in the present Denmark, he will have some linguistic difficulties: the runes have changed since Dan's times! Mercury must therefore be his interpreter. Mercury first undertakes a preparatory research trip. On his return he informs Jove that Christian is even greater than his fame suggests. Rank him among the high gods, he says; he is the greatest on earth. Jove orders Aeolus and the sun to equip King Dan with a chariot of clouds and to light up his path. At the end King Dan turns to the real king present in the hall, Christian, and congratulates him, even on behalf of Jove, and praises Denmark. The geniuses of joy and love promise the king rich pleasures, and four heroes perform a sword dance. Mars, Fama and Victoria honour the king, and five warriors execute a martial dance, banging their shields together in a way that produces the royal coat of arms, amid the fanfare of trumpets. The king was at once the main subject and the main spectator. He was no longer performing. He was the justification of it all. He was the centre of the event without participating in it.

These were closed performances, reserved for a limited circle to attend on one specific occasion. A similar opera, *Der vereinigte Götterstreit* ('The settled Controversy between the Gods'), was performed to celebrate the king's forty-fourth birthday in 1689. A theatre had been erected in the garden of the castle Sophie Amalienborg in the capital. The pompous performance was clearly inspired by the grandiose stagings of *Le Roi Soleil*. The hall was magnificently packed with royal symbols and laid out as an enormous arbour. The ceiling was decorated as a heaven with golden stars: the theatre was a microcosm; the drama was cosmic. Divine forces paid homage to, and congratulated, his Majesty. Their descent from Mount Olympus to the greatest of all heroes, King Christian, was accompanied by music, fireworks, and cannons. Apollo and Mars quarrelled about whether martial glory or peaceful joy should dominate the realm. In the end they agreed that armed peace serves the country best. All Danes should praise the eternal reign of Christian, commanded Jove. The gods ascended among roars of cheers and the sounds of trumpets and timpani.

The success was so great that the king decided to have the performance repeated four days later for an audience that included even people of lower ranks. When Mars started his praise of the heroes of former times, an oil lamp exploded. All the dry leafage caught fire immediately. The audience panicked. The doors opened inward. In a quarter of an hour around 180 people perished in the flames. The fire spread to the castle, which burned down to the ground. For decades the clergy used this incident as an argument concerning the dubious nature of theatre as an art form. The remarkable point is however the effects of repetition of the performance. Such court performances were related to the occasion upon which they were performed. When repeated they were detached from their context and assumed the status of theatre, valuable for its own aesthetic qualities. The absence of the king implied a step from rituality to theatricality.

The royal funeral in 1699 represented a total theatre, theatrical in all aspects and throughout the space of performance and audience. The royal castle was illuminated with coloured lamps in the shape of skulls. In the palace yard was placed a triumphal arch, and in the palace square stood columns with flaming bowls. The navy in the port was illuminated. While the king's dead body was carried through the town, his symbolic image was displayed in an enormous scene of apotheosis placed on the top of the Chancellery and illuminated from behind: the deceased king steering his triumphal chariot over the clouds. It is not difficult to find models for this in the imagery of the *Roi Soleil.*

Concluding Remarks

The Long Baroque

The *querelle entre les anciens et les modernes*, in the form of the fight for a contemporary imagery, implied a critique of the metaphysical conception of power. The longevity of expressions of absolutism was nonetheless remarkable. One could talk about a 'long Baroque'. In conclusion an attempt shall be made to pursue the main expressions of royal power, the Christian, the Norse and the Roman, into the eighteenth century.

The premises and practices of the anointment lived on. At the anointment of Frederik IV in 1700 the throne was compared to the throne of God. The queen was compared to Mary who sat at the feet of Jesus and listened. It was not until the late eighteenth century that the conception of kings as earthly gods began to appear anachronistic. Nevertheless, even then, the conceptual and ceremonial apparatus remained intact, even though the autocratic system was moving from one-man government to bureaucracy.

The earliest thorough performative displays of the Norse dimension are found in the Hamburg Opera's productions of panegyric operas by Reinhard

Keiser with subjects taken from, for example, Saxo.[21] In 1721 Keiser and
the company were rewarded with an engagement at the royal court of Copenhagen. In 1723 Keiser produced *Ulysses* which praised the royal couple
by depicting them in the ideal guises of Ulysses and Penelope. The context
implied a complex and interactive role-playing. Frederik IV, the head of the
church, was a former practitioner of bigamy: his present queen was an ex-
mistress to whom he had earlier been married 'by the left hand', a manoeu-
vre that was sanctioned by learned theologians. No contradiction was perceived between this and the idealised presentation of king and queen as
Ulysses and Penelope. The Lord's anointed managed to live in parallel realities. Frederik was sovereign.

The Norse dimension, reflecting a specific national identity, co-existed
with conventional classical references and depictions of the kings as great
and generous emperors. In a 'Temple of Virtues' for the deceased Christian
VI in 1746, the king's coffin was surrounded by Justice and Peace, personified by Norse heroes Magnus Lagabøte and Frode Fredegod. The temple
itself was Doric! Frederik V supported Paul Henri Mallet's work on Northern history and mythology, which had a considerable European impact in
the second half of the century. It was meant to show the North as the realm
of freedom, as opposed to the South. Although the increasing focus on
Norse themes suggested a weakening of the homogeneity of European culture, the performative consequences of that trend primarily took place on
the theatrical stage, as dramas and operas, whereas the appearance of royal
pomp was still deeply rooted in Romance fashion and culture.

In 1770-1772 Denmark was *de facto* governed by Christian VII's re-
formatory German physician Johann Friedrich Struensee. In the end Struensee was arrested, and, with reference to the sixth book of the *Danish Law*
from 1683 and the twenty-sixth paragraph of the *King's Law* from 1665, he
was accused of having offended the king's sacrosanct person and misused
power which belonged to royal authority. He was accused of *crimen laesae
maiestatis*, condemned to death and executed with a detailed and ritual cruelty that aroused horror in enlightened Europe. The execution was meticu-
lously staged, and the staging was published in various written and illustrated versions. While the king, Christian VII, was mentally ill, and

---

[21] In 1702 he presented *Regner*, about a Swedish princess and the Danish Prince.
Although Nordic, the princess prays to Venus. In 1706 Keiser produced *Die listige
Rache des Suenos*, presenting the Norwegian city of Bergen with columns and laurels, and an illuminated Roman triumphal arch for King Sven and his admiral Hulde-
ricus. Irene was shown in the clouds surrounded by the Graces and the patron spirits
of Denmark and Norway with Mars in chains at their feet. Later, in Copenhagen, he
created, for example, *Othin*.

completely unable to govern, his power and person were sacred: Struensee had offended God.

The celebratory play *Cereris og Thetidis Strid* ('The Quarrel between Ceres and Thetis'), performed in 1774, written by the illustrious poet Johannes Ewald, on the occasion of a wedding in the royal house, is an almost anachronistic, conventional celebration of Christian VII's happy regime which creates blessing and prosperity in growth, art and wisdom. It mixes Roman mythology with references to 'Skjoldungen' and similar Norse subjects. The idea is that Ceres and Thetis, that is, the earth and sea, quarrel about who 'supplies the greatest wealth to the North'. Even if Ceres has granted the country riches and rapture, Thetis insists that she herself has brought an 'even greater treasure to the North', namely the princess Frederikke of Mecklenburg-Schwerin. The theatrical costume worn, for example, by Vertumnus, the god of the seasons, was a complete repetition of the symbolic Baroque 'Roman' costume worn by kings and actors (fig. 6). The depiction of the king as a superhuman metaphysical figure demonstrates, together with the heroic costumes, that it made no difference if the divine ruler was a poor and scared schizophrenic madman.[22] Regardless of Christian's awareness or behaviour, he embodied royalty.

In 1784 the crown prince took power, even if the insane king was still the formal absolute ruler. After the prince's participation in a short military campaign in Sweden in 1788, the Danish king was praised like this: 'Thanks be to You, that You gave us this Your Son! (...) the people (...) thank You, as mankind praises the Father of the Universe for the Redeemer.'[23] The parallelism between the royal and the heavenly father and son was still intact and apparently near at hand. The national euphoria almost automatically gave rise to another element of continuity, the image that had survived all cultural transpositions: the sketch for a monument of the crown prince's victory shows the image not of a contemporary or Norse or Christian hero, but of a Roman emperor.

---

[22] This convention for the appearance of heroic figures was even seen in Ewald's tragedy *Balders død* (*Balders's Death*) from 1778, which takes place among Norse gods, where we recognize the conventional Roman classical costume as *the* heroic imagery. The visual reference is to a heroic dimension which implies the regime's official mythology.

[23] Holm, E., *Om det Syn paa Kongemagt, Folk og borgerlig Frihed, der udviklede sig i den dansk-norske Stat i Midten af det 18de Aarhundrede (1746-1770)* (Copenhagen 1883) p. 58.

The Constant Prince

There are no sharp distinctions between rituality and theatricality in the beginning of the period treated here. People of high rank performed in the context of activities which affected and modified reality. By contrast, later on, when the entirety of societal life had been ritualized, the tendency was that professional performers executed the impersonations, albeit still in celebrative, ceremonial ways. After that, a 'secularization' meant that heroic pomp appeared on stage as pure theatre, while the ruler simply embodied metaphysical power. The distinction between ritual and theatre becomes more explicit; although not complete: on the one hand the stage might be used for the celebration of royal glory; and on the other hand, to those who denied metaphysical notions of power, the official performativity seemed deprived of meaning, that is pure and senseless 'theatre'.

In addition, *grosso modo* one could say that in the first period up to introduction of absolutism, in the period of the wars of religion, Christian notions were central; in the next phase, dominated by fatal wars with Sweden, Roman elements became dominant; and in the final period, with growing complications in relation to the German domain, the Nordic theme acquired increasing importance, although it did not impact upon the ruler's own performance. The Norse dimension is, firstly, a proof and legitimization of the regime's antiquity, gradually implying that the Nordic dynasty is comparable to the classical empires, and finally passing into a conception of Nordic history, culture and mythology as even more valuable and powerful than the Southern cultures.

Theatre dealt with a basic need for spectacle, to such a degree that it maintained the metaphysical, divine, overtones. It is an interesting fact that the heroic costumes of the royal figures in their symbolic identity correspond to the costumes of serious drama, and that there is no distinction between 'Roman' and 'Norse' imagery in relation to this. The visual conventions (costumes) for the elevated heroic characters are homogenous: they appear as Baroque 'Romans', just as the royal figures do. Splendour was rooted in the Baroque understood as an intensified version of the Renaissance, itself a re-enactment of Antiquity. Thus the idea and appearance of splendour implies the magnificence and spectacle of Antiquity. Splendour shares this characteristic with the church, especially the Catholic one. Divine royalty is Baroque.

Concerning the commonplace 'the king', it thus turns out that three levels can be observed. Firstly, there is a general idea of the ruler as a paternal, superhuman figure; that idea is not affected by the fundamental changes of the legal basis of kingship. Secondly, we see a theoretical, legislative conception of the ruler which undergoes drastic transformations in the period. And, finally, there is the appearance of the king, which, although to begin with might have implied roleplaying, was very much related to splendour, to the magnificence and spectacle of Antiquity, and to religious connotations.

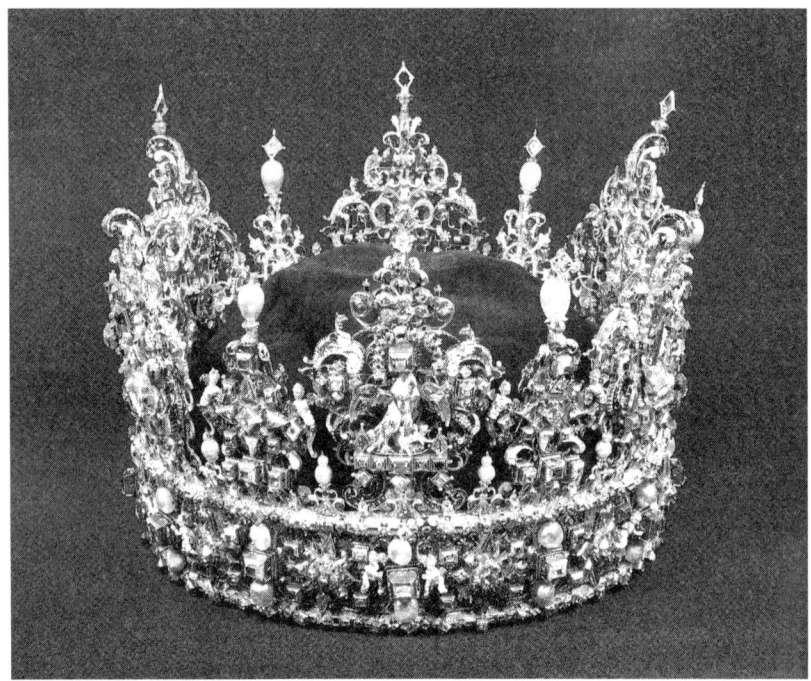

1. Dirich Fyring: the crown of Christian IV with allegories of royal virtues. Gold, enamel, diamonds and pearls, 1596. The Chronological Collections of the Danish Kings, Rosenborg, Copenhagen.

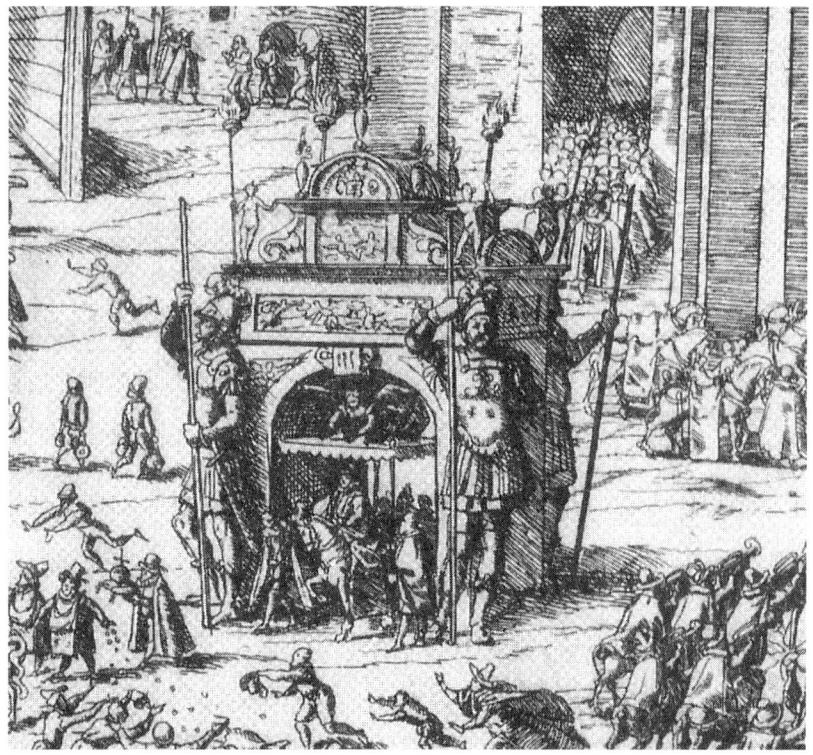

2. Triumphal arch for the crowning procession of Christian IV. Engraving by Philip Uffenbach in August Erich, Klarlige oc visse Beskriffuelse, Copenhagen 1598. Detail.

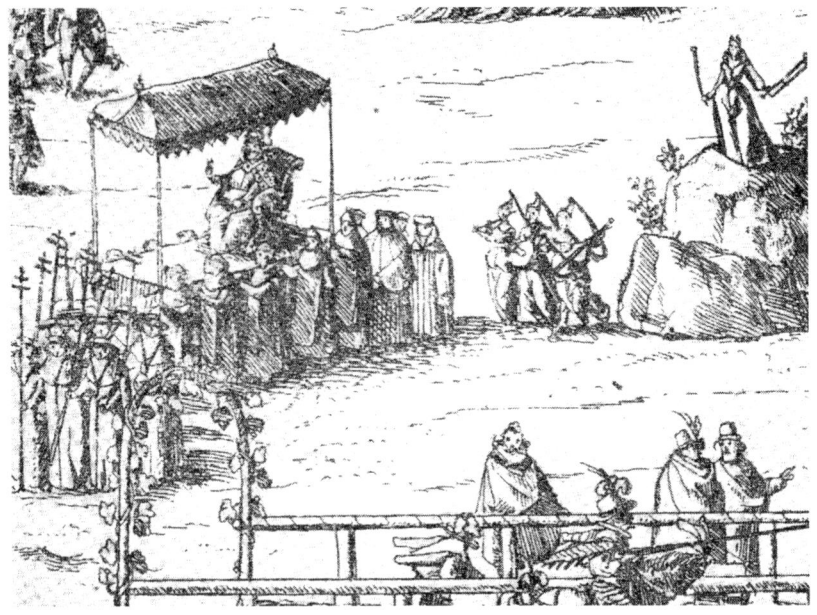

3. Christian IV performing as pope Sergius IV during the crowning celebrations.
Engraving by Philip Uffenbach in August Erich, Klarlige oc visse Beskriffuelse,
Copenhagen 1598. Detail.

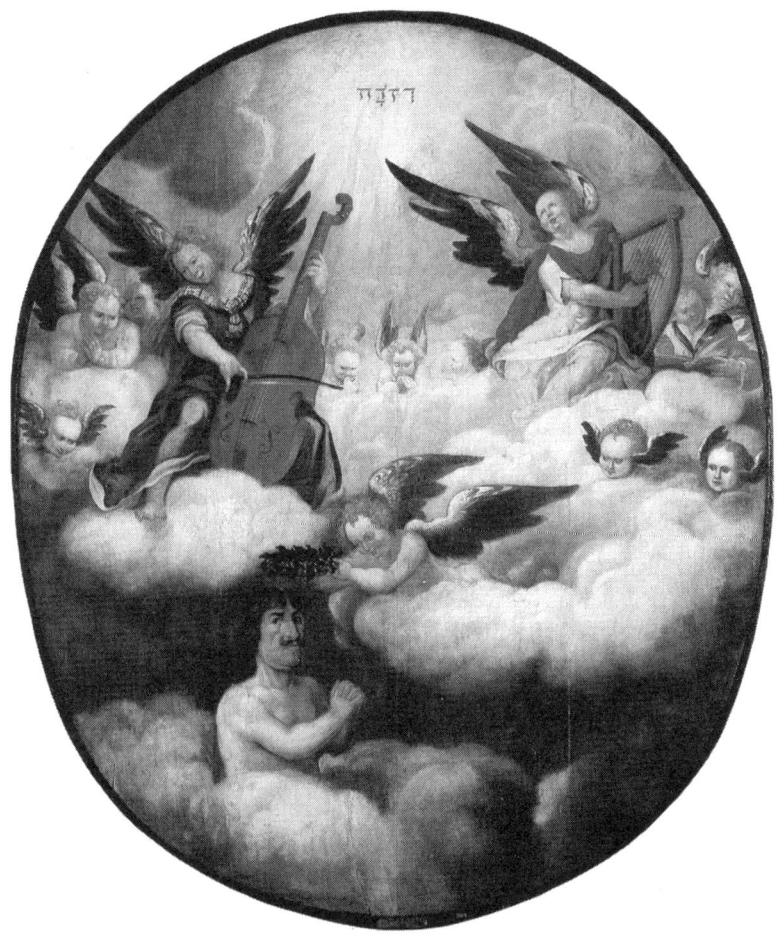

4. Anonymous: *The apotheosis of Christian IV*. Oil painting, ca. 1644. The Chronological Collections of the Danish Kings, Rosenborg, Copenhagen.

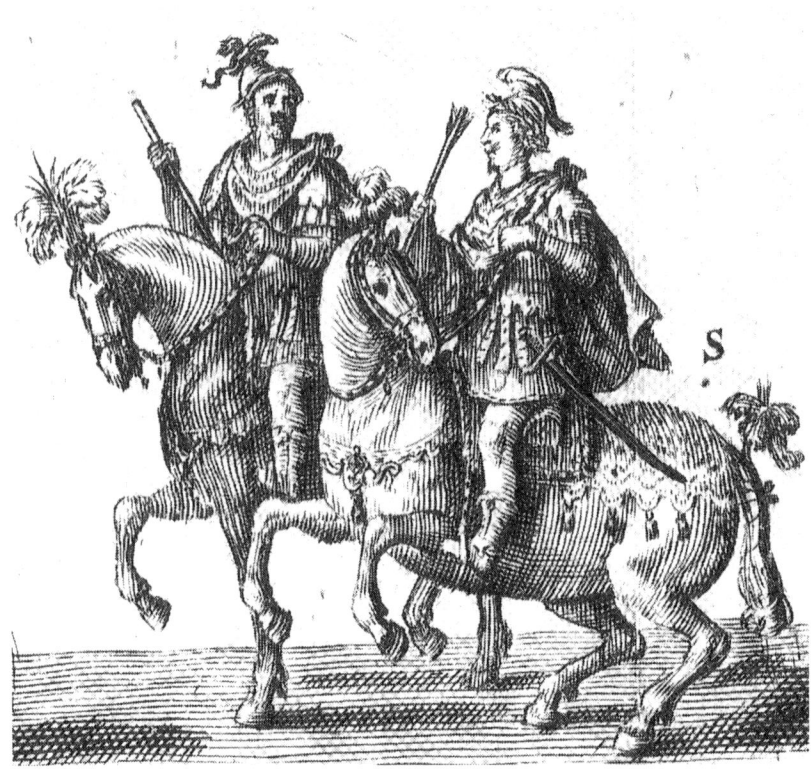

5. Christian IV and the prince-elect as the two Scipios at The Great Wedding, 1634. Engraving by Crispin de Pas II in Jørgen Holst, Triumphus Nuptialis Danicus, Copenhagen 1648. Detail.

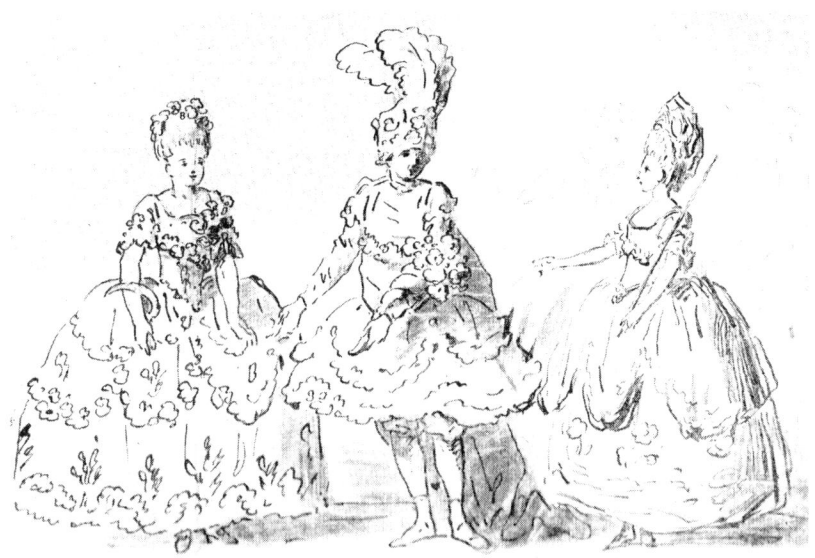

6. Ceres, Vertumnus and Thetis wearing 'roman' costumes in a celebration play at the royal theatre of Copenhagen, 1774. Drawing by Peter Cramer, 1774.

THE 'NETHERLANDISH BEEHIVE' (1608)

PUBLIC OPINION AND IDENTITY AS A COMMONPLACE IN
DUTCH ANTI-PEACE PROPAGANDA

Vincent van Zuilen

Honourable, dearly beloved Reader. A good Friend requested that I should gather all [booklets] on the subject of Truce or Peace that have been published recently. Because there are many enthusiasts, he said, who greatly seek after them in order to have them bound together, but are not sure whether they already possess them. Yes, even the Booksellers do not know what has been published so far. Therefore, I have put together and described all those I could get in this Dialogue. I call it the *Netherlandish Beehive* because it contains so many good warnings, sweet as the taste of honey, which may please all the lovers of the Fatherland. [....] God save our Netherland[s] from all quarrels and discord.[1]

In these words an anonymous author and publisher introduced a popular Dutch pamphlet, *Den Nederlandtschen Bye-Korf* (*The Netherlandish Beehive*), which appeared in 1608 amidst the largest pamphlet war the Netherlands had ever seen. The occasion at hand was the peace negotiations between the States General of the United Provinces and the ambassadors of the sovereign Archdukes of the Habsburg Netherlands, who also acted on behalf of the King of Spain. The official negotiations started in May 1607, and only after almost two years of hard bargaining did they result in a truce of twelve years, starting in April 1609. The negotiations proved to be so lengthy and tiresome due to the following three deal-breaking issues. The Dutch demanded a formal recognition of their political and religious free-

---

[1] *Den Nederlandschen Bye-korf: Waer in Ghy lieden beschreven vindt/ al tghene dat nu wtghegaen is/ op den Stilstant ofte Vrede/ zeer nootzakelijc om te lesen van alle Liefhebbers des Vaderlandts...* (s.l., 1608), Catalogue Knuttel no. 1474, [p. 2]. Hereafter I will refer to it as the *Beehive*. As I will point out later on, 'Netherlandish' should not be confused with 'Dutch'. The former refers to the entirety of the Netherlands, the latter to only the northern provinces constituting the Dutch Republic. Importantly, this author, like many others in his day, referred to the Netherlands in the singular: Netherland, suggesting a stronger sense of unity.

dom, as well as of their 'natural' right to the profitable overseas trade with the Indies.[2]

When the *Beehive* appeared, at some point in late spring 1608, Dutch society was agitated by countless rumours, and numerous pamphlets speculated on the outcome of the negotiations. In less than two years, over 250 different pamphlets about this particular event are known to have been published, whereas for the previous forty years of pamphleteering the annual average was in all probability no more than twenty to thirty different pamphlet publications on particular topics. Although the total production of these propagandistic booklets is hard to estimate, it seems safe to assume that the author of the *Beehive* did not exaggerate the volume of printed political texts that swamped the Dutch reading public in 1607 and 1608. Since the success of propaganda depends largely on its discussion of current events and its speedy communication of them, pamphlets are usually considered to be disposable consumer goods with only a relatively short life expectancy. From this point of view, it is telling that for almost each individual pamphlet mentioned in the *Beehive* four or more different editions or reprints have survived today. On these grounds, the pamphlets should be regarded as political best sellers,[3] and even more strikingly as functional collectors' items: 'worthy to keep safe, [because] one day they might refresh our memory'.[4]

According to C.E. Harline, the pamphlets printed during the truce negotiations mark an important transition in Dutch political culture. From 1607 onward, pamphlets became 'a commonplace element in Dutch political life'.[5] Not only did the number of pamphlets increase explosively in these years, they also confronted the States with a large-scale campaign of criticism for the first time. With only a single exception, all these pamphlets opposed the prospect of peace or truce with the King of Spain and his allies. Whereas most of the printed propaganda during the first decades of the Dutch Revolt was either directly or indirectly state-sponsored, it seems safe to assume that from the turn of the century pamphleteering increasingly became the product of private initiative.[6] While most authors remain anonymous, this assumption is supported by the increasingly rich diversity of literary styles and genres that might appeal to all social groups in society.

---

[2] The best overview of these negotiations is still W.J.M. van Eysenga, *De wording van het Twaalfjarig Bestand van 9 april 1609* (Amsterdam, 1959).

[3] C. E. Harline, *Pamphlets, Printing, and Political Culture in the Early Dutch Republic* (Dordrecht, 1987), p. 236.

[4] *Beehive*, [p. 2]

[5] Harline, *Pamphlets*, p.11.

[6] Harline, *Pamphlets*, p. 34, pp. 46-56.

Dialogues between various kinds of people, poems, songs, dreams, and rid-dles became the predominant printed form in which to convey political messages, ideas, and convictions. While the decision-making processes in the Dutch Republic remained the exclusive domain of only a small group of regents, these more popular genres enhanced the role of public opinion in Dutch society in two ways.

First, in these pamphlets and particularly in the dialogues, the image of a passive, uninformed, and silent majority, incapable of understanding the fine art of politics, evolved into that of an actively involved community of people, whose opinions on state affairs should matter to the government. While in the traditional essayistic pamphlets the population was usually por-trayed in a subordinate role, the dialogues dealt with politics from the per-spective, interests, and daily experiences of humble tradesmen, artisans, farmers, soldiers, sailors, and so on. Although the conversations depicted were fictitious, they were part of highly recognizable situations, which en-abled any individual easily to relate the abstract principles and conse-quences of politics to their own personal life. The frequent use of common sayings and proverbs, humorous remarks and comments, everyday language and sometimes stereotypical regional dialects, also help to explain the ap-peal of essentially political dialogues, poems, and songs. By deploying the propagandistic techniques described above, the pamphleteers could more convincingly mobilize the support of the general public to further their spe-cific goals. Furthermore, from the early 1600s onward, pamphleteers more explicitly encouraged an attitude dreaded by any government in early mod-ern Europe, namely that the common man should feel free to express his opinion and to debate politics in public.[7]

Second, by converting complicated theories about state sovereignty, law, liberties, international trade, diplomacy, and theology into simpler forms, pamphleteers fulfilled a bridging function between the worldview and knowledge of the political and intellectual elites on the one hand, and those of popular culture on the other. As the author of the *Beehive* states, his selection of pamphlets consists of 'descriptions or whatever you might like to call them ... [They] reveal many secrets of state the common man does not know about'.[8] Thus, pamphleteers integrated privileged information and theories into existing popular patterns of thought, images, experiences, and

---

[7] *Ibidem.* Cf. P. Arblaster, '"Dat de boecken vrij sullen wesen": Private Profit, Pub-lic Utility and Secrets of State in the Seventeenth-Century Habsburg Netherlands', in: Koopmans, J.W., ed., *News and Politics in Early Modern Europe (1500-1800)*, Groningen Studies in Cultural Change, XIII (Leuven, Paris, Dudley Ma., 2005), pp. 79-95.

[8] *Beehive*, [p. 6]

general knowledge related to the war in the Netherlands. In turn, the addition of 'insiders'' information to conventional perceptions in one pamphlet could lead – as it often did – to a further discussion of these political commonplaces in other publications. Consequently, as I will show with reference to the case of the *Beehive*, in propaganda fixed interpretations of commonplaces could be transformed into new ones.

If we define commonplaces as 'non-elastic culturally sanctioned modes of thought and organisation of knowledge within a given community', the pamphlets of 1607-1609 raise fundamental questions regarding their use as a propagandistic tool. As Frans-Willem Korsten argues in this volume, commonplaces must have had a double, often self-contradicting potential in the sense that they confirmed existing convictions while also paving the way for change.[9] In the case of early modern printed propaganda, such as the Dutch pamphlets of 1607-1609, this seems to have been exactly the case. As the pamphleteers sought the support of the largest possible audience – that is, of all social segments of society – in order to intervene successfully in the political decision-making process, they addressed a huge, diverse, and anonymous public. To convince each and every individual – whose personal affiliations the pamphleteer could not possibly know – he needed examples and argumentation that were either actually valid or cleverly presented as such. Either way, the case of the *Beehive* and the pamphlets of 1607-1609 may illustrate to what extent commonplaces – that is, fixed or conventional modes of (political) thinking – were applied to a new situation.

Pamphlets and Public Opinion

The *Beehive* consists of a dialogue between a publisher from Holland (the author himself) and a Flemish bookseller, discussing the enormous demand for the 'countless' pamphlets that were published in a short period of time concerning the potential truce. Both men express their expectation that they will make good, possibly even quadruple, profits from gathering, binding and selling the most popular pamphlets. In the process, they mention the contents, prices and general importance of over thirty texts, including clearly argued essays on politics, religion and economics; invented dialogues between various kinds of people; poems; songs; dreams; riddles; and government documents related to the negotiations.

Thus the *Beehive* is introduced as a commercial enterprise devised by two clever business associates who have noticed the public's enthusiasm for

---

[9] 'God as Keystone of the System of Commonplaces: The Case of Joost Van Den Vondel's plays', pp. 1-24 in this volume.

information concerning the peace talks which had 'already lasted over a year, and still we do not see the outcome of it'.[10] The sheer lengthiness of the negotiations apparently made many people wonder what was causing a delay.[11] Could it be that the States were contemplating proposals which went beyond the original terms of war or peace, and which the people should know about? Furthermore, in the preceding decades, negotiations had either been called off or had resulted in provisional treaties that were violated shortly afterwards. Between 1600 and 1606, the States had firmly rejected any overture by the enemy, so why discuss peace terms in 1607? Could it have anything to do with the fact that Spain had concluded separate peace treaties with Holland's foreign allies, France (1598) and England (1603), which left the Dutch isolated in the face of an enemy which they might no longer be able to resist on their own?

The negotiations, forty years after the beginning of the Dutch Revolt, also raised the question of whether or not the original goals of the war had been met. Whereas the majority of the regents thought that the political and religious autonomy of the Dutch Republic was secure, dependent only upon the formal assent of the King of Spain and the archducal sovereigns of the southern provinces, the pamphleteers pleaded differently. They argued that the Spanish could not be trusted and would strike again in the future. Equally important, the pamphlets often reminded their public that the southern Netherlands, allies in the 1570s and 1580s, were still subjected to the yoke of tyranny. A peace treaty would imply a definite division of the Low Countries into two separate states, each with a political and ideological system of its own. Consequently, what many pamphleteers considered to be a distinct cultural community – a commonwealth of provinces that shared a common past of mutual interdependency, interests, and experiences – would be cut in half forever. While the province of Holland was prospering at present, the pamphleteers stressed that the States still had a moral obligation to continue the war, not only to honour their alliance with the inhabitants of the Spanish Netherlands, and to safeguard the security of the Free Provinces, but also to restore the God-given unity of the old commonwealth, upon which depended the prosperity of each separate province.[12]

---

[10] *Beehive*, [p. 5].

[11] *Proeve Des nu onlangs uyt-ghegheven Drooms/ off t'samen spraack tusschen den Coning van Hispanien ende den Paus van Roomen* (s.l., [1608]) (Knuttel no.1401), [p. 6].

[12] Cf. V. van Zuilen, 'The Politics of Dividing the Nation? News Pamphlets as Vehicle of Ideology and National Consciousness in the Habsburg Netherlands (1585-1609)', in: J.W. Koopmans, ed., *News and Politics in Early Modern Europe (1500-1800)*, Groningen Studies in Cultural Change, vol. XIII (Leuven, Paris, Dudley Ma., 2005), pp. 61-79.

As soon as the news about the negotiations became public, pamphleteers capitalised on lurking fears and uncertainties in order to mobilise public opposition against the States' presumed peace policy. As mentioned above, these writers tried to influence their readers by making them aware that a peace treaty would affect everyone dramatically. The commercial aspirations of the makers of the *Beehive*, the remarks of other pamphleteers related to public opinion, and the response of state officials illustrate the appeal of the pamphlets of 1607-1608. Within two or three months after its first publication in around May 1608, at least two updated and revised editions of the *Beehive* appeared.[13] The *Beehive* was a political enterprise. Although the author paid his respects to the government, his selection of pamphlets all either rejected any treaty with Spain and its allies explicitly, or could be interpreted as doing so. Most of these pamphlets expressed a deep-seated distrust of the apparent Spanish desire for a peaceful solution. The latter was perceived as just another trick to appease the Dutch until Spain regained its full strength and was able to strike again. Others feared a restoration of the Catholic Church, which in turn would eventually lead once more to the persecution of Protestants. Some pamphlets from the early years of the Dutch Revolt were added in order to remind readers that earlier attempts to reach a peaceful solution with the King of Spain and his allies in the Netherlands had failed. Peace with Spain was impossible by definition. Some pamphlets even suggested that some of the leading politicians in Holland had either been bribed by Spanish agents or were selfishly hoping to increase their personal trade profits by means of the peace treaty. The fact that the States had been willing to negotiate with the arch-enemy in the first place was propagated as proof in itself that at least part of the political elites, notably the rich merchant class of Holland's commercial centres such as Amsterdam, were jeopardizing everything that the people of the Netherlands had accomplished and suffered for severely in forty years of war.

The three known editions respectively advertise 30, 33, and 37 individual pamphlets, 28 of which were officially banned by the States of Holland and the General States in special placards of 28 and 29 August 1608. Considering the renowned freedom (albeit only relative) of the printing press in the Dutch Republic – during the entire seventeenth century only about 150 books were specifically forbidden[14] –, the government showed particularly little leniency in this case. Anyone who could be connected to the printing, selling, spreading, or even owning of a copy of the *Beehive* or any of the

---

[13] Cf. W. P. C. Knuttel, ed., *Catalogus van de pamfletten-verzameling, berustende in de Koninklijke Bibliotheek*, Vol. I (1486-1620) (The Hague, 1899), pp. 291-293.

[14] I. Weekhout, *Boekencensuur in de Noordelijke Nederlanden. De vrijheid van drukpers in de zeventiende eeuw* (The Hague, 1998), p. 60.

other condemned pamphlets would suffer severe penalties.[15] A far more extraordinary measure against a particular pamphlet was the States' order to their official printer to publish *Pieces mentioned in the 'Beehive' approved by the States*.[16] This clearly demonstrates the extent to which the success of the *Beehive* worried the States, even though they refrained from commenting on it directly. The resolution of the General States of 23 August 1608 states that booklets such as the *Beehive* had a damaging effect on the reputation of the state and the good of the commonwealth. According to the States, these pamphlets had been published for no other reason than to incite the community against the lawful government.[17]

The pamphlets often depict ordinary people talking about the negotiations in an everyday situation at home, in the street or while travelling by boat from one place to another. Time and again, the pamphleteers refer to people who read, share and discuss a variety of discourses, dialogues, and dreams. Apparently, pamphlets were generally available and part of everyday life. It is never suggested that the people do not read or buy books; they are given pointers about which books it is necessary to read.[18] For example, in a pamphlet where Pieter visits his friend Pauwels, he is not surprised to find him reading several booklets. He merely inquires whether there is anything new or interesting in these ones. Pauwels replies that they contain interesting facts and personal experiences related to the peace talks, which

---

[15] *Resoluties Staten van Holland* (s.l., s.d.; copy University Library Leiden), 20 August 1608, pp. 202-205.

[16] *Stucken gementioneerd in den Byenkorf die byde ... Staten Generael ... toeghestaen ende niet verboden worden ...* (The Hague, 1608) (Knuttel no. 1477). The texts include some of the documents and correspondence by the Archdukes, the King of Spain, and the General-States prior to the formal opening of the negotiations; a missive by the Emperor arguing that he should be included as a impartial mediator; a letter by the Prince of Orange and the States of Holland to King Philip II (1572); the famous Act of Abandonment of 1581; and, finally, an essay by the administrators of the East Indies Company pleading (quite redundantly) that the States should never renounce the Dutch claims to free trade with the Indies.

[17] *Resolutiën der Staten-Generaal van 1576 tot 1609*, XIV (1607-1609), Rijks Geschiedkundige Publicatiën 131 (The Hague, 1970), p. 624.

[18] The *Beehive* itself was meant in part as a catalogue or prospectus of propaganda. In the dialogue the Hollander says he will explain the contents of the pamphlets to the Fleming 'in the style of peasants because I am one of the 'blunt' people ('botte gheslacht'). Being 'blunt' was considered a (stereo)typical attribute of the people of Holland. In Holland itself people took pride in this reputation, interpreting it as meaning they were down-to-earth, simple yet pure.

help us, 'the common people, who have a short memory', to understand better what goes on in the Hague.[19]

In a dialogue between a Burgher who claims to have read all the tractates on the peace, a Nobleman who resides in government circles, a humble Boatman, and a Peasant, people with different social backgrounds openly discuss current politics on a track-boat. Even as the Burgher seems appalled that the Peasant and the Boatman share their views in public, the latter refuses to keep silent: 'Why should I hold my tongue, as I can buy books on this matter everywhere [?]'.[20] In conclusion to the discussion that follows, the Boatman expresses the wish that the conversation be published like all the others, whereas the Burgher thinks that there is already too much print in the world. Ironically, the author of this dialogue finishes with a short poem that may reflect the reality of propaganda and commerce: 'A poor horseman sat at the helm rudder and listened. He repeated the conversation to the printer, and thus it was printed in order to make some money.'[21]

Similarly, in the Testament of War of 1608, a personified War is dying and says farewell to all the people, of both high and low rank, who have served him so well. Demonstrating that almost every profession had benefitted from and still relied economically on a continuation of the war, he explicitly appreciates the efforts of writers in winning the hearts of the people to the cause of war. Once War is gone, he says, the writers will have to revert to walking the streets like peddlers to make a living.[22]

Some pamphlets discuss the situation in the Netherlands from the perspective of the enemy and even suggest that the Dutch have an international reputation for being literate, informed and always ready to debate politics in public. A dialogue between King Philip III and his chief negotiator, the friar Jan Neyen, depicts the frustrations of the Spanish court at their failure to lure the Dutch into a treacherous peace. Neyen explains to His Majesty that the Dutch simply cannot be fooled because 'everything we plan in private is revealed to them in all those dreams'. The envoy even expects that the

---

[19] *Discovrs Van Pieter en Pauwels/ Op de Handelinghe vanden Vreede* (s.l., 1608) (Knuttel no. 1456), [pp. 1-2].

[20] *Schuyt-praetgens, Op de Vaert naer Amsterdam/ tusschen een Lantman, een Hovelinck, een Borger, ende Schipper* (s.l., 1608) (Knuttel no. 1450), [pp. 4-5]. On this pamphlet also cf. Harline, Pamphlets, pp. 199-208.

[21] *Schuyt-praetgens*, [p. 8].

[22] *Het Testament vanden Oorloghe* (Knuttel no. 1409), [p. 5]: 'Writers simultaneously win the hearts of the people and make a living. Without war the writers will have to walk the streets like humble peddlers.'

King's new instructions will be sold in print on the streets even before he returns to the Netherlands.[23]

Another pamphlet 'reveals' the opinions of the Catholic cardinals, bishops, priests and religious orders concerning a treaty with the Dutch 'heretics' who are all literate, know the Bible and the psalms by heart, and seem aware of everything that happens in the Netherlands, England, France, Germany, and other countries. The author presents his pamphlet purposely 'in rhyme so Everyman may see'.[24] However, as another pamphleteer noted, there is one great disadvantage to this form of communication, namely that the people often find it so pleasant to read and sing these texts that they tend to miss the political warnings these pamphlets convey. Although his own Dream-vision was deliberately published as a comic play with songs meant to be to sung, the poet therefore reminds his audience that singing without contemplation is nothing but childish amusement.[25]

A rare example of the private reception of pamphlets is found in contemporary handwriting on the inside cover of *Considerations on the Peace in the Netherlands*. According to an anonymous reader, a certain burgomaster of Amsterdam who strongly opposed the prospect of peace wrote this pamphlet. In vain this regent had handed out his considerations during a meeting of the States of Holland and, soon afterwards, the text appeared in print and was sold to the people by peddlers on the street and in the bookshops.[26] Taken together, these examples give the impression that in the early seventeenth century pamphleteering had become an industry that provided many people in Holland with an income. Even though the witness cited above stresses that taking politics to the streets is contrary to 'a decent Dutch conscience', he implicitly admits that it had become common practice to do so.[27]

---

[23] *Raetsel* (Knuttel no. 1418) [pp. 1, 7]. This pamphlet bares the same pseudonym 'Yemandt (someone) Adams' as the *Beehive*.

[24] *Bulle Oft Mandaet des Paus van Roomen* (s.l., s.d.) (Knuttel no. 1444), [p. 7]. Some authors explicitly mention public performances of such pamphlets that made the public literally see what they described. The author of *Hovt en beleght. Een oudt Schipper van Monickendam* (s.l., 1608) (Knuttel no. 1472), [p. 5] addresses his audience as 'you spectators'.

[25] *DROOM-GESICHT eenes metter Herten tot GODT op-getrockenen mensches* (s.l., 1607) (Knuttel no. 1408), [p.7]

[26] *Consideratien vande Vrede in Nederlandt gheconcipieert* (s.l., 1608) (Knuttel no.1448a), [p. 2]. The handwriting is dated 'In April 1609'.

[27] *Ibidem.*

The Multifunctional Metaphor of the Beehive

The metaphor of a beehive was a well-chosen title for a pamphlet. Its use was multifunctional and could easily appeal to people of different political and religious persuasions. The image of a beehive represents a harmonious society, whose inhabitants are small individually but strong in their numbers. All bees work together industriously for the common good of their hive, and therefore can be associated with virtues such as diligence, piety, loyalty, and concord. In return, the commitment of the 'bees' is rewarded with prosperity sweet as the taste of honey. Like the Dutch, who depend on international trade, the bees fly out in search of nectar in all kinds of flowers, some of which turn out to be rich in nectar, while others prove to be poisonous. Like the bees which have to defend their hive against spiders, wasps, and flies, the Dutch also have 'natural' enemies who are envious of their prosperity. Furthermore, the beehive had a long tradition in literature and iconography as a classic symbol of hope. Being one of the seven cardinal virtues, hope was often depicted as the Roman goddess Spes who can be identified by fixed attributes such as broken chains, an anchor, and a beehive. Closely related to the virtue of hope, bees were also associated with the changing of the seasons. By resuming activity in spring, the bees herald the arrival of better times to come.

In the Netherlands in the sixteenth century the metaphor of the beehive was a frequently used commonplace in political and religious books and pamphlets to represent an ideal and pure community. In 1569, Philip of Marnix, a well-known adviser of William of Orange, and an important Calvinist ideologist of the Dutch Revolt, published his famous *Beehive of the Holy Roman Church* in order to refute the claims of Catholicism to be the community of the true Christian faith. After his death in 1598, Marnix was remembered for, amongst other things, the sweet rhetoric and eloquence of his *Beehive* that had frustrated 'the foul ambitions of the Pope'[28] In 1586, pamphleteers in favour of the English alliance described the Netherlands as a rich bouquet of flowers, home of the bees, who for their protection must swarm to the noble English rose rather than to the French lily.[29] In 1601, an anti-Spanish pamphlet instructed its readers that it was not enough to

---

[28] M. Zverius, *Claeg-dicht Over de doot vanden ... Heere Philips Marnix van St. Aldegonde. By maniere van tsamensprekinghe* (Leiden, 1600) (Knuttel no.1156), [p. 6].
[29] *Brevis narratio Triumphi quo a Senatu populogue Traiectensi... Robertus DudlAEus Comes LeicESTRIVS...* (Utrecht, 1586) (Knuttel no. 763). *Ghelyck als die Joden brvyt worden door Coningin Hester* (Utrecht, 1586) (Petit catalogue no. 443), [p. 4]: 'The poor native bees can no longer bear the insufferable Spanish flies'.

slaughter the venomous spiders, but rather they must behave like true little bees that 'are medicinal for some, and a pest to others'.[30] In 1595, one the most important polemicists in the Habsburg Netherlands, the Jesuit Johannes David, stated that the 'heretics' in Holland were wrongly accustomed to comparing themselves to bees: bees, he argues, are pure and virginal creatures, whereas the 'heretics' behave like spiders. Sometimes they succeed in nesting in the sweet honeycomb of Christianity, but still they are nothing but a poisonous 'corrupting brotherhood'.[31] So, one and the same commonplace was applied by both Protestant and Catholic propagandists to convince their readers of their own moral superiority.

The dynamic use of commonplaces such as the metaphor of the eternal struggle between the virtuous bees and the evil spiders, gained strength in anti-Spanish Dutch propaganda for another rather obvious reason in the first decade of the seventeenth century. Since the Spanish army in the Netherlands was led by the Italian banker Ambrosio Spinola, and since *spin* means spider in Dutch, almost all pamphleteers made use of this pun in 1607 and 1608. *The Dream of the Spiderhead*[32] *and the Little Bee* (1608) consists entirely of an elaboration on the lengthy stay of the negotiators in The Hague, including no other than general Spinola himself, by means of a tale of the bees and the spiders. The author claims to have seen in a dream how a weakened 'Spider-head, so very attached to his money' had made his web in The Hague as a final resort to catch the little bees. Although the bees suspected that the spider just wanted to spy on them, patiently waiting for the right moment to attack, they nonetheless trusted in its promises of good faith. Thus, the spider was able to poison the bees' flowers and honeycomb gradually at his leisure.[33]

Just as nature has inspired both political thought and popular literature throughout history, similarly in early modern pamphleteering the identification of states, rulers, and peoples with particular animal species was indeed a commonplace. The comparison of mankind with the animal kingdom provided authors with virtually infinite possibilities to address a complicated matter in a recognisable fashion. The basic premise of this mode of thought is that in nature all creatures, man and animals alike, are divided and defined by fixed patterns of behaviour. Accordingly, just as animals can be

---

[30] *Toetssteen, Waer aen men waerlick beproeuen mach, hoe valsch ende ongefondeert* (s.l., 1603) (Knuttel no. 1230), [p. 11].

[31] [David, J.] *Kettersche Spinnecoppe* ... (Brussels, 1595) (Wulp, Catalogus, no. 812), pp. 15, 143-150, 253-254.

[32] Which could both be interpreted as: 'He who has a head like a spider' and 'He who is the head or leader of the spiders'.

[33] *Vanden Spinnenkop ende t'Bieken* (s.l., s.d.) (Knuttel no. 1463a).

grouped by the characteristics of their species, so too humanity is divided
into nations, each with specific distinguishing features which irrevocably
determine their ambitions and behaviour. In other words, the policies of
each government reflect the specific innate and unchangeable virtues and
vices of their nation. By examining past experiences with particular nations,
future relations too become predictable. This worldview of fixed identities
as a constant in history can be conveniently employed in political propaganda irrespective of the actual matters at hand. Nowadays we tend to consider these assumptions about national stereotypes to have been superseded,
but in the early modern period national characteristics functioned as a
model for assessing present circumstances.[34]

Another excellent example of the dynamic application of this commonplace is found in a Dutch pamphlet mentioned in the *Beehive* that was first
published in 1586 and 1587 in several Dutch, French, and Latin editions. At
the time, the rebels were forced on to the defensive after the loss of their
strongholds in Flanders and Brabant. Moreover, internal political and religious frictions, general war-weariness amongst the population, and rumours
of secret peace negotiations led the pamphleteer to remind his fellow compatriots that, however bleak the situation might be, a true lasting peace with
the Spaniards would be literally impossible on 'natural' grounds. His analysis of the political and military situation starts with an extensive exposition
of the mechanisms of national attributes in general. As every nation
('Natie') is given a diversity of language, customs, ways of life, and com-
plexion, each one has a special and irresistible inclination to fulfill its particular desires and affections. The French are said to be disorderly, impa-
tient, and frivolous, the Italians pretentious, simulating, vain, and cunning,
and the Spaniards swollen with pride, ambitious, condescending, and vin-
dictive. As history shows, the Spanish will neither give up their compulsive
ambitions to found a universal Kingdom nor *ever* forgive those who cross
them.[35] Interestingly, the pamphleteer offers a warning to both the inhabitants of the Dutch Republic and the conciliated Provinces in the south, since
Spain will eventually revenge the Revolt on all the 'Nederlanders', including the loyalists and the Catholics. Therefore, if the Netherlanders in general wish to avoid ruin and annihilation they must immediately settle their
differences and stand united again as 'old friends, allies, and compatriots'.[36]

From this perspective, it is worthy of note but no coincidence that the
Beehive in 1608 is structured as a dialogue between a Hollander and a
Fleming. In Holland several influential interest groups preferred a 'just war'

---

[34] Zuilen, 'The Politics of Dividing the Nation', pp. 61-79.

[35] *Het alghemeyn eynde* (Knuttel, no. 765), passim, esp. [pp. 3-5].

[36] *Ibidem*, [pp. 11-14].

to a 'harmful' peace. For obvious reasons this war faction included reformed ministers, military leaders such as count Maurice of Nassau, and of
course the large minority of immigrants from the southern provinces. In the
late 1580s and early 1590s no fewer than around 150,000 people migrated
from Flanders, Brabant and the Walloon provinces to the main cities of Holland and Zealand. There, their numbers ranged from 25 to 50 percent of the
urban population.[37] Amongst these refugees were circa 250 highly skilled
and experienced printers, binders and booksellers who in their exile found
not only new employment but also an expanding market. Around the year
1600 probably half of all the printers in Holland were born either in Flanders or Brabant. Indeed, in some towns and even some provinces in the
north the very first printer was a refugee from the south.[38] A dialogue between an author and publisher from Holland and a Flemish bookseller was a
credible situation. Together they advertised the *Beehive* as a collection of
good and useful warnings for all who love '*the* Fatherland' and '*our* Netherland' in the singular.[39] This implies that the metaphor of the beehive not
only represents an ideal society in general, but also signifies the inhabitants
of the Low Countries as a national community in a more modern sense. If
so, this contradicts the assumptions shared by many historians that the majority of early modern people only shared a local sense of national identity
as they usually spent most of their lives in the same village, city, or immediate region they were born.[40] Such a view does not explain the huge interest in a multitude of pamphlets demanding the prolongation of a war that
would make no sense to a strictly local minded audience.

  Finally, the commonplace metaphor of the beehive also referred to the
vast multitude of pamphlets that appeared on the subject of the truce negotiations. It should be remembered that bees were a familiar metaphor in dis-

---

[37] J. Briels, 'De Zuidnederlandse immigratie 1572-1630', in: *Tijdschrift voor geschiedenis* 100 (1987), pp. 331-355.
[38] J. G. C. A. Briels, *De Zuidnederlandse boekdrukkers en boekverkopers in de Republiek der Verenigde Nederlanden omstreeks 1570-1630. een bijdrage tot de kennis
van de geschiedenis van het boek* (Nieuwkoop, 1974), pp. 7, 12-27
[39] *Beehive*, [p. 2].
[40] S. Groenveld, '"Natie" en "patria" bij zestiende-eeuwse Nederlanders', in: van
Sas, N.C.F., ed., *Vaderland. Een geschiedenis vanaf de vijftiende eeuw tot 1940*,
Reeks Nederlandse Begripsgeschiedenis I, (Amsterdam, 1999) pp. 55-81 (pp. 63-
67). For more recent views on this matter, see A. Duke, 'The Elusive Netherlands:
The Question of National Identity in the Early Modern Low Countries on the Eve of
the Revolt', *Bijdragen en Mededelingen betreffende de Geschiedenis der Nederlan-
den* 119 (2004), pp. 10-38; and J. Pollmann and A. Spicer, eds, *Public Opinion and
Changing Identities in the Early Modern Netherlands. Essays in Honour of Alastair
Duke*, Studies in Medieval and Reformation Traditions 121 (Leiden, 2007).

cussions of commonplacing: just as bees made honey from nectar gathered from a variety of flowers, writers might collect together commonplace materials from a variety of flowers in order to construct something new. And, just as its natural counterpart contained bees, the *Beehive* should be considered as a collection of pamphlets that shared all the features of natural bees: each individual exists solely to serve and to protect the interests of their commonwealth, and to sting when threatened. The question at hand is how the pamphleteers of 1607 and 1608 defined the community that they, with only a single exception, hoped to protect from a peace treaty or truce that would affirm the de facto status quo of two separate Netherlandish states, hence 'national' communities.

The Double Potential of a Common National Identity

As shown in the previous section, the persuasiveness of propaganda depends on the author's ability to present his readers with general images, examples, and arguments to which they could all, to some extent, relate. As commonplaces must be a fundamental ingredient in propaganda, pamphlets can be used to deduce to what extent 'the people' could identify themselves as members of a distinctive national community. Since the twenty-eight privately-authored pamphlets mentioned in the *Beehive* were published anonymously, it is hard to establish the influence of the personal backgrounds of the authors on the contents of their writings. However, three of these pamphleteers have been identified as Protestant exiles from the Spanish Netherlands. Since historians generally assume that most propaganda in the years of the truce negotiations was just the product of disgruntled Flemish refugees, their pamphlets may serve as a starting point for the analysis of content.

The *Pleasant Discourse* by Dr Nicolaes Mulerius (1564-1630) from Bruges must have been particularly popular. It appeared in both prose and rhyme, and was added to several other pamphlets in 1608. The pamphlet consists of a dialogue between St. Peter and St. James, that is, between the pope and King Philip III, who discuss the failure of their joint efforts to establish world domination. Since even their control over the 'oppressed Netherlands' is slipping away, St. Peter advises St. James to lure the Dutch 'heretics' into a temporary peace. Interestingly, Mulerius refers to the unity of all the Netherlands by calling the rebels in the northern provinces one half of a people.[41] Moreover, it was to be feared that Holland's increasing

---

[41] Mulerius, *Waerachtich ende ghenoechlijck discours* (s.l., 1608) (Knuttel, no.1411a) [pp.4-5]. On Mulerius cf. L. Elaut, 'Nicolaus Mulerius uit Brugge, de eerste medische hoogleraar te Groningen (1564-1630)', *Scientiarium historia. Drie-*

sea power would soon lead to Spain's complete loss of the riches deriving from the West and East Indies. The fact that Mulerius' mother was buried alive by the Inquisition in 1568 goes some way towards explaining why he depicts the war in the Netherlands predominantly as a religious struggle between the greedy forces of evil and those who, like St. Mark, are protected by the 'Shield of the Gospel'.[42]

Of course religious arguments and anti-Spanish sentiments had dominated the propaganda of the Dutch Revolt since the 1560s, but by 1600 the endless repetition of these arguments in countless pamphlets resulted in an increasing identification of the Dutch as God's new chosen people, rather than a mere display of similarities between the Dutch and the Israelites.[43] This comparison between the Protestants in the Netherlands and the biblical people of Israel is explicit in the writings of another exile. J.W. Migoen (d. 1609?), the son of a Lutheran schoolmaster from Antwerp, worked as a printer, bookseller, almanac maker, and French teacher in Rotterdam and Gouda. In the title of his pamphlet, a dialogue between two common men discussing another printed dialogue, Migoen addresses his audience as 'all loyal patriots, *especially* those who are born in the Free Provinces'. In this pamphlet the King of Spain declares that the inhabitants of that 'tiny country' of the Netherlands must be like the former Israelites, who grew stronger the more the Pharaoh oppressed them. More importantly, the comparison should teach the Netherlanders in general that God sent the Spanish as a punishment for their sinful ways. Migoen urges his readers to note that God will, therefore, grant eternal peace only if they can sincerely call out: 'O Israel, that is you Netherlanders, and you Netherlander, you are no longer depraved'.[44]

Without a doubt, the merchant Willem Usselincx (1567-ca.1647) wrote the most carefully considered pamphlets about the negotiations. After his journeys through Castile, Portugal and the Azores, Usselincx settled as a fairly wealthy man in Amsterdam in 1591. In the following years his overseas experiences inspired him to gather support for the foundation of a Dutch West Indies Company. On the brink of realising this plan – several committees in the Estates General had been studying his ideas since 1605 –

---

maandelijks tijdschrift voor de geschiedenis van de geneeskunde, wiskunde en natuurwetenschappen 1 (1959), pp. 3-13.

[42] *Verhael Vande Occasie* (Knuttel, no.1457), [p. 3].

[43] G. Groenhuis, *De Predikanten. De sociale positie van de gereformeerde predikanten in de Republiek der verenigde Nederlanden voor +/- 1700* (Groningen, 1977), pp. 79-105.

[44] *Proeve*, [p. 8]. On Migoen cf. O. F. M. van Heel, *De Goudse drukkers en hun uitgaven* IV (Gouda, 1952), pp. 6-9; Briels, *Zuidnederlandse boekdrukkers*, pp. 364-365.

the final decision was, amid the truce negotiations, indefinitely postponed in February 1608.[45] Then, Usselincx decided to influence public opinion in a series of pamphlets in which he hoped to demonstrate that a continuation of the war and the foundation of a West Indies Company were of vital importance to the economy, and hence to the security and autonomy of the Netherlands. In the first of his pamphlets, probably written in January or February of 1608, Usselincx emphasises the God-given right of all nations to trade freely. As the 'Netherlandish nation' inhabits only a small country, it depends heavily on the fulfilment of its natural inclination to explore the seas. The greater part of this pamphlet consists of detailed descriptions of Dutch maritime presence across the world, of good Dutch relations with native populations, and of the rich diversity of spices and products of the Indies. Usselincx maintains that, as long as the King's negotiators retain the restoration of a Spanish monopoly on this lucrative trade as a condition for peace, the States ought to refuse to negotiate at all.[46]

Instead, the States agreed to prolong the provisional truce for eight months. In the following months, Usselincx produced several additional pamphlets in which he shifted his attention more and more to the immediate interests of the people of the Netherlands themselves. In summary, he argues that peace with Spain will strengthen the economic position of the enemy, causing foreign merchants to withdraw from the Netherlands. Consequently, as Dutch trade and industry decrease, the people will become impoverished, dissatisfied, and divided. Ultimately, as discord spreads, the country will be hopelessly vulnerable. In his most extensive survey of the present situation, *Further Thoughts*, Usselincx gives many examples from the first two decades of the Revolt to emphasize the mutual interdependence of the provinces of the general Netherlandish commonwealth. Since the enemy is also aware of this interdependence, the Spanish peace proposal should be considered as yet another attempt to create jealousy, partiality, and hatred between the Netherlanders.[47] According to Usselincx, the enemy has succeeded in changing Spain's war of conquest in the Netherlands into a

---

[45] J. F. Jameson, *Willem Usselinx: Founder of the Dutch and Swedish West India Companies*, Papers of the American Historical Association, II, no.3 (New York, London, 1887), pp. 31-37; C. Ligtenberg, *Willem Usselinx* (Utrecht, 1914), pp. 18-26.

[46] *Memorie vande gewichtige redenen die de Heeren Staten generael behooren te beweghen om gheensins te wijcken vande handelinghe ende vaert van Indien* (s.l., s.d.) (Knuttel no.1431), passim. Usselincx is responding to a similar pamphlet written by the administrators of the East Indian Company: *Discovrs by Forme van Remonstrantie* (s.l., 1608) (Knuttel no.1428).

[47] *Naerder Bedenckingen, Over de zee-vaerdt* (s.l., 1608) (Knuttel no. 1441), passim, esp. [p. 18].

civil war between people who share a common 'fatherland'. Quite contrary to the convictions of many modern historians, Usselincx and many other pamphleteers describe the emotional bond of people with their homeland in terms of what I would like to call a composite fatherland, a fatherland of fatherlands. On the one hand, most of the refugees of the 1560s had originally fled from their fatherland to England or Germany, but after some years they settled 'in Holland and Zealand which they consider to be their fatherland too. But even though the refugees are welcomed here, their opinions are ignored as if they were French, English, Germans, or other foreigners. However, this is their fatherland just as Brabant, Flanders and the other oppressed Netherlands are *our* natural fatherland too'.[48] Of course, being himself an immigrant from Antwerp, Usselincx is personally affected by the debate in Holland about the future of the southern provinces. Still, the idea of the Netherlands as a single body is completely taken for granted and serves as one of many arguments intended to convince the public in Holland. Apparently his notions of 'freedom of the entire fatherland', bonds of 'brotherhood' and 'good Netherlandish blood' do not require further authorial comment.[49]

Most of the pamphleteers of 1608 whose identities remain unknown recognised the public's general desire for peace, but expressed their concerns that the people were too easily tempted by the promises of an untrustworthy enemy. The sense of togetherness expressed by refugees like Mulerius, Migoen, and Usselincx is also found in most of the other pamphlets of 1608. While a liberation of the Spanish Netherlands was not often regarded as in itself reason to continue the war, the pamphleteers frequently insert examples of the old alliance with the cities of Flanders and Brabant with little explanation or comment. Even the *Discourse of a Hollander and a Zealander* says that the interests of the Free Netherlands are best protected when Flanders remains a buffer zone, and that the loss of 'Artois, Hainault, Flanders and Brabant are still too fresh in our memories to forget'.[50] In a dialogue called a *Catechism* which primarily deals with religious arguments, the question of what a truce will bring is answered simply with: 'the fate of Bruges… iron, fire, flames, and blood'.[51]

---

[48] *Ibidem*, [p. 27].

[49] *Vertoogh, hoe nootwendich, nut ende profijtelick het sy voor de vereenighde Nederlanden te behouden de Vryheyt van te handelen op West-Indien* (s.l., 1608) (Knuttel no. 1442), [p. 20].

[50] *Copye van een Discours tusschen een Hollander ende een Zeeuw* (s.l., s.d.) (Knuttel no. 1454), [p. 2].

[51] *Catechismvs. Dialogvs oft Tzamensprekinge ghemaect op den Vrede-handel. Ghestelt by Vraghe ende Antwoordt.* (Knuttel no. 1415), [p. 8].

Although the intended public is never defined other than as readers or good patriots, the pamphlets' warnings seem to be aimed especially at the younger generation who probably had never even seen a Spaniard or Italian. This becomes clear if we consider that most of the narrators in the pamphlets are older men whose recollections of past experiences with the enemy seem intended to highlight the idea that the Spanish leopard cannot change its spots. This is the case in *An Old Shipmaster From Monnickendam*, a pamphlet published in at least eight different editions indicating it must have been particularly popular.[52] The author of *This Miraculous Tiding* describes himself as a man of old age who remembers clearly how the Spanish violated various agreements in past decades.[53] The Nobleman in another dialogue recalls his services to the prince of Orange in the early 1580s, but sighs 'that almost all the old Beggars are gone now'.[54] In another dialogue between two neighbours, Jan considers Louis de Requensens and Don Juan of Austria, governors in the 1570s, as examples of Spanish deceivers 'of our time'.[55] The selection of pamphlets written in 1568 and 1572 in the *Beehive* are intended further to strengthen or revive a sense of continuity of events since the early days of the Dutch Revolt.[56]

Concluding remarks

While the protests against peace were ignored by the authorities (who concluded a Twelve Years' Truce in April 1609), they did serve to establish pamphleteering as a common practice in the Dutch Republic. In turn this enhanced public debate on subjects normally reserved for the political elites. In order to influence the general public convincingly, pamphleteers often reflected current political opinions and repeatedly made use of the historical experiences from the Dutch Revolt that they considered to be a fixed

---

[52] *Hovt en beleght. Een oudt Schipper van Monickendam* (s.l., 1608) (Knuttel no. 1472).

[53] *Dees wonder-Maer end' Prophetsije wis* (s.l., s.d.) (Knuttel no. 1465), [p. 1].

[54] *Schuyt-praetgens*, [p. 7]: *Geusen* (beggars) was the nickname for the Dutch rebels in the 1560s.

[55] *Buyr-praetjen: Ofte Tsamensprekinge ende Discours* (s.l., s.d.) (Knuttel no. 1526), [p. 7]. He also recalls the suffering of all the poor refugees of the 1560s and 1570s. Ibidem, [p. 16].

[56] *De Artijckelen ende besluyten der Inquisitie van Spaegnien* (s.l., 1568) (Knuttel no. 156); *Sendbrief. In forme van Supplicatie aen die Coninclicke Maiesteyt van Spaengien* (Dordrecht, 1572) (Knuttel no.213). These texts were written from the perspective of the Netherlands as a confederate unity but, as the author(s) of the *Beehive* state(s), they remained valid as a good warning against the perpetual Spanish hatred of the Netherlands.

part of the collective memory of society. The argumentations were overall highly homogeneous and inelastic, but the application of such fixed commonplaces as national stereotypes, religious morality, and solidarity proved to be both multifunctional and dynamic over time. Twenty years after the de facto separation of the Netherlands in the mid-1580s, the notion of a general Netherlandish identity or sense of togetherness had still not lost its propagandistic appeal or its ability to stir the general public against a peace treaty with Spain. However, most likely due to the absence of the actual violence of war in the province of Holland since the late 1580s, an increasing generation gap, and the politico-economic pragmatism of the regents in Holland may have combined to produce another identity reduced to the new commonwealth of seven 'free' Dutch or northern provinces.

BETWEEN COMMONPLACE AND MYTH

WILLIAM OF ORANGE AS FATHER OF HIS COUNTRY

Jan Bloemendal

When I was a school boy in the sixties and early seventies I was told about the history of my country, the Netherlands.[1] I got the impression that 'we' were a Protestant nation, founded by the 'Father of our country', William of Nassau, William of Orange, or William the Silent, who was a member of the German Nassau family, who was by heritage Prince of Orange in France, who was called William the Silent because he never showed his true feelings, and who was Prince of Holland by God's grace. The Nassau had close connections with the Netherlands. William was killed at 2 pm on July 10th 1584, by a Frenchman, Balthasar Gerards, after his proscription by the Spanish king, Philip II.[2] Soon after the assassination the myth spread that the Prince was the *pater patriae* who united his people, that he was the leader of the Eighty Years War and that he liberated the Netherlands from Spanish tyranny and led it to independence, even though this was not quite true. At the time of his death the Spaniards were still in power, and William himself was highly controversial, accused of being a turncoat in religious matters, starting as a Lutheran, but becoming a Roman Catholic or a Calvinist when it seemed expedient. And certainly not all his military operations were successful. So how could this myth of the 'Father of his country' become so persistent that it became a commonplace?

---

[1] Cf. J. Bloemendal, '"Mon Dieu, mon Dieu...". Aspecten van literatuur en werkelijkheid in D. Heinsius' *Auriacus, vie Libertas saucia*', in: *Bulletin Geschiedenis Kunst Cultuur* 5 (1996), pp. 91-107; Heinsius*, Auriacus, sive Libertas Saucia*, ed. Bloemendal; J. Bloemendal, 'Rond der Vader des Vaderlands. Oranje, Heinsius en Leiden', in: eds. K.L. Enenkel, Sj. Onderdelinden and P. J. Smith, '"Typisch Nederlands". De Nederlandse identiteit in de letterkunde' (Voorthuizen, 19990, pp. 11-25. The present paper focuses on the history of the concept of *pater patriae* with regard to William of Orange and the concept is related to the discussion of commonplaces and to questions regarding Christian tragedy.

[2] An inspiring, but somewhat misleading book is Jardine, *The Awful End of Prince William the Silent. The first assassination of a head of state with a hand-gun.* William was no head of state, but *stadholder* (deputy) of the real 'head of state', the Spanish king.

At the outset, it is necessary to examine what in this context is meant by a 'myth' and a 'commonplace'. The term 'myth' has been used very flexibly. In classical Greek 'mythos' signified any story or plot, whether true or invented.[3] In modern use, the word 'myth' often refers to one story in a mythological system, that is, in a system of hereditary stories of ancient origin which were once believed to be true by a particular social group. The term has also been extended to denote supernatural tales that are deliberately invented by their authors (for example the 'Myth of Er' by Plato). Since the work of Roland Barthes, the word 'myth' has been able to denote a system of signs which in their connections confirm ideology. Finally it can be used for signifying any widely held fallacy ('the myth of progress', 'the myth of the American dream').[4] In this paper it will be used in the last sense.

One can look at the ontology of myth, but also at its function. Sem Dresden in his essay on myth gives this working definition: 'By myth I understand in the first instance a sacred tale, which had a religious function in a certain community but which also functions socially.'[5] The 'myth' of William of Orange as the *pater patriae* also had such a social function, legitimising the 'reign' of the family of Orange[6] and offering the newly founded state a kind of unifying object of identification.[7]

Is it too bold to define the use of a persistent myth as a 'commonplace'? Ann Moss, in her contribution to the first volume in this series, writes: 'Commonplaces are cultural material with both past and present currency (...). They refer to opinions commonly accepted as valid.'[8] When defined thus, 'myth' in the sense in which I use it, has something in common with the concept of commonplace: an opinion that is 'commonly accepted as valid'. Just like a commonplace a myth has 'both past and present cur-

---

[3] A survey in, for instance, Abrams and Harpham, *A Glossary of Literary Terms*, pp. 178-180

[4] R. Barthes, *Mythologies* (Paris 1957), see also A. Leak, *Barthes. Mythologies*. London 1994). See also J. Bloemendal and P. Smith, 'Inleiding', in: *idem* (Eds), *De Muze en de Mythe. Over de literaire verwerking van het verleden* (Amersfoort, 2007), pp. 7-8.

[5] S. Dresden, 'Thomas Mann and Marcel Proust. On Myth and Antimyth', p. 27.

[6] Juridically, the house of Orange had no hereditary succession, but in fact William of Orange's sons Maurice and Frederic Henry were elected stadtholder.

[7] Since 'the Prince' had given his life for his country, others were implicitly or explicitly summoned to devote themselves too to the Low Countries, and the state in a sense was legitimized by William's death.

[8] A. Moss, 'Power and Persuasion. Commonplace Culture in Early Modern Europe', in: D. Cowling and M.B. Bruun (eds.), *Commonplace Culture in Western Europe in the Early Modern Period,vol.I: Reformation, Counter-Reformation and Revolt*, (Leuven, 2010), pp. 1-14.

rency', since it is embedded in the past, and valid in later times, which are then 'the present'. In other words: a commonplace can become a myth, when it gets a social or a religious function in the present. So the commonplace or myth of William of Orange as the *Pater Patriae* has its roots in the past, that is: in the image of William that arose during his lifetime. It got however most of its value in later times, when it had a function in the historiography of Leiden University and the legitimization of the United Provinces.

In early modern times, as Moss shows, commonplace had a stricter sense of quotations from earlier authors. Erasmus in his *De duplici copia verborum ac rerum* (1512) advised pupils to compile such a store of wisdom in a notebook. Such a commonplace book could be used as a weapon in the struggles between reformist movements and Roman-Catholic orthodoxy.[9] Moreover, the commonplace books arranged and classified the information stored in them, thus offering an internal legitimization of the system presented in them.

The 'myth' of William of Orange as the 'Father of his Country' is not a 'commonplace' in the sense of a heading in a notebook with *loci* from authors from Antiquity, the Middle Ages and the Early Modern period, although it would be possible to make such an entry with quotations on *pater patriae* from diverse authors and works.[10] However, these quotations would mention some of the persons called *pater patriae* without giving any *sententiae* about them. It is therefore no surprise that in the *Polyanthea nova*, the famous commonplace book by Josephus Langius, there is no entry for *Pater patriae* or anything similar. Under the small 'heading' *Pater* there is a sen-

---

[9] In terms of intertextuality, this is very interesting, since one should question whether the intertexts related to the commonplace book, and to the texts that are produced with such a commonplace book at hand, are all part of intertextuality. In other words: if a quotation used in some text is found in a commonplace book, should all the quotations on the same page of that book, as well as the texts from which these quotations are taken, be considered to engage in intertextuality?

[10] Such a lemma could offer, for example, Cicero's *Republica* 1.64 (quoting Ennius, Annals 1.112-113); *Pro Sestio* 121 (where Cicero in all modesty indicates that others call him *pater patriae*); Florus, *Epitoma de Tito Livio* 2.154 and 182; Manilius, *Astronomica* 1.7 and 925; Martialis, *Liber spectaculorum* 3.12; Juvenal, *Satires* 8.244; Ovid, *Epistulae ex Ponto* 1.1.36; *Fasti* 2.127 and 637; *Tristia* 2.39 and 181; Seneca, *De clementia* 1.14.2; Suetonius, *Augustus* 58.1; Tertullian, *Apologeticum* 34; Lactantius, *Divinae institutiones* 1.15.31 (quoting Ennius/Cicero); Eusebius (in the translation by Rufinus), *Historia ecclesiastica* 8.17.2 and 9.8.15; Orosius, *Historia adversum paganos* 7.13.3 and 7.14.1; Aurelius Victor, *Liber de Caesaribus* (= *Historiae abbreviatae*) 1.6; *Epitome de Caesaribus* 13.14; N.N., *Historia Apollonii regis Tyri* 50; Isidorus, *Chronicon* 273; John of Salisbury, *Policraticus* 8.19 (Webb 2, 369.13 and 20); Petrus Damianus, *Carmina*, Carmen metricum 99.4.

tence by Plato linking father and fatherland, but in another way. The entry *Patria* is longer, but does not mention the concept of *pater patriae* either. Nonetheless, the myth of the *pater patriae* can be seen as a commonplace in the sense that it comprises a set of notions including love and care, authority and sovereignty. The concept could have been listed in a commonplace book, and the entry could have offered a 'system' of values and qualities of the *pater patriae*.

Whether it was listed as a commonplace or not, William of Orange was given the title 'Father of his Country' already during his lifetime, as a letter from the world of diplomacy from 1577 shows, alluding to the Prince as the '*Pater Patriae*, for so they commonly call and accompt him'.[11] Even before that, Janus Dousa (1545-1604), one of the founding fathers of Leiden University, used the term in his *Nova Poemata* of 1575:

> But you, for whom all the Netherlands
> long with all their solemn pledges as their protector,
> and above all Leiden,
> o Father of your Country, and its guardian,
> avert the danger from your people.[12]

Here the honorary title is linked with Leiden and its Academy, founded by William of Orange in 1575 as a reward for the city's courageous attitude during the siege by the Spaniards in the preceding year. It is also associated with the people he took care of in an affectionate way.

Soon after William's death the title was authorised, so to speak, in an epic written by the Haarlem poet Georgius Benedicti Wertelo, *De rebus gestis Guilielmi, comitis Nassovii* (1586), in two books (1264 hexameters). It is an epic in a fully Virgilian style, but the Prince is put in a Christian context. God granted him the title:

> Dutchman, God does not begrudge glory to him
> whom He wanted to be the Father of his Country.[13]

---

[11] W. Davison to F. Walsingham, Brussels, 29 September 1577; quoted from Van Dorsten *Poets, Patrons and Professors*, p. 33.

[12] *Tu vero, votis quem sibi tam diu / Suspirat omnis Belgica vindicem, / Prae caeterisque Lugodunum, / O patriae Pater, atque custos / Auerte genti perniciem tuae.* Dousa, *Nova poemata* 1575 [= 1576], fol. A viij^{vo}. With thanks to Chris Heesakkers.

[13] *O Belga, nec enim laudem Deus invidet illi, / Quem patriae patrem voluit.* (Benedicti, *De rebus gestis* 1.664- 5).

In the second book of this epic a poetic description is given of William's murder. After his death William of Orange ascends to heaven, that is, Religion takes his soul there in a chariot of fire.[14] *Pater patriae* is presented as a God-given title, in which the word *patria* designates a geographical and political entity: William of Orange defended the Netherlands, especially the northern parts.

When the student of Leiden University Daniel Heinsius (1580-1655) in 1601 wrote a history drama about William of Orange, he followed the same path as his patron Janus Dousa and Benedicti, another former Leiden student. In his Latin tragedy *Auriacus, sive Libertas saucia* (*Orange, or the Wounding of Liberty*), published in 1602, he presented the murder of the 'Father of his Country'. In this tragedy, it is the character of Libertas who, wounded, says farewell to the country and its citizens. The death of the prince will cause the fall of the Netherlands: 'Citizens, the country and the Father of the country must be buried'.[15] In her speech, Libertas uses the term 'Father' as one of a number of forms of praise: William is the 'support of the country' and 'that famous heart of the world, the great saviour of the Dutchmen'.[16] Before this threnody is sung, William is portrayed as a thoroughly Stoic hero who holds his emotions in check through his *constantia*. He says:

> The lofty mind
> of a brave man is such, that he does not yield
> to any destroying attack of wicked fate,
> or leave his place,
> relying on his virtue and strength.[17]

But although he controls his emotions, he is not inexorable, for:

> He gives in
> to the tears and idle complaints of women,
> and only grief and sighing of the weaker vessel
> softens his invincible heart.[18]

---

[14] Of course this alludes to ascensions like that of Elias, 2 Kings 2:11.

[15] *Tumulanda cives paria et patriae est pater*, *Auriacus*, l. 1996.

[16] *Patria fulcrum*, *Auriacus*, l. 1989, and *cor illud orbis, magna Belgarum salus*, l. 2050. The term *Belga* is used for an inhabitant of the Low Countries, including what is now Belgium and the Netherlands.

[17] Talis herois viri / Mens alta, nullis quae labascit improbae / Sortis ruinis, aut loco cedit suo / Virtute nixa, viribusque [...]. *Auriacus*, ll. 1533-36.

Thus Heinsius combined, on the one hand, an interest (typical in Leiden) in Dutch history and its role in forming a nation state with, on the other hand, the rise of a Stoic philosophy that had found its ultimate expression in Lipsius's treatise *De constantia*, published in the same year that William of Orange died. In the play Heinsius adopted classical concepts, including *patria* and *pater patriae*, and adapted them to his drama. It might seem surprising that William is presented as a Stoic hero rather than as a Christian one, although Stoic virtues were not unusual at the time. Christians should control their emotions but not so much with reference to Reason as with reference to God's salutary presence in the world, and because in Christian history only three moments really matter: the Creation, Christ's Death and Resurrection, and his Second Coming and Final Judgment. But in *Auriacus*, it is not these major events that are mentioned, or even hinted at, but Fate and Chance. In another sense this tragedy might be called Christian, in the sense that it 'intensifies' in the way Burcht Pranger uses the word. Pranger indicates that one of the features of Christian tragedy is to 'intensify' feelings and the sense of life, that are no longer seen in a human context, but viewed in the light of the transcendental world and of God.[19] Since (earthly) history does not matter, it is a problem to write tragedy in the Christian tradition. After all, the vicissitudes of sovereigns and rulers that form the subject of tragedy do not matter, and the sad ending that occurs so often in tragedy is incompatible with Christianity, since the end is always happy. The Dutch playwright Pieter Cornelisz Hooft put it thus in his *Theseus en Ariadne*:

> The great God makes everything
> happen for better.
> Therefore, it is an act of folly
> of injudicious people,
> to consider an event that seems to be
> an immediate harm as a damage
> before they see well
> whether it was a detriment or an advantage.[20]

---

[18] Lachrymis / Vanisque cedit faeminarum questibus: / Invictaeque unus pectora enervat dolor / Gemitusque sexus impotentis / *Auriacus*, ll. 1536-39.

[19] B. Pranger, *The Artificiality of Christianity*, p. 37 suggests that it must be the condensation of 'intense sadness and intense joy' that constitutes the tragic in Christianity. See also B. Pranger, *De kunstmatigheid van het Christendom*, pp. 9-15, and the contribution by Frans-Willem Korsten pp. 1-24 in this volume.

[20] 'Om beter alle quaet / De grote Godt laet schieden. / Des ist een sotte daet / Van onbescheyden lieden, / Tot achterdeel te dieden / Het schijnbaer letsel ras, / Al eer sy recht bespieden, / Oft schaed' of voordeel was.' (Hooft, *Theseus en Ariadne*, ll. 1371-

In favour of a dramatic concept of tragedy is the notion that Christians are in a sense obliged to realise the Kingdom of God on earth. The attempts to do so will fail and this very failure may be seen as the fundamental tragedy of mankind, as Paul puts it in Romans 7.15: 'Not what I would, that do I practise; but what I hate, that I do.' In my opinion, this is a possible solution for the problem set by George Steiner: 'But tragedy is that form of art which requires the intolerable burden of God's presence. It is now dead because His shadow no longer falls upon us as it fell on Agamemnon or Macbeth or Athalie.'[21] For, whether one interprets the words of Paul in a Christian or in a non-Christian way, the understanding of man's weakness in doing wrong, even when knowing what is right, remains a human tragedy.

Seen thus, the commonplace of the *pater patriae* implies both William of Orange and God himself. William is God's representative on earth, who sacrifices his life for his countrymen, just like God's unique son Jesus Christ had done. In William, it is God who protects and legitimizes the Netherlands, and thus, God is, again, the ultimate commonplace. His sovereignty, represented by William's sovereignty, is the ultimate concern of Heinsius's tragedy, linked to the Low Countries. But then the question arises: to which Low Countries?

Of course it is tempting to combine the presentation of *Auriacus* with the propaganda after Prince Maurice's successful 'ten years' (1588-1598), reaching its climax in the battle of Nieuwpoort-Newport (1600).[22] The radiance of the father shines upon the son and the splendid deeds of the son outshine the father's, one is inclined to think. But Maurice's role in the play is too small for that. He is only introduced after the end of the drama, in an inserted leaflet, as a kind of *deus ex machina*, who says he will revenge his

---

78), see P.C.Hooft, *Theseus en Ariadne*, ed. Witte, pp. 107-108. The lines are a part of the final choral ode. The very last words of the song – and of the play – repeat this thought, but then in an admonishment to Princes: 'Dus Princen leeft in vrede, / Vertrouwend anders niet, / Dan, dat wat Godt oyt dede, / Om beter is gheschiedt.' (Therefore, Princes, live in peace, trusting only that what God ever did, has happened for better, vss. 1439-42, ed. Witte, p. 110). The same idea is expressed by Hooft's contemporary Bredero in a song called 'O hoofdeloose sinnen': 'O dol en dom vermeten! / O sotheyt sonder voet! / Ick waande wat te weten, / Maer mijn boerachtigh bloet / Heeft in der daet bevroet, / Dat niemant kan voorkomen, / 't Geen Godt heeft voorgenomen, / Die 't al om beter doet.' (Oh, foolish and stupid audacity! O folly without foot! I thought I knew something, but my peasant blood has in fact experienced that nobody can prevent what God has resolved, who does everything for the better.).

[21] G. Steiner, *The Death of Tragedy*, p. 353.

[22] See, for example, S. Groenveld, 'De man met de loden schoenen. Een levensschets', in: ed. K. Zandvliet, *Maurits. Prins van Oranje.* (Amsterdam-Zwolle 2000), pp. 13-35, esp. pp. 23-26.

father. This also affects the sense of tragedy, and could have done so in a Christian way as mentioned above, but it does not. Heinsius added the scene only reluctantly and at a late stage, without including any Christian notion, explicit or implicit.

In its turn the tragedy spawned imitations in the vernacular and in Latin in which the concepts of 'father', 'country' and *pater patriae* received interpretations particular to these other plays. In this part of my essay, I will outline and evaluate instances of the development of these concepts and of the myth or 'commonplace' of *pater patriae* in the dramas. It will become clear that its constituent concepts of *pater* and *patria* are not univocal, but rather open to several interpretations. The 'commonplace stores', the several lemmata, contain diverse elements, qualities and values that are linked to these concepts.

Let us start with the concept of *patria*. In Auriacus it is the fatherland and its protection that form the motives for Auriacus' acts. *Patria* is one of the key concepts in the play. But the concept is not unambiguous. It gets several interpretations, depending on which character invokes it. A chorus of Flemish exiles sings or speaks the first choral odes. For them Flanders is their homeland:

> Paternal soil,
> Paternal soil, rocks and grottoes
> Shadowy valleys,
> Paternal soil, Flanders, drink in
> Our laments.[23]

But for them not only Flanders, but every land that is free of Spanish hegemony is their home:

> For us is a fatherland
> Everything that the cruel Spaniard does not know.[24]

One must realise that the boundaries of Flanders then did not match the present ones. The river Schelde was the eastern boundary, and the province

---

[23] *Patria tellus / Patria tellus, saxaque et antra / Et cognatae vallibus umbrae / Patria tellus, Flandria, nostros / Imbibe questus* (*Auriacus* 238-42).

[24] *Patria est nobis / Quicquid saevus nescit Iberus* (*Auriacus*, ll. 632-3). Later Heinsius used the same motif in his poem on the death of admiral Van Heemskerck: 'Al daar gij niet en zijt, daar is ons vaderland' (Our fatherland is wherever you are not, transl. JB).

also included what are now parts of Northern France, near Dunkirk (Duinkerken) and Cambrai (Kamerijk). The city of Antwerp was not part of Flanders but of Brabant with its capital Brussels. Ghent, Heinsius' native town, was a Flemish city.

The choral songs after acts III and IV are sung by native Hollanders. Their *patria* remains implicit, but they sing the praise of their people. For the Hollander, however, his country means something more than that: 'His country is every land and every sea, his country is everywhere and nowhere.'[25] So *patria* seems to have a geographical basis, being the city or region where someone was born. For the Prince of Orange, his country encompasses both 'North' and 'South' seen as a *res publica*, a state of general interest, an institute serving the common interest. Besides this geographical denotation, *patria* also connotes affection, the dearly beloved country. The early modern public – although it must have been limited, in view of the highly stylised Latin of this sophisticated play – will have agreed with these interpretations.

But these are not the only ways in which *patria* is dealt with. The concept also gets – fully in line with the learned public it addresses – a Stoic interpretation. In a dialogue between William's wife Louisa (Louise de Coligny) and an old man, the latter tries to console her with the argument that a prince is protected by the love of his people. When Louisa objects that William was born in Germany, the *senex* says:

> Who only assigns him his own country
> Encloses the mind of a prince within too narrow
> Boundaries:
> (...)
> You ask about the native soil of a lofty prince?
> He is born in the world, every soil
> Is his country, and only the whole is his limit.
> His magnanimous ardour, his heroic courage
> Reaches in his own as far as all countries.
> (...)
> Every prince is citizen of the whole world
> And at home everywhere.[26]

---

[25] *Patria huic tota est humus, est et aequor. / Patria huic nusquam est et ubique* (*Auriacus*, II, 1781-2).

[26] *Angustiore principis mentem viri / Mens coercet, patriam quisquis suam / Assignat illi (...) / Natale magni principis quaeris solum? / In orbe natus ille, patria est ei / Quaecunque soli, terminusque quicquid est. / Seseque terris aequat unus omnibus / Generosus ardor ille et herous vigor. (...) / Ubique civisille et inquillinus est / Quicunque princeps.* (*Auriacus*, II. 576-8; 585-9; 607-8).

In *Auriacus* the character Libertas gives William of Orange the title 'Father of his Country' in her final lamentation about the Prince, in which *patria* has been given political, geographical and emotional connotations:

> Burghers, you have to bury both your country and the Father of your Country.[27]

The Leiden rhetorician and captain in the army of Prince Maurice, Jacob Duym, in his adaption of Heinsius's *Auriacus* gives the concept of *pater patriae* a far more Christian interpretation. In his *Het Moordadich Stvck van Balthasar Gerards* (*The Audacious Murder committed by Balthasar Gerards*, 1606) William of Orange is a Calvinist martyr.[28] Immediately at the beginning of the tragedy this becomes clear:

> God who reigns over Heaven and Earth,
> Who turns everything just as He wants,
> Who gives life and laws to every one,
> (...)
> He has given lustre to our House and descent
> With brave and courageous Princes (...).[29]

In Duym's 'commonplace store' the myth of William of Orange is used in the early seventeenth-century Netherlandish debate about whether the war against the king of Spain should be continued or whether a treaty or even a lasting peace should be sought. The States General and their Great Pensionary Johan of Oldenbarnevelt were in favour of peace, since this would lead to trade and prosperity; on the other hand, Maurice was not eager to dismiss his troops, which would weaken his position. Duym is very clear about his point of view on the matter. The play ends with the poet ('Dichtstelder') who tells the audience that they have witnessed the hatred and wickedness of the Spanish. The Spaniards thought that the Netherlands would remain without a head of state, but:

> Praise and above all hail to the Lord
> (...)
> who has chosen the young hero, Count Maurice,

---

[27] *Tumulanda, cives, patria et patriae est pater* (*Auriacus*, l. 1996).

[28] Edition in Duym, *Het Moordadich Stvck*, ed. Serrarens and Wijngaards.

[29] *De goede God die d'Aerd' en Hemel oock regeert, / Die alle saken recht, naer sijn begeerte keert, / Die elck het leven gheeft, en ygelick stelt wetten, / (...) / Hy ist die ons huys, en onse afcomst heeft verciert, / Met soveel Princen goet, vroom van hert en ghemoed (...)*, Duym, *Het Moordadich Stvck*, ll. 55-57, 64-65.

and summoned him to serve his country and the Lord's States.[30]

In the tragedy, the chorus is formed by 'citizens'. The first choral song is sung by 'veel ghevluchte Vlaminghen' (many Flemish who have fled), the second one by 'veel ghevluchte Brabanders' (many Brabranders who have fled). Duym does not forget his place of birth, Louvain, and explicitly encompasses the Southern Netherlands in his play. But the Northern provinces are included, too: the third choral ode is sung by 'menichte van Hollanders' (a crowd of Hollanders).

Duym did not use the term 'father of his country' explicitly, but the Freedom of the Country ('Vrijheyd des Lands') as a character expresses the common grief about the loss of the Prince and calls him 'the bravest Hero in the world' ('des werelds vroomsten Held', l. 1173), 'this worthy Prince' ('desen waerden Prins', l. 1181) and 'your good Stadtholder' ('u Stadhouder goet', l. 1191), but she also names him in terms that express aspects of the idea of a 'Father of his country': 'your refuge' ('u toevlucht', l. 1203) and 'his country's liberator' ('den verlosser s'Lands', l. 1205).

The concept of *pater patriae* has its origin in Roman literature and society, so it could have been stored in commonplace books, while in their turn the Roman concepts *pater patriae* or *parens patriae* had Greek, Hellenistic and native Roman roots.[31] In the Republic the title was granted unofficially to men who had saved the state at a crucial moment. Cicero claimed the title for his allegedly brave actions against Catilina; in Marius's case it was given to him because he had successfully ended the war against the Cimbrians; and Sulla earned it because, due to his victory, the wives and children of the *nobiles* had returned safely to their husbands and fathers. Further Pompey and Caesar received the title. The term connoted affection, partly because of the association with the *patria tutela*, the protection that the father gives his children, but it also implied power, since it also alluded to the *patria potestas*, the authority of a father. Under the Roman Empire the emperors almost automatically were given the title, without a specific action associated with it. In the early modern period, these particular affective connotations of *patria tutela* and *patria potestas* were supplemented with political and philosophical elements: princes were presented as their coun-

---

[30] *Maer ghelooft sy den Heer en boven al ghepresen, / (...) / En heeft den jongen Held, Graeff Maurtiz uytghelesen / Nu verweckt tot s' Lands dienst en s' Heeren Staten last.* Duym, *Het Moordadich Stvck*, ll. 1327, 1330-1331.

[31] See Alföldi, 'Die Geburt der kaiserlichen Bildsymbolik ... *Parens patriae*'. Cf. Bloemendal, 'Rond de Vader des Vaderlands', pp. 21-22.

tries' support, as protectors of political freedom or unity, and as inhabitants of the entire world in a Stoic sense.

Not only the Princes of Orange were given this title. Joost van den Vondel assigned it to Johan van Oldenbarnevelt in his famous poem: 'Het Stockske van Joan van Oldenbarnevelt, vader des vaderlands' (*The Little Cane of Johan van Oldenbarnevelt, Father of his Country*). The concept was used – unsurprisingly, one is inclined to say – in other contexts too. In nineteenth-century Holland with its fascination for the national past, poems were written about the 'Vader des Vaderlands' (*Father of his Country*), see, for example, IJsbrand Dirk Muller Massis, *Lied gewijd aan den Vader des Vaderlands* (*Song, Devoted to the Father of the Country*, Utrecht 1884) and Wilhelmus Albertus Terwogt, *De Vader des Vaderlands in zijn leven en werken geschetst voor het Nederlandsche volk*, (*The Father of his Country, in his Life and Works sketched for the Dutch People*, Maassluis 1884-1887), both ministers of the Dutch Reformed Church. In addition, historical paintings on this subject matter were made.[32] In the 1960s, the commonplace was used in Protestant circles, to stress the unity of God, the Netherlands and Orange ('God, Nederland en Oranje'). This underlined the idea that the House of Orange always had been Protestant, and would always remain so. The nation was – and in fact still is – governed by a mostly Protestant (or former Protestant) establishment, that took and takes positions in the administration, but also in the civic and business communities.[33] In this atmosphere, the myth and commonplace was part of the campaign, so to speak, for retaining the *status quo*. William of Orange was, in this view, a Protestant leader of the revolt against the Roman-Catholic Spaniards, and by doing so he was the 'Father of his Country' installed, so to say, by God himself. The present monarchs present themselves as descendants of William, even though they in fact descend from another branch of the family. Thus the commonplace is still, implicitly, used to legitimize the position of the House of Orange in the Netherlands. Thus, it still tries to link 'God, the Netherlands, and Orange', where God is a kind of ecumenical, but primary Protestant Lord. Indeed, William the Silent as the Father of his Country is a commonplace with a tenacious duration.

Whether it is correct or not to label the myth of the *pater patriae* as a commonplace, it certainly has some characteristics of commonplaces. The idea of

---

[32] See, for instance, De Haan, *'Vaderlandsch trots'* and Jensen, *De verheerlijking van het verleden.*

[33] It is telling that in 2007 a Dutch cabinet was installed in which both the prime minister and the deputy prime ministers were educated at the (Protestant) Free University.

the *pater patriae* was accepted in the early modern Netherlands if not generally then at least by some people. This sort of accepted view is one of the characteristics of a commonplace. The idea of the *pater patriae* can be used in contradictory ways, as we have seen. William of Orange and his son Maurice could be labelled as *patres patriae* but so could the latter's opponent Johan van Oldenbarneveldt. In this sense, the notion was politically inconsistent.

But there is more to say. This essay makes clear that myths as well as commonplaces are taken from one context into other ones and therefore every time get new meanings. Whether a quotation – or commonplace or myth – is listed in one entry of a notebook or in another, and whether it is used in one new context or another, will vary. People using such a commonplace book for their conversation, and authors consulting it for their literary works, add new contexts, and new meanings, but they take with them the old contexts and their meanings, too. Both commonplaces and myths get their meaning from both the present and the previous contexts. As a result, the intertextuality of commonplaces and myths is even more intricate than other forms of intertextuality. For a wide range of denotations and connotations rings in them, from their first context in the 'original' text, via the 'secondary' context in the commonplace book, to the 'final' context in the text that 'quotes' them. This affects the 'source' text, the 'intermediate' text, and the 'receiving' text. But also, the wide range of feelings that are attached to this kind of commonplace – born in the *inventio* of ancient rhetorical theory, developed in commonplace books and 'commonly accepted as valid' – are present in these texts.

Especially the shared 'commonness' of commonplaces and myths means that they unify people. He who has a different opinion, has to cope with a stronger or weaker social pressure; (s)he who agrees, feels himself or herself at home. But such a process of inclusion also means exclusion, in the case of the commonplace of William of Orange as the Father of his Country, foreign people are excluded, but also in the nineteenth and twentieth centuries the Roman Catholics within the Netherlands will have felt themselves put out of action by this rather Protestant commonplace or myth. This leads us to a difference between a commonplace and a myth. In order to be effective, a commonplace should be more or less 'commonly accepted', a myth may be falsified without becoming ineffective. Think of the 'myth of the American dream'.

All these kinds of consideration make myths and commonplaces always new and fresh. I have experienced this as a scholar, and as a school boy, who was taught that God, the Netherlands and Orange as the Father of his Country were inextricably bound up with each other in a threefold cord; while a commonplace in the 1960s, this idea now has become a myth.

KING AND COUNTRY LIFE

THE RUSTIC SCENE AS A DRAMATIC COMMONPLACE
IN EARLY MODERN SPANISH *COMEDIAS*

Rina Walthaus

After a period of imperialistic policy and great expansion, the Spanish monarchy, from the late sixteenth century onwards, was confronted with a great political and economic decline. In Spain, as elsewhere, the consolidation of the power of a king, who pretended to be the worldly representative of God, was a matter of constant concern. The need to build up an image of God-given greatness through propaganda that would persuade and convince both foreign powers and the Spanish people itself, was felt by the seventeenth-century Spanish Habsburg monarchs and by ministers or *privados* such as the Count-Duke of Olivares. Important tools for official propaganda and mass persuasion were the arts (both permanent and ephemeral), public festivities, royal entries and exequies. No stone was left unturned in efforts to create the illusion of greatness and power in a period that was not so glamorous at all. Visual arts, architecture (the palace of Buen Retiro), literature and music were all exploited in a display of multimedia propaganda in which allegorical, heraldic, mythological, cosmic, biblical and sacred symbolism were widely used.[1]

Theatre was another multimedia art that was just as important a tool for propaganda and persuasion accessible to the common people. While the seventeenth century in Spain was an age of serious political, economic and social decline, the theatre, like the other arts, reached its Golden Age. Court theatre, public theatre and religious theatre in the open air constituted an immense machine that, apart from its primary function to instruct and to entertain, could be used, and was used, for political, religious and moral teaching and persuasion. The *autos sacramentales*, performed in the open air during the religious festivities of Corpus Christi, were accessible to a broad audience in the streets; here the Christian order and the great dogmas of

---

[1] See, for instance, my article 'The Sun and Aurora: Philip IV of Spain and his Queen-consort in royal festival and spectacle', in: M. Gosman, A. MacDonald and A.J. Vanderjagt, eds., *Princes and Princely Culture 1450-1650*, II (Leiden/Boston, 2005), pp. 277-308.

Counter-reformation Catholicism were visualized in order to convince the people of their truth and significance. The public theatres (*corrales*), where an immense number of profane and religious plays were performed, offered a so-called national theatre: people of all social classes came to see the plays (*comedias*), since the entrance fees diverged from an expensive *aposento* for the happy rich to a low budget seat or stand for the less wealthy. Thus, this public theatre for the *vulgo* as promoted by Lope de Vega,[2] can be seen – like TV nowadays – as a a sort of mass medium *avant la lettre* and a public platform for discussion and exploration of all kinds of social and political questions: romantic issues such as love and honour, but also serious themes of current interest. Therefore, where early modern Spanish mass persuasion is concerned, there was no better place to influence public opinion than the *corral*.

This is also true for the issue of royal power, which is amply discussed in early modern Spanish literature, including drama. In many sixteenth- and seventeenth-century plays, the role of the king and, with that, themes such as good and bad rulership or the abuse of power, is put upon the stage, sometimes as the main theme of a play, in other cases as a secondary element. While on the one hand such plays can function as a kind of dramatic *speculum principis* for the king and the powerful (and as such can include some implicit prudent advice or even criticism, an element that must appeal to the audience in the public theatre), on the other hand there is the unavoidable confirmation and glorification of royal power, as a message for the audience that a good ruler means order, peace and justice for his kingdom. Lope de Vega, for instance, well-known as a dramatist who seeks the approval of his audience, is – in spite of all the apparently 'democratic' elements in his plays – nonetheless an ardent defender of the monarchy. In fact, in Spanish Golden Age drama there is political persuasion in two directions: both to the king and powerful (this in a very discrete and implicit way) and to the audience of common people. Since this volume about the consolidation of God-given power concentrates upon the top-down attempt to retain control, this essay will focus on this latter aspect.

With regard to the issue of political propaganda aimed at the masses and the role of commonplaces as a tool of persuasion, it is interesting to examine some Spanish *comedias* that dramatize a political conflict of authority (a political clash between nobility and royal power or between powerful

---

[2] '... que es forzoso / que el vulgo con sus leyes establezca / la vil quimera de este monstruo cómico...', Lope de Vega, *Arte nuevo de hacer comedias en este tiempo*, ll.148-150, in J.M. Rozas, *Significado y doctrina del 'Arte Nuevo' de Lope de Vega* (Madrid, 1976), p.186.

and powerless) and where royal power appears connected with the lower stratum of society: the powerless country people, the rural and rustic world of farmers, peasants or shepherds. In these plays, then, rustic scenes with country people acting in their rural setting, are combined with other scenes that take place at the highest level of power and – the focus of this essay – king and country people meet on the stage.

In general, rustic scenes with shepherds, farmers and peasants enjoyed a great popularity in the seventeenth-century Spanish genre of *comedia*. According to Noël Salomon in his extensive and classic study of this topic, the frequency with which Spanish dramatists brought country life, its rustic people, its songs, its costumes and folklore onto the stage was unique in western Europe.[3] The presence of shepherds in literature and drama has, of course, a long and rich tradition: a narrative of idyllic and rustic representations goes back to the classic bucolic pastoral (Theocritus, Virgil, Horace and Ovid) and is developed further through different forms of medieval drama (such as *Officium pastorum*) and Renaissance pastoral plays (Guarini's *Il pastor fido*). Spanish drama, however, from the fifteenth century onwards and through Juan del Encina's *églogas* in particular, had developed a less idealised and more popular form of pastoral drama that offers a more quasi-realistic vision of actual country life, with 'down-to-earth' rustic characters (farmers and peasants more than shepherds): a 'counter-pastoral' that differs from the conventional Renaissance 'Arcadian' pastoral. This last form, characterised by a conventionalised and distant Arcadian and Golden Age setting with refined 'philosophical' shepherds, is represented in early modern Spain in poetry and narrative romance such as Garcilaso de la Vega's eclogues and Jorge de Montemayor's *La Diana*.[4] In Spanish Golden Age drama, however, this pastoral time and space was actualised, suggesting a more or less concrete and 'actual' country life, which, of course, is no less a literary representation and idealisation. Therefore, it is important to distinguish the Spanish *comedia pastoril* (López Estrada) or

---

[3] 'En ningún otro teatro europeo, en ninguna otra época, encontramos un ejemplo de tal insistencia, por parte de los dramaturgos, en poner en escena al campo y a sus gentes, sus canciones, sus trajes, sus costumbres y hábitos, sus personajes folklóricos', N. Salomon, *Lo villano en el teatro del Siglo de Oro* (Madrid, 1985), p. 9. This study was first published in French: *Recherches sur le thème paysan dans la 'comedia' au temps de Lope de Vega* (Bordeaux, 1965). The author states that with Lope de Vega 'el motivo villanesco se instituyó como uno de los temas mayores de la literatura dramática' (*ibid.*).

[4] For a discussion of convention in Spanish pastoral romance see P. Fernández-Canadas de Greenwood, *Pastoral Poetics: The Use of Conventions in Renaissance Pastoral Romances* (Ann Arbor, Mich., 1981, diss.).

comedia de villanos (Salomon)[5] from Renaissance pastoral drama such as Guarini's *Il pastor fido*.

Thus, in this development in Spanish drama, the shepherd – the proper character for a pastoral – had become less present, making way, in seventeenth-century plays, for the peasant and farmer, as a simple or comic rustic character (the *bobo*, the *simple*, the *gracioso*)[6], or as a high-standard and idealised *villano digno*[7]. It was this rustic form that, from 1600 onwards, triumphed in Spain over traditional pastoral, as if, according to Salomon, 'from the sixteenth century onward, people had enough of the false bucolics in the style of the pastoral romances and poetry, because of its lack of realism and its topics'.[8] As various scholars have pointed out, this dignification of the farmer in drama must also be seen in the context of the concrete socio-economic circumstances in seventeenth-century Spain, where the rural sector met with great problems such as the emigration of farmers; so the Crown, being conscious of the importance of this sector for the economic recovery of the monarchy, intended to win or maintain the adhesion of wealthy farmers.[9] Moreover, Salomon observes that this idealisation of farmers and village life that we find in so many *comedias*, reaches its peak

---

[5] See F. López Estrada, 'La comedia pastoril en España' in: M. Chiabò and F. Doglio, eds., *Origini del dramma pastorale in Europa* (Viterbo, 1985), pp. 235-256; and Salomon, *Lo villano*.

[6] See A. Hermenegildo, *Juegos dramáticos de la locura festiva: pastores, simples, bobos y graciosos del teatro clásico español* (Palma de Mallorca, 1995).

[7] I take this term from Salomon, who, in *Lo villano*, distinguishes four main types of the rustic countryman: the comic, the exemplary and useful, the pintoresque and lyrical, and the dignified ('villano digno').

[8] 'como si, pasado el siglo XVI, las falsas bucólicas al estilo de la novela y del romance pastoril hubieran cansado por su irrealismo y sus tópicos' (Salomon, *Lo villano*, p. 14).

[9] According to J.A. Maravall, 'Conseguir la adhesión de un grupo social como el que esos labradores y otros semejantes representan es uno de los concretos objetivos del teatro barroco. (...) Después de 1600 son muchos los que ven en ellos la única fuerza capaz de sacar del atolladero a la monarquía española, lo cual había de llevarlos no a adquirir un papel social directivo, pero sí a convertirse en objeto de preferente atención por quienes tenían en su mano la dirección y gobierno de la sociedad. (...) es sobre 1600, aproximadamente – por tanto, coincidiendo con una crisis tanto económica como social – cuando el villano, además de continuar dando el tipo cómico del rústico, se reviste también de la figura del campesino rico, poseedor de gran hacienda, correlativamente ejemplo de virtudes personales y sociales y mantenedor – con frecuencia, muy explícitamente – de una doctrina conservadora con respecto a la Monarquía y a su esquema básico de compartimentación' in *Teatro y literatura en la sociedad barroca* (Madrid, 1972), pp. 69 and 74-75. See also by the same author *La cultura del barroco* (Madrid, 1980[2]) and Salomon, *Lo villano*.

precisely in the period that the farmer San Isidro Labrador was canonised as patron of Madrid (1622): 'El villano ejemplar que propone por lo general esta comedia es hermano en algún grado de este Isidro que recibe en el mismo momento una aureola religiosa'[10] (The exemplary farmer presented in this *comedia* is something like a brother of Isidro, who at this precise moment, receives a religious aureole).

Hence, the rustic scene in drama had become a convention. What I wish to argue, then, is that in the series of plays studied here, such rustic scenes, relying on a long and well-known literary and dramatic tradition of shepherds, peasants and farmers, and referring as they do to the well-known literary-philosophical topos of the pure and idyllic country life as a framework, function as a dramatic commonplace,[11] which as such persuades, appealing simultaneously to the ears and to the eyes of the audience. In the present essay, I aim to demonstrate how in a selection of plays in which royal power is introduced into the rustic world of the village or, just the reverse, rustic scenes are introduced into plays that pivot upon rulership and royal power, the rustic scene, presenting a certain conventionalised pattern, is, thus, 'instrumentalised' as a commonplace to reinforce the image of royal authority as a guarantee for peace, justice and harmony by stressing the intimate link of the sovereign with that lower stratum of society: life in nature and the village. On the one hand this reflects a Renaissance neoplatonic vision of universal harmony, where a *circuitus spiritualis* unifies high and low and man in nature is idealised as morally better.[12] On the other hand, however, it must also be linked to the specific socio-economic situation in early modern Spain, as I have explained above. Moreover, farmers were thought to represent the 'pure' Old Christians, a point that is sometimes voiced with pride by farmers in the plays, such as, for example, by

---

[10] Salomon, *Lo villano*, part II, chapter II, p. 195.

[11] I take the notion of 'commonplace' in a wider sense, as it was defined in the proposal for the present workshop 'The Role of Commonplaces in Western Europe (c.1450-c.1800)': 'The notion of a commonplace – in this context – denotes metaphors with an established semantic meaning, ritualized figures, or other kinds of figures, types or patterns which are considered sufficiently manifest and unequivocal so as to serve the communicative means.'

[12] As, for instance, in the neoplatonic vision of Fray Luis de León, who in the chapter 'Pastor' in his *De los nombres de Cristo* states that 'la vida pastoril es vida sossegada y apartada de los ruydos de las ciudades y de los vicios y deleytes della. (…) el [amor] pastoril, como tienen los pastores los ánimos senzillos y no contaminados con vicios, es puro y ordenado a buen fin; (…) Y ayúdales a ello también la vista desembaraçada, de que contino gozan, del cielo y de la tierra y de los demás elementos; que es ella en sí una imagen clara, o por mejor dezir, una como escuela de amor puro y verdadero' (*De los nombres de Cristo*, Madrid, 1977, pp. 221-223).

Peribáñez: 'Yo soy un hombre, / aunque de villana casta, / limpio de sangre, y jamás / de hebrea o mora manchada' [I am a man and, though born a farmer, I have pure blood, which was never tainted by Moorish or Jewish blood] and by the old farmer Giraldo in Vélez de Guevara's *La serrana de la Vera*: 'soy un labrador, / con honrrado nazimiento, / cristiano viejo y onrrado'[I am a farmer, of honest origins, Old Christian and honest].[13] These rustic scenes, notwithstanding their variety, show a certain pattern that suggests the idea of *menosprecio de corte y alabanza de aldea* (the denouncement of the court and the praise of village life), a commonplace since the publication of the sixteenth-century bestseller on this topic by Fray Antonio de Guevara.[14]

My corpus includes *comedias* from the first half of the seventeenth century in which rural life and royal power are connected in different ways. In some of these, rural life is in the foreground, the village being the setting of the main action of the play, where farmers and peasants are the protagonists (as, for example, in Lope de Vega's *El villano en su rincón* and Calderón's *El alcalde de Zalamea*) or in which the protagonist is a nobleman who lives incognito as a farmer in a village (Rojas Zorrilla, *Del rey abajo ninguno* or *El labrador más honrado, García del Castañar*). In other plays the main action develops on the highest levels of political power and the scenes of country life are introduced as a short rustic intermezzo (Tirso de Molina's *La prudencia en la mujer* and *La república al revés*). The kings in question are mostly monarchs of Spain's national past (Enrique III in *Peribañez y el Comendador de Ocaña*, the Catholic Kings in *Fuenteovejuna*, Alfonso VII in *El mejor alcalde, el rey*, all three plays written by Lope de Vega, Felipe II in Calderón's *El alcalde de Zalamea*, the Catholic Kings in Vélez de Guevara's *La serrana de la Vera*, Alfonso XI in Rojas Zorrilla's *Del rey abajo, ninguno*, María de Molina in Tirso de Molina's *La prudencia en la mujer*). In some cases it is a foreign king. *Comedias* in which farmers and rural life play central roles but in which no kings are involved, are not my focus, since I am concerned in this essay with the connection between royal

---

[13] Lope de Vega, *Peribáñez y el Comendador de Ocaña*, ed. by A. Zamora Vicente (Madrid, 1969), p. 134; L. Vélez de Guevara, *La serrana de la Vera*, ed. by E. Rodríguez Cepeda (Madrid, 1967), p. 49. About the so much debated issue of the purity of blood in Golden Age Spain see, among many other studies, Salomon, *Lo villano*, part II, chapter. III, and the classical studies in this debate: A. Castro, *De la edad conflictiva* (Madrid, 1961) and A.A. van Beysterveldt, *Répercussions du souci de la pureté de sang sur la conception de l'honneur dans la 'comedia nueva' espagnole* (Leiden, 1966).
[14] Fray Antonio de Guevara's *Menosprecio de corte y alabanza de aldea* was published in 1539.

power and rustic scenes, and the persuasive effect of this combination. Furthermore, I have restricted this study to the genre of the seventeenth-century *comedia nueva*. Although the religious and allegorical *autos sacramentales* may offer interesting material as well, this genre – because of its specific Counter-reformation context and its religious purpose of the celebration of the Eucharist at the festivities of Corpus Christi – is too complex to be combined with the study of the profane socio-political *comedias* in the limited space of the present essay.

I will focus, then, on two main questions. Firstly, what conventional elements characterise these rustic scenes so that they can be instrumentalised as a commonplace, as a communicative tool recognizable and attractive for the audience in the public theatre, so that persuasion will be achieved? And, secondly, in what way do they suggest to the audience the blessings of God-given royal power?

To begin responding to the first question, one should observe that this rustic world in seventeenth-century Spanish *comedias* presents basically two types of rustic characters that both have their literary tradition: the simple and comic peasant (shepherd) as an element for laughter and the more serious *villano digno*, the idealised farmer of high moral standards who plays a central role in the play. This double representation corresponds to two contrasting semantic layers of rusticity: on the one hand, the traditional disdain for the simple-minded rustic countryman and, on the other, the prestige of the classical shepherd from the pastoral tradition as the embodiment of spiritual harmony. Both types of characters have recognizable common or rustic Spanish names (such as Juan, Sancho, Bras, Laurencia, Pascuala, Gila) instead of the sophisticated poetic names (such as Galatea, Sireno, Salicio, Nemoroso) used in the pastoral novel or lyrics.

Furthermore, the rustic setting is endowed with what we could call, anachronistically, a certain *couleur locale*,[15] which is achieved through the introduction of folk motifs, folk song and dance – an element that must have appealed strongly to the audience. Lope de Vega's play *Peribáñez y el Comendador de Ocaña*, for instance, offers some splendid scenes of rural wedding festivities and scenes of harvesters in which popular lyricism, folk motifs and images of rural fertility abound.[16] Folk song, music and dance such as the *folía* and *trébole* are performed on the stage.[17] While marriage –

---

[15] For a discussion of elements of folklore in these plays see 'El villano pintoresco y lírico', part III in Salomon, *Lo villano*, pp. 365-622.

[16] According to I. Arellano, 'se insiste en estas imágenes de abundancia campesina en un conjunto cromático que evoca los bodegones pictóricos del Barroco', , p. 190.

[17] The *folía* and *trébole* were very popular dances in Lope's time. According to the seventeenth-century dictionary of S. de Covarrubias (1611) the *folía* 'es una cierta

quickly settled in a few final lines – is the conventional happy ending of most Spanish Golden Age *comedias*, symbolising the restoration of order at the end of the play after a period of disruption and disorder, the rustic wedding scenes in plays like *Peribáñez* and *Fuenteovejuna* have a different function; these offer an idyllic and folkloric setting of spring-festivities full of *couleur locale*, a space of rustic harmony and epithalamium that will be disrupted by the vile acts of a nobleman. Other plays similarly include rural celebrations that create an ambience of local festive joy.

Another favourite method of creating an illusion of 'real' rusticity is the occasional use of a conventionalised popular dialect (*sayagués*[18]) spoken by the simple and comic peasants in the play – a linguistic tool that therefore may be seen as a rustic commonplace in itself, as it was a frequent device in Spanish literature to create such an illusion of rustic simplicity. Notwithstanding these simple and quasi-realistic elements, rustic life and morals are idealised: virtue dominates in these characters and in their rural world. In the confrontation with powerful nobles, it is usually the nobleman who functions as the villain of the play, while the *villano* is morally superior. So the topic or commonplace of *menosprecio de corte y alabanza de aldea* (contempt for the court and praise of the village) is implicitly imbedded in the deep structure of the play and is eventually confirmed; in some cases it is voiced most explicitly, as in Lope de Vega's *El villano en su rincón*. Where the political issue of royal power is concerned, an essential point here is that these honest and virtuous farmers, who in some plays come to revolt or even to murder their noble master, show an unconditional love and faithfulness to the legal and just king. When they see the king in person, they admire his appearance as an icon of beauty and light, a sun, and here comic rusticity and serious adoration can fuse, as in Lope de Vega's *Peribáñez*:

Inés	¡Pardiez, que tengo de verle,
	pues hemos venido a tiempo
	que está el Rey en la ciudad!
Costanza	¡Oh, qué gallardo mancebo!

---

dança portuguesa, de mucho ruido; porque ultra de ir muchas figuras a pie con sonajas y otros instrumentos (…) y es tan grande el ruido y el son tan apresurado, que parecen estar los unos y los otros fuera de juyzio. Y assí le dieron a la dança el nombre de folía de la palabra toscana *folle*, que vale vano, loco, sin seso, que tiene la cabeça vana' (*Tesoro de la lengua castellana o española*, ed. M. de Riquer, Barcelona, 1993, p. 603).

[18] A stereotyped form of rustic dialect that was used in Golden Age drama to produce an effect of comic simplicity.

Inés	Este llaman don Enrique
	Tercero.
	(...)
Casilda	¿Que son
	los reyes de carne y hueso?
Costanza	Pues, ¿de qué pensabas tú?
Casilda	De damasco o terciopelo.
(...)	
Inés	Los reyes son a la vista,
	Costanza, por el respeto,
	imágenes de milagros.[19]

[Inés: By God, I have to see him, since we have arrived in time, for the king is in town!

Costanza: Oh, what a handsome young man!

Inés: They call him Henry the Third.

(…)

Casilda: So kings are of flesh and blood?

Costanza: Well, what did you think?

Casilda: Of damask and velvet.

(…)

Inés: Kings are for our eyes, Costanza, by respect, images of miracles.]

and in *Fuenteovejuna:*

Laurencia	¿Aquestos los Reyes son?
Frondoso	Y en Castilla poderosos.
Laurencia	Por mi fe, que son hermosos :
	¡bendígalos San Antón![20]

[Laurencia: Are these the kings?

Frondoso: Yes, and they are powerful in Castile.

Laurencia: My God, how beautiful they are. May St. Antony bless them.]

and in *El mejor alcalde, el rey:*

Pelayo	Mucho tienen los reyes del invierno

---

[19] Lope de Vega, *Peribáñez*, p. 48

[20] Lope de Vega, *Fuenteovejuna*, ed. by F. López Estrada (Madrid, 1973²), pp. 176-177.

> que hacen temblar los hombres.
>
> (...)
>
> Pelayo   Los reyes castellanos
> deben de ser ángeles.
>
> Sancho   ¿Vestidos no los ves como hombres llanos?[21]

[Pelayo: Kings are much like winter, for they make people tremble.

(...)

Pelayo: The kings of Castile must be angels.

Sancho: Don't you see them dressed like common people?]

But before the humble villagers the king himself becomes more human and does not refrain from speaking directly with them.[22]

Our next point, then, is the persuasion process and the propagandistic effect of this union of king and country life on the stage: in what way do such plays or episodes suggest to the audience the blessings of God-given royal power that reaches and protects the lowest strata of society? In plays such as *Peribáñez*, *Fuenteovejuna*, *El mejor alcalde, el rey* (all three by Lope de Vega), *El alcalde de Zalamea* (Calderón), *La serrana de la Vera* (Vélez Guevara) and *Del rey abajo, ninguno* (Rojas Zorrilla), where the main setting is the village and where farmers and peasants play the main roles, the disruption of this – down-to-earth as well as idealised – rustic world comes from a powerful nobleman who abuses his power in unjust and cruel acts, often driven by sexual lust in a topical combination of power, sex and violence.[23] It goes without saying that it is not the noble class as such that is criticised in the plays, nor is the system of hierarchical order which constituted early modern society. It is a specific noble individual who is criticised, punished and condemned for his villainous behaviour. In this

---

[21] Lope de Vega, *El mejor alcalde, el rey*, ed. by J.M. Díez Borque (Madrid, 1974), pp. 191 and 194.

[22] '¿No veis cuán apacible, / cuán humano es el Rey? Que los leones / son graves con los graves animales, / y humildes con los tiernos corderillos' (Lope de Vega, *El villano en su rincón*, ed. by J.M. Marín, Madrid, 1987, p. 118)

[23] *Peribáñez*, *Fuenteovejuna*, *El mejor alcalde, el rey* and *El alcalde de Zalamea* have been characterised as plays of rustic honour ('comedias de honor villano'). Although in Rojas Zorrilla's *Del rey abajo, ninguno* the farmer García, whose honour is threatened in the same way, turns out to be a nobleman, the situation is, in fact, the same, because the noble 'villain' of the play thinks he is dealing with a humble farmer. *La serrana de la Vera* has a different outcome, but here as well it is the social power of a military captain which makes possible the sexual conquest of the peasant girl Gila.

way, order and justice are restored at the end of the play (sometimes in a rather spectacular way) and the political system stays intact. Thus, in *Peribáñez y el Comendador de Ocaña*, the peaceful village life, which is symbolised by the lyrical and rustic wedding scene at the beginning of the play, is disrupted by the powerful Comendador don Fadrique. This nobleman, driven by passion for the beautiful newly married village woman, wife of Peribáñez, firstly tries to seduce her[24] and then intends to violate her, but the brave Peribáñez prevents this, saving his wife and his honour by killing the Comendador. When the news reaches the royal court, the king (Enrique III) wants to execute the farmer, but when king and queen hear from Peribáñez how it all happened, the queen sympathises with the farmer. Her tears are proof that he had acted justly: 'Que he llorado; / que es la respuesta que basta / para ver que no es delito, / sino valor' (p. 136) [For I wept and that is the answer that suffices to see that it is not a crime, but courage]. Peribáñez's act is further justified by the fact that, shortly before, the Comendador had given him the rank of captain and knight in order to send him away to the war – just as David did with Uriah – thus, clearing the way for the sexual conquest of the farmer's wife. So royal authority pardons Peribáñez. The bond between monarch and farmers is reciprocally confirmed[25] when king and queen reward Peribáñez and his wife with gifts and honours, and the farmers, on their side, sanction the king's title of 'The Just': 'Con razón todos te llaman / don Enrique el Justiciero' (p. 137) [With reason all the people call you Henry The Just].

Lope's *Fuenteovejuna* dramatises the sufferings of the village Fuente-ovejuna under the cruelty and misbehaviour of Comendador Fernán Gómez, who tries to seduce and even violate the women of the village. After the rape of Laurencia during her wedding, the villagers finally revolt and kill the Comendador. Again, in the context of the hierarchically structured society of early modern Spain, this is a critical and doubtful act; therefore, as in *Peribáñez*, the dramatist has framed a further justification by making the Comendador himself a rebel who attacks the authority of the Catholic Kings. The village people, while revolting against their legal noble master,

---

[24] In this play, the idea of 'menosprecio de corte y alabanza de aldea' echoes in the famous verses with which Casilda rejects the advances of the Comendador : 'más quiero yo a Peribáñez / con su capa de pardilla, / que al Comendador de Ocaña / con la suya guarnecida' (p. 74).

[25] With regard to the aspect of reciprocity, which is essential in the relationship between monarch and subject, see Richard Maber's essay 'The Sun King and his subjects: reciprocity in a commonplace of power' pp. 25-39 in this volume.

honour their kings.[26] In the final scenes, then, the Catholic Kings appear on the stage together with the village people. The kings sanction their deed, pardoning the village by force of the circumstances, since the murder was a collective action of the villagers. The farmers, again, express their loyalty to their kings: 'Señor, tuyos ser queremos. / Rey nuestro eres natural, / y con título de tal / ya tus armas puesto habemos' (p. 178) [Sir, we want to be yours. You are our natural king and with that title we have already displayed your coat of arms].

In *El mejor alcalde, el rey* the final solution in favour of the village people is even more spectacular. Here, similarly, a powerful nobleman rapes the fiancee of an honest farmer just before his wedding. While in *Peribáñez* and *Fuenteovejuna* the king appears only at the end of the last act to dispense justice as a *deus ex machina*, in this play the king (Alfonso VII of León) is already involved by the second act, where he tries to protect the farmer,[27] but cannot prevent the rape. At the end of the play, then, the king comes to the village to bestow justice and to restore honour and peace for the farmers. In a *coup de théâtre* the king, firstly, forces the nobleman to marry the humble peasant girl violated by him and then, immediately after this, the king orders the nobleman to be executed. As a consequence, the peasant girl – her honour restored – becomes a rich widow and, as such, marries her fiancee. Restoring thus honour, justice and peace, the king is represented and praised as the best judge, 'el mejor alcalde', as indicated in the title of the play.

A similar case of honour is dramatised in Calderón's *El alcalde de Zalamea*, where the farmer Pedro Crespo, who has just been appointed 'alcalde' (mayor and judge[28]), orders the execution of the noble captain who has raped his daughter. Here again, this action, though not completely be-

---

[26] Here the music and song by the farmers in *Fuenteovejuna* must have appealed to the common people in the audience: '¡Muchos años vivan / Isabel y Fernando, / y mueran los tiranos ! [...] / ¡Vivan los Reyes famosos / muchos años, pues que tienen / la vitoria, y a ser vienen / nuestros dueños venturosos ! / ¡Salgan siempre vitoriosos / de gigantes y de enanos, / y mueran los tiranos!' (pp. 154-155).

[27] At different moments the king expresses his loyalty and accessibility to the poor people: '¿quién a ningún pobre la [puerta] resiste?' (p. 190) and 'porque el pobre para mí / tiene cartas de favor' (p. 211).

[28] The seventeenth-century dictionary of Covarrubias, *Tesoro de la lengua castellana*, gives an interesting explanation of the title *alcalde*, which also echoes the traditional idea of comic rusticity: 'nombre arábigo, el que preside y govierna en algún lugar; dizen que de *cahed,* que vale presidente y governador. [...] los preeminentes son los de Casa y Corte de su Magestad y los de las Chancillerías, y los ínfimos los de las aldeas, los quales, por ser rústicos, suelen dezir algunas simplicidades en lo que proveen, de que tomaron nombre alcaldades.'

yond dispute, is sanctioned by King Philip II ('Bien dada la muerte está; / que erró lo menos no importa / si acertó lo principal'[29] [Putting him to death was right, for it does not matter if he failed in a detail, if he acted rightly in the main thing] and mutual loyalty is confirmed: the farmer praises the king's justice and the king honours him with the permanent title of 'alcalde'.

In *Del rey abajo, ninguno*, by Francisco de Rojas Zorrilla[30], scenes at the royal court of King Alfonso XI (who is preparing a military campaign against Muslim Algeciras) alternate with scenes of rustic country life. The main dramatic conflict of the play is a case of honour in which the protagonist García is involved, since a nobleman of the court tries to seduce his wife, and García, due to a misunderstanding, thinks that it is the king himself who threatens his honour. The subsequent dilemma (honour vs. loyalty to the king) is solved in the final anagnorisis, in which true identities are revealed and García takes revenge by killing the nobleman. What interests us in the context of this study, however, is the idyllic representation of rustic life, which echoes the topos of *beatus ille* and introduces folk motifs, popular elements and a combination of serious and comic rusticity similar to that we have seen in the previous plays. And again, it is a nobleman who brings disorder. Kings and farmers appear together on the stage, where not only the serious 'farmer' García speaks with the monarch (who does not know yet that this farmer is a nobleman in disguise), but also his rustic servant stands beside the queen speaking in a rather comical way in his popular *sayagués* dialect.

While Luis Vélez de Guevara's *La serrana de la Vera* (based on popular folk ballads) also offers a rural setting in which rustic country people and royal authority appear in direct contact, the ultimate fate of the female protagonist, the *serrana*, however, is different. Already in the first act, during the rustic festivities celebrated in Plasencia in honour of the visit of the Catholic Kings, the villagers and the monarchs are brought together on the stage. The country people adore their kings and the legendary *serrana* Gila in particular falls in love with queen Isabel, in whom she sees a role model for her own unconventional ('varonil') aspirations and to whom she even expresses her adoration:

> Que de bos, alta señora,
> a muchos días que estoy
> enamorada, (…)

---

[29] Calderón de la Barca, *El alcalde de Zalamea*, ed. A. Cortina (Madrid, 1971), p. 208.
[30] F. de Rojas Zorrilla, *Del rey abajo, ninguno*, ed. B. Wittmann (Madrid, 1996).

Vos tenéys gentil presona,
y malaia yo si miente
en quanto dize de vos
la fama, y que si onbre fuera,
por vos sola me perdiera,
y aun así lo estoy, ¡por Dios!³¹

[For I have been in love with you, High Lady, for many a day. (...) You look so
lovely and damned me if I lie in all what Fame tells about you, and if I was a
man, I would die for you alone, and even now I would, by God.]

Again, it is a lustful nobleman who brings about the catastrophe. Gila, in
spite of her exceptional physical and mental strength, falls victim to him,
being deceived, seduced and abandoned. To take her revenge on men and
society she becomes a bandit, robbing and killing men (among these her se-
ducer) in accordance with the ballad sources. At the end of the play she is
captured and the king cannot but sanction the execution imposed on her by
law. However, this is not without a deep compassion for the fate of the
peasant girl expressed by queen Isabella: 'Pena me a dado, / sabiendo que es
muger [...] A mí me enterneze el alma' [It gives me sorrow, knowing that
she is a woman. She raises tenderness in my soul] (pp. 147 and 151).

In Lope de Vega's *El villano en su rincón* the main theme is a different
one. Here it is not a case of loss of honour due to a seduction or rape of a
village woman by a nobleman, but the topic of *beatus ille* itself that is
dramatised. The protagonist, Juan Labrador (John the Farmer), embodies
this conception of life and reminds us of the classical Diogenes who scorned
the power and wealth of Alexander the Great. The farmer praises, like a philosopher, his simple life in the village, in his small and humble setting,
called 'rincón', where he feels like a king in his kingdom. Although he wor-
ships the monarch of his country from a distance and he shows a perfect
loyalty, he avoids the physical presence of king and court, insisting upon the
commonplace idea of *beatus ille* and *menosprecio de corte y alabanza de
aldea* in very explicit terms:

Yo tengo en este rincón
no sé qué de rey también;
(...)

---

³¹ L. Vélez de Guevara, *La serrana de la Vera*, pp. 77-78. The reaction of the queen
a little later is no less emotional: 'Enamora / verla tan valiente y bella' (p. 80).

Soy más rico, lo primero,
porque de tiempo lo soy;
que solo si quiero estoy,
  y acompañado, si quiero.
Soy rey de mi voluntad,
no me la ocupan negocios,
y ser muy rico de ocios
es suma felicidad.[32]

[I have something of a king as well on this humble spot (...) Firstly, I am richer, for I am rich in time; I am alone if I so wish and I have company if I so wish. I am king of my will, which is not troubled by occupations, and being rich in leisure is the greatest blessing.]

Intrigued by the behaviour of this farmer, the king decides to visit him incognito. In the simple village house the king has dinner with the farmer and in return he invites Juan Labrador for a dinner in the palace. Thus, in two scenes, king and farmer are seen having dinner together on the stage, in solidarity. The king learns that even in a humble place a man can feel as happy as a king; the farmer, too proud of his simple life far from the court, comes to recognize that he was wrong in avoiding the king's presence. At the same time, it is demonstrated to both Juan Labrador and the audience in a most concrete way that the monarch is a sun whose light reaches the most humble and smallest place in society: 'Mira al Rey, Juan Labrador; / que no hay rincón tan pequeño / adonde no alcance el sol. / Rey es el sol' (p. 200) [Look at the King, John the Farmer, for there is no setting so small and hidden that it is not reached by the sun. The sun is King][33] Once again, their mutual bond is confirmed at the end when the king honours the farmer and the farmer serves the king.

All these plays, then, represent rural country life and rustic country people from a very positive perspective, which is idealised without being Arcadian and which makes use of 'realistic' down-to-earth or even comic elements. The most idealising factor is, in fact, that visual bond between country people and royal authority. While the play may show a rebellion against a bad powerful nobleman, and even his murder by the country peo-

---

[32] Lope de Vega, *El villano en su rincón*, p. 153.
[33] The imagery of the king as sun was interpreted in a different way by Juan Labrador in the beginning of the play: 'Servirle y no verle quiero, / porque al sol no le miramos / y con él nos alumbramos, / pues tal al Rey considero. / No se deja el sol mirar, / que es su rostro un fuego eterno' (*ibid.*, p. 109).

ple, there is no question of revolution, and nor can there be in this seven-teenth-century context; instead, political hierarchy and royal authority are clearly confirmed. The return of peace and justice stems from royal author-ity: the king (or king and queen as a couple). In return, the country people, from the beginning, adore their kings.

Such unconditional love for king or queen also characterises the village people in other plays of my corpus, which similarly focus upon a conflict of power, but in which the dramatic action develops mainly in the highest reaches of political power at the court: *La prudencia en la mujer* and *La república al revés*, both composed by Tirso de Molina. Both *comedias* deal with the issue of rulership, a mirror for princes taught by recourse to the positive example of María de Molina in *La prudencia en la mujer* and the negative example of the tyrant Constantino in *La república al revés*. In both plays, it is the good ruler (María de Molina and Empress Irene, Constan-tino's mother) who appears connected with rustic country life, where she finds the loyalty that failed at the court. The rustic scene is a short comic intermezzo which, nevertheless, functions as an important metaphor of vir-tue and simple happiness in sharp contrast with the court where the main action is set. In *La prudencia en la mujer*, the rustic intermezzo appears at the end of the play, where the queen, after retiring from the ambitious and deceitful royal court where she was surrounded by ambitious and base no-bles, finds a peaceful welcome in the countryside among shepherds of the most simple sort. Their simple, even silly, conduct and their popular dia-lect[34] are a source of laughter, but behind their comic simplicity there is real loyalty (they even protect their queen when she is threatened with capture by the authorities). Again, their mutual bond is explicitly confirmed when the queen honours the shepherds and these rustic *sayagués* speaking people declare 'y siendo reinesa, es justo / c'agamos su voluntá' [since she is 'queenness' it is just that we do what she wishes].[35] A similar reciprocity can be found in *La república al revés*[36], where in the first act the villagers receive their empress with an abundance of rustic gifts, the description of which suggests a horn of plenty. The empress, in return, rewards the shep-

---

[34] For instance, they address the queen as 'reinesa' (creating a feminine form of the feminine word *reina*) and 'su maldad' (her Badness) instead of 'su Majestad' (her Majesty).

[35] Tirso de Molina, *La prudencia en la mujer*, in: *Obras dramáticas completas*, III, ed. by B. de los Ríos (Madrid, 1958), pp. 893-951; p.945. The word 'reinesa', which I have translated by 'queenness', is a comic invention by the farmer, which adds a feminine ending to a word (*reina*) which is already feminine.

[36] Tirso de Molina, *La república al revés*, in: *Obras dramáticas completas*, I, ed. by B. de los Ríos, (Madrid, 1946), pp. 375-428.

herds by exempting the village from taxes; she praises country life as better than the ambitious life at the court.[37] So, while in these two political plays the rustic scenes (here of shepherds) constitute short and secondary inter-mezzos, they, nevertheless, show a similar connection of monarch and country life as we have observed in the previous plays. While the king may be the sun whose light reaches and protects all corners of society, his own image in these dramas is no less illuminated or coloured through this ritual-ised association of the monarch with a rustic life that, due to a long tradi-tion, suggests a world of truth and innocent harmony.

The possibility of bringing together king and country people in a play and on the stage is an element made possible by the very nature of the genre of the Spanish Golden Age *comedia nueva*, since this genre does not main-tain the traditional 'classical' norms of drama and usually combines the tragic and the comic. Lope de Vega, in his *Arte Nuevo de hacer comedias en este tiempo* (1609) with much irony rejects the traditional idea that royal authority should not be introduced into comedy, in spite of the fact that, as he tells us, breaking this classical rule once provoked the anger of king Philip II:

> Elíjase el sujeto, y no se mire
> (perdonen los preceptos) si es de reyes,
> aunque por esto entiendo que el prudente
> Filipo, rey de España y señor nuestro,
> en viendo un rey en ellos se enfadaba,
> o fuese al ver que al arte contradice,
> o que la autoridad real no debe
> andar fingida entre la humilde plebe.[38]

> [Choose the subject and do not mind (may the precepts pardon you) if it is about kings, though I have heard that for that reason the prudent Philip, king of Spain and our lord, when he saw a king in the play, got very angry, either be-cause he saw that this was against the rules of drama, or because royal authority must not be represented among humble people.]

The separation of the tragic and the comic, and, with it, that of high and low characters, would be returning to the old classical comedy, which, accord-ing to Lope, would be unnecessary since 'en España le hacemos mil agrav-

---

[37] 'En la quietud / del campo que viste Abril / sí tendré [life and health], que en el palacio, / donde la ambición se bebe, / la más larga vida es breve', *ibid.*, p. 392.
[38] Lope de Vega, *Arte nuevo*, ll. 156-164, p. 186.

ios, / cierren los doctos esta vez los labios' [in Spain we offend it a thousand times, so let the learned academics hold their tongue now]. [39]

As a consequence, a typically tragic character, the king, and characters which usually figure in comedy, such as the shepherd, farmer and peasant, can be introduced into the same play and appear together on the stage. The plays discussed here show the king alongside and joined with country people in an image of apparently 'democratic solidarity'. It is striking that the mixed form of Spanish *comedia nueva* (or tragicomedy), with this mixture of characters from the highest and the lowest social classes, flourishes precisely in a period when God-given royal power had to be consolidated and when it was important to persuade the common people of the blessings of that system, blessings that are shown to extend to even the most humble men and women in that pyramidal top-down structure. While the *corrales* in Spain functioned as a kind of platform where questions of current interest were discussed and people of all classes could be reached, a new dramatic genre had developed as well: the *comedia nueva*, an anti-classical form that united the tragic and the comic, bringing high and low characters together on the stage, with royal authority appearing alongside, and in dialogue with, farmers and peasants. The new, hybrid, structure of the *comedia nueva* surely was a good instrument for such political mass persuasion, showing how top and bottom could be, and should be, united.

As various scholars have pointed out, such a union or 'solidarity' of king and rural characters on the stage must not be interpreted as a kind of 'democratic' idealism *avant la lettre*, as, for instance, the great nineteenth-century critic Menéndez Pelayo thought. On the contrary, it is the confirmation and consolidation of royal authority that is at stake here, just as Díez Borque observes with regard to Lope de Vega: 'Lope preaches, from the stage, conformity, in a society structured by class, with everybody in his place, and only in the case of abuse (personal dignity) is it possible to make the interests of the vassal prior to those of his lord'.[40] The vertical distance that separates the king, on the top of the pyramidal structure of the Spanish

---

[39] *Ibid.*, ll. 172-173, p. 187.

[40] 'viene a predicar Lope, desde las tablas, la conformidad, en una sociedad estamental, de cada uno en su puesto y sólo ante el abuso (dignidad personal) es posible anteponer los intereses del vasallo a los del señor' (J.M. Díez Borque, introduction to his edition of Lope de Vega, *El mejor alcalde, el rey*, p. 94). With regard to Lope's *Fuenteovejuna*, Arellano observes as well that 'La dimensión revolucionaria de *Fuenteovejuna*, que señalaron los críticos del XIX es muy discutible (...) en el esquema ideológico de la obra lopiana no quepa hablar propiamente de carácter revolucionario, sino de afirmación de la potestad del soberano' (Arellano, *Historia del teatro*, pp. 191-192).

monarchy, from the lower strata of the common rural people, is bridged briefly and temporarily in the scenes discussed here, where the king appears united with or participating in rustic life, in dialogue with the people of the village and confirming peace and justice. What we see, then, in these plays is a temporary switch from the vertical axis of (normal) hierarchical order to a more or less horizontal level, which does not imply an anachronistic 'democratic' equality, but only a temporary, though very appealing, image of union. Nevertheless, it is important to bear in mind the visual power of such a scene, in which king and peasants appear together, united on the stage, on the same horizontal level, offering an image of mutual solidarity and harmony: a very convincing message, as it is transmitted, simultaneously, to the ears and to the eyes of the audience. In such a strategy of persuasion, then, the rustic scene is instrumentalised as a dramatic commonplace, that, referring to the well-known topos and framework we have discussed above, reinforces the political argument or propaganda of royal authority as a guarantee of peace and order.[41]

The other side of the semantic field of rusticity as literary or dramatic convention – that is, the traditional social disdain for the simple-minded, uncivilised or even rude spirit and conduct of the shepherd or peasant – is not entirely absent, latently slumbering to appear ocasionally at the surface, as, for instance, in *Peribáñez*: '¡Que un tosco villano sea / desta hermosura marido!' [That a rough, simple countryman is the husband of such a beauty!][42] and 'Los azadones, / ¿a las cruces de Santiago / se igualan?' [The spade, does it equal the cross of Santiago?]. Or in *La Serrana de la Vera*, where queen Isabel the Catholic observes: 'Tal vez suele agradar una villana / como tosco manjar, que por antojos / da el arto del faysán al apetito' [Sometimes a countrywoman tastes very well as a simple meal, when the appetite is spoiled with pheasant and the like].[43] Such expressions of disdain, which mark the distance that separates high and low, monarch and countryman, though scarce,[44] are, in fact, a sort of dissonance that undermines the dominant idyllic vision that the play aims to give of the bond be-

---

[41] It is worthy of note here that in his edition of *El mejor alcalde, el rey*, of 1974, Díez Borque already mentions incidentally the idea of the farmer as commonplace ('lugar común'): 'No se trata solamente de la dignificación del labrador rico [...] En nuestro caso estamos ante la repetición de un *lugar común*, modelo de vida y conducta' (Díez Borque, ibid., p. 100; italics mine).

[42] Lope de Vega, *Peribañez,* p. 20 and p.133

[43] Vélez Guevara, *La serrana de la Vera*, p. 146.

[44] According to J. Rodríguez Puértolas, 'en España dicho desprecio no alcanzó nunca los límites de otros países europeos' (in 'El campesino en la comedia del Siglo de Oro', in: *De la Edad Media a la edad conflictiva* (Madrid 1972), p. 326.

tween king and farmer. This tension or dissonance, originating from the different layers of the rustic topos in literary and dramatic tradition, may be related as well to that dynamic of contradiction and dissonance proper to commonplaces as discussed by Frans-Willem Korsten in this volume.

As I observed at the beginning of this essay, we must not overlook the fact that these plays allow some critical recommendations to the sovereign as well. Tirso de Molina, for instance, includes very explicit advice to princes in his *La prudencia en la mujer* and *La república al revés*. Such advice to princes, in a long *speculum principis* tradition, is another commonplace that appears in various seventeenth-century dramas. Situated between, on the one hand, king and powerful authorities (sometimes the dramatist's patrons) and, on the other, a heterogeneous audience that encompasses common people as well, the dramatist must appeal to both. That means persuasion at different layers, in different directions, up and down. Since this volume focuses on the 'top-down' strategies of persuasion, the interesting question of 'bottom-up' persuasion remains outside the scope of the present study. It is, nevertheless, important to recall here that many a Golden Age dramatist knew well how to negotiate within the narrow framework of political and religious norms and censorship, and knew how to express an implicit political criticism as well.

PERFORMING PAPAL AUTHORITY

PROCESSION AS A COMMONPLACE IN
SEVENTEENTH CENTURY ROME

Mårten Snickare

> **common** – Of a public or non-private nature. (…)
> Of or belonging to the community or a civic authority.
>
> **place** – Orig., an open space in a town, a market-place. (…)
> A position or situation in space or with reference to other bodies.
>
> Shorter Oxford English Dictionary, 2002

1. *The procession: structure and communitas*

The *procession* was the single most important, and versatile, form of public ritual in early modern Europe. A distinct group of people, moving in a more or less strict order along a predetermined route, watched by as well as watching other people standing alongside, was the quintessential way of manifesting – or rather dramatizing – such different things as a victory, the death of a sovereign, the accession of a ruler, the establishment of diplomatic relations, a princely wedding, the punishment of a criminal, or the piety of the faithful.

The potency of the procession as ritual form can be explained along two lines. The first is anthropological, and goes back to the writings of Arnold van Gennep and, later, Victor Turner. In his ground-breaking study from 1909, Van Gennep coins the concept *rite de passage*, referring to all kinds of rites that accompany important transitions in the life of a human (or a group of humans), from one state, age, or social position, to another.[1] These social or mental passages are often dramatized as a physical passage (that is, a procession), in which the individual departs from his or her present position and passes a threshold or a gate, before he/she gets incorpo-

---

[1] A. van Gennep, *Les rites de passage: étude systématique des rites* (Paris, 1909).

rated in a new place, socially as well as topographically. In Van Gennep's terms, the entry of a Roman triumphator can thus be understood as a passage from the state of war to the state of peace, the triumphal arch serving as a *limen* between the two states. Elaborating on Van Gennep's theory of passage and liminality, Victor Turner points to the tension, or even contradiction, implicit in the processional form: on the one hand it is a manifestation of *structure*, the individual participant conforming to the overall hierarchical order, playing his or her allotted role. On the other hand it is a performance of *communitas*, offering the possibility of belonging, and transcendence, away from mundane time and space.[2] It might be argued that this very tension contributes to the vitality and versatility of the processional form.

Another way of explaining the importance of the procession is historical. Every procession in early modern Europe in some way alludes to, and draws its strength from, two historical models, or commonplaces: the triumphal entry in ancient Rome, and the entry of Christ into Jerusalem. These two archetypal processions are themselves closely intertwined in that Christ's entry took place within the context of the Roman Empire and could be interpreted as an inversion, or even a mockery, of the Roman triumph. In that way they also illustrate Turner's distinction between structure and *communitas*: While the Roman triumph might be defined as the foremost manifestation of supreme power and hierarchical structure, Christ's entry is rather a performance of humility, togetherness and the overthrowing of hierarchies. Finally, the two historical models emphasize the fact that every procession, in one way or another, is about both worldly power and sacred transcendence.

If we turn to early modern Rome, the links to these processional commonplaces become particularly manifest, even tangible. Firstly, the cityscape was (and to some extent still is) marked by physical remains of the ancient triumph, such as triumphal arches and processional streets. Secondly, with the strengthened power of the Papacy, and the grandiose building schemes launched by Popes such as Julius II or Alexander VII, Rome was gradually established as the incontestable centre of the Christian world, and the stage for its most extravagant ritual performances – many of them in the form of a procession. At the centre of these performances was the Pope, the Vicar of Christ. Antiquity and Christianity were thus the two dominant fields of force in which power and authority were negotiated and enacted. However, the relation between the two was not without tension and complication. Even if Antiquity was the primary model for art, architecture, rheto-

---

[2] V. Turner, *The Ritual Process. Structure and Anti-Structure* (London, 1969).

ric, or law, it also belonged to the time before Christianity. The Caesars and citizens of ancient Rome were, for all their glory, pagans, worshipping false gods and persecuting early Christians. Combining these two ritual commonplaces – the Roman triumph and the entry into Jerusalem – could thus be described as an instance of the ambiguity, dissonance, and incoherence that Frans-Willem Korsten points out as characteristic of Baroque aesthetics and politics.[3]

2. The Possesso: continuity and transformation

An occasion at which this complex relationship between Antiquity and Christianity in general – and the Roman Triumph and Christ's entry in particular – was acted out to an eminent degree, was the so-called Possesso, a procession by which a newly elected Pope took possession of the city of Rome. Ancient ruins and remains were incorporated in the processional staging; symbols of Antiquity and Christianity were juxtaposed, intertwined or contrasted with each other. The Possesso was also an event in which the potential for both structure and communitas, inherent in the processional form, was mobilized.

The Possesso could be defined as the last act in a ritual cycle devoted to maintaining the continuity of the papacy after the decease of a Pope – the three preceding acts being the funeral of the deceased Pope, the conclave in which the new Pope was elected, and the coronation. Originating in the 8th century, the Possesso procession more or less followed the same route for a thousand years: starting from the Vatican, crossing the Tiber at Castel S. Angelo and continuing along what eventually became known as Via Papale;[4] then skirting the Capitol, Forum and the Colosseum before arriving at the Lateran, where an elaborate ceremony took place, which included the Pope receiving the keys as Bishop of Rome and successor to Saint Peter, and, finally, giving Benediction from the Loggia.[5] However, if the external form was remarkably invariable, the meaning of the procession gradually changed, as the power relations between the Pope and certain groups in society shifted. During the Middle Ages and early Renaissance, the Pope's

---

[3] F.-W. Korsten, 'God as Keystone of the System of Commonplaces. The Case of Joost van den Vondel's Plays', pp. 1-24, chapter 1 in this volume.

[4] The Via Papale more or less corresponds to today's Via dei Banchi Nuovi and Via del Governo Vecchio, skirting the southern end of Piazza Navona and then continuing towards the Capitol.

[5] On the history of the Possesso, see F. Cancellieri, Storia de' solenni possessi de' sommi pontefici (Roma, 1802); R. J. Ingersoll, The Ritual Use of Public Space in Renaissance Rome, (University of California, 1985, unpublished dissertation).

secular power was put at stake during the *Possesso*, literally as well as symbolically. The procession was frequently attacked by groups of citizens, or by henchmen to one or the other of the city's petty princes. To choose a safer route was not an option: in order to claim his authority the Pope had to challenge the city's power centres and local leaders, by way of passing through their territory. The procession was thus a performance of unstable power relations. Papal power over the city could not be taken for granted; every new Pope had to prove his right, and ability, to it.

From the late fifteenth century onwards the supremacy of the papacy was undisputed. The ritual and real threat against the Pope during the *Possesso* was gradually replaced by an unchallenged display of pomp and splendour, the former competitors for power becoming incorporated in the ceremony. As Richard Joseph Ingersoll maintains in his discussion of the *Possesso* of Alexander VI in 1492, 'From this moment on the *Possesso* was defined from the papal point of view; the triumph rather than the trial, became its organizing metaphor'.[6] This was also the time when the parallels to the ancient triumph, implied in the *Possesso* from the start, became more and more pronounced. Ephemeral triumphal arches were erected along the route, carrying inscriptions comparing the greatness of the Popes to the Roman Caesars. During the sixteenth century the ancient triumphal arches of Septimus Severus and Titus were incorporated in the procession, furnished with temporary inscriptions and emblems covering the original ones. From the *Possesso* of Pius V in 1566, the procession passed over the Capitol, terminal point of the ancient triumph, and symbolic centre of the city of Rome; at the top of the hill, the Pope was greeted by the city's civil government in an unmistakable performance of new power relations.

The *Possesso* processions of Alexander VI in 1492, Julius II in 1503 and Leo X in 1513 have been described as the most elaborate and sumptuous, the former passing through no less than thirteen ephemeral triumphal arches.[7] After that, and especially after the Council of Trent, the splendour and magnificence allegedly decreased. This might be true to some extent, but one must be attentive to the rhetorical gestures and figures in the contemporary sources, particularly the official printed relations of the events. In the political and religious climate of the Counter-reformation, it became a commonplace to stress the frugality and piety of the Pope, a fact that at least partly explains the recurrent accounts of the Pope preventing the erection of another triumphal arch, and ordering the money thus saved to be distributed among the poor.

---

[6] Ingersoll 1985, p. 197.
[7] Ingersoll 1985, pp. 196-208; see also Cancellieri 1802.

3. *Depicting the Possesso*

There also seems to have been a gradual shift in emphasis in the staging of the procession, certain elements (for example ephemeral triumphal arches) losing their importance while others becoming increasingly pronounced. One remarkable example is the depictions of the processions, pictures that should not primarily be regarded as visual documents of the rite, but rather as integrated parts of it, extending its range in space and time. Before the late sixteenth century, there only exists one known depiction of a *Possesso* procession, viz. a fresco at the Hospital of Santo Spirito, showing the *Possesso* of Sixtus IV in 1471.[8] Starting with the *Possesso* of Sixtus V in 1585 the depictions, particularly engravings, become more and more frequent. During the seventeenth and eighteenth centuries practically all *Possesso* processions were represented in engravings; sometimes there are several depictions of one and the same *Possesso*.[9] They all follow an established pictorial scheme, ultimately derived from ancient bas-reliefs: a line of people and horses winding to and fro from the lower to the upper parts of the picture, sometimes with depictions of well-known buildings or monuments inset to indicate place and route.

The relation between ritual event and pictorial representation is complex. Quite often engravings were produced before the event they represent; they were commercial products, intended as souvenirs, and the ritual event itself was probably the best opportunity to sell them. One example is an engraving of the *Possesso* of Alexander VII in 1655, published by Giovanni Battista de Rossi (fig. 1).[10] It is known that the Pope, as a rhetorical gesture of humility, prevented the erection of two triumphal arches; in the picture it is clearly visible how the anonymous engraver first represented these arches and then erased them from the copperplate, thus adjusting the engraving to the new situation. Sometimes the publishers cut the costs by re-using an old, engraved copperplate, only adjusting details such as the name and portrait of the Pope in question. Another engraving of the *Possesso* of Alexander VII, published by Giovanni Giacomo de Rossi, was re-issued with small alterations, first as a representation of the *Possesso* of Clemens IX in 1667,

---

[8] Ingersoll 1985, p. 195.

[9] In what is probably the most complete collection, at the Museo di Roma, there are 24 engravings depicting 16 different possesso processions between 1605 and 1769. The collection further includes 23 engravings of triumphal arches erected for possesso processions from 1605 to 1775, and four portraits of Popes riding in possesso. See the database at www.museodiroma.comune.roma.it.

[10] 'La solennissima Cavalcata fatta in Roma per l'andata di n. Sig.re Papa Alessandro VII', etching 242 x365 mm, ed. G.B. de Rossi, Museo di Roma (inv. GS 99).

and then again as a depiction of the *Possesso* of Innocence XII in 1692 (see fig. 3 below).[11] That this was a frequent practice is indicated by the title of an unusually elaborate engraving representing the *Possesso* of Clemens X in 1670: 'Nuovo disegno dell'ordine tenuto nella solenne cavalcata...', thus emphasizing that the design for the engraving was new and not re-used (see fig. 5 below).[12]

As these examples show, the engravings should not be regarded as straightforward visual documents of the events they represent. But still, or just for that reason, they say a lot about how the *Possesso* was conceived, which elements of it were considered particularly important and meaningful, and how the understanding of the rite changed over time. In what follows, I will take the pictorial representations of the *Possesso* as a point of departure for a discussion of two essential and interrelated issues: the interaction, or reciprocity, between the participants in the procession and the people alongside the processional route; and the interplay between the architectural space where the rite takes place, and the bodily motions of its participants. Finally, I will touch upon the intense, but ambiguous, relation to Antiquity as enacted in the *Possesso*.

4. *The participants: shifting roles and crossing gazes*

The procession as a ceremonial form involves two groups of people: on the one hand the persons moving in the procession and, on the other, the people standing, sitting or moving alongside. But to distinguish these groups as participants versus spectators, or actors versus audience, is possible only with certain reservations. Firstly, it must be emphasized that there is no physical border between the space of the participants and the space of the spectators; nothing comparable to the proscenium arch that separates stage from auditorium in the Baroque theatre. Both groups share the same ceremonial space, consisting of streets and squares, delimited by buildings, and

---

[11] L. Rouhier, 'La Cavalcata con le sue Cerimonie del Pontefice nuovo quando piglia il Possesso a Santo Giovanni Laterano', etching 363 x 495 mm, ed. Giovanni Giacomo de Rossi, Museo di Roma (inv. GS 100), re-issued as inv. GS 116, and inv. GS 164. It is worth noting that the Pope's name is not included in the title of the print, perhaps a deliberate choice by the publisher to facilitate future re-use.

[12] Giovanni Battista Falda, 'Nuovo disegno dell'ordine tenuto nella solenne cavalcata dal Palazzo Vaticano alla Basilica Lateranense per il Possesso preso da Nostro Signore Papa Clemente Decimo il di VIII giugno MDCLXX', etching 340 x 483 mm, ed. Giovanni Giacomo de' Rossi, Museo di Roma (inv. GS 128). In S. Tozzi, *Incisioni barocche di feste e avvenimenti* (Museo di Roma, 2002), this engraving is erroneously catalogued as representing the *Possesso* of Innocence XI in 1676.

dignified by help of ephemeral decorations such as draping, carpets, garlands and triumphal arches. Secondly, during the procession the roles of actor and audience are not fixed. Gazes are exchanged in all directions; the people along the processional route do not seem to be there just to see, but also to be seen.

A first glance at one of the earliest engravings, representing the *Possesso* of Leo XI in 1605, might give the impression that the people beside the procession play a passive, diminutive role (fig. 2).[13] Spectators gathered outside the Lateran in the upper right-hand corner are represented as a remarkably anonymous crowd: obviously smaller in size than the participants in the procession, and more vaguely drawn, with heads shaped as blank ovals. However, a more attentive look at the engraving reveals traces of people outside the procession taking an active part in the performance, interacting with the procession and the Pope. In the lower right-hand corner, the procession is seen passing through a triumphal arch labelled 'L'Arco dei Fiorentini in Banchi', which means that it is erected at the expense of the group of Florentine bankers living in the area south of Ponte S. Angelo. In that manner, this financially and politically influential group pay their homage to the Pope at the same time as they ostentatiously draw attention to themselves and their wealth. A little further, just where the Pope is shown passing in his sedan chair, there is an *apparato*, or a decoration commissioned by the erudite Sienese merchant Marco Antonio Ciappi; a kind of stage covered by gold brocade and red damask and inhabited by sculptures representing *Carità*, *Giustizia* and *Abbondanza*. From the mouth of a nude man, a representation of the river Arno, wine is pouring in a grandiose gesture of wealth and generosity, directed towards the procession as well as the spectators.[14]

After passing another *apparato*, erected at the expense of a Cardinal, and a triumphal arch at the Capitol, commissioned by the Senate of Rome, the procession arrives at the Lateran in the upper right-hand corner, received by the 'Clero Lateranense'. The Clergy is represented as equally important as the participants in the procession; they are drawn in the same size and with the same precision and clarity. To sum up, the engraving presents the

---

[13] 'La solenniss.ma cavalcata fatta in Roma per landata di n.s. Papa Leone XI al Possesso d. S. Gio. Laterano', etching 243 x 378 mm, ed. G.A. de' Paoli, Museo di Roma (inv. GS 48).

[14] A detailed description of the *apparato* is included in *Relazione del Viaggio fatto dall S. di N.S. P. Leone XI. nel pigliare il Possesso a S. Gio. Laterano con la descrittione degli Apparati, Archi, Trionfi, et Inscrittioni*, ed. Guglielmo Facciotto (Roma, 1605); republished in Cancellieri 1802, pp. 161-167 (on Ciappi's apparato, see Cancellieri 1802, pp. 165-166).

Possesso as an event characterised by visual exchange between, on one hand, the Pope and his company in the procession, and, on the other, politically and economically influential groups and individuals in the city. It also gives the impression that the latter draw attention to themselves, not so much by means of their own ostentatious presence, but rather through elaborate artistic decorations along the route. The visual, artistic whole of the ceremony thus appears as the result, not of one single stage designer, but rather of many different initiatives.

Fifty years later, in an engraving of the *Possesso* procession of Alexander VII, some significant changes are perceptible (fig. 3).[15] Most remarkable is the absence of triumphal arches and other *apparati*, the engraving thus visually underlining that the Pope 'prohibí espressamente al Senato e al P. R. gli Archi trionfali e ogni altra pompa inutile' (...explicitly prohibited the Senate and citizens of Rome [from erecting] triumphal arches or any other unnecessary pomp).[16] As much as a rhetorical gesture of humility, this might also be interpreted as a manifestation of power and control, the Pope in this way drastically limiting the opportunities for citizens or groupings to display their wealth and social status, along the processional route. On the other hand, spectators of different kinds play a more significant role than in the earlier engraving. In the lower left-hand corner, next to Castel S. Angelo, a group of people stand and watch the procession. They appear well dressed, the men wearing wide-brimmed hats, and a few of them seem to be engaged in conversation. Outside the Lateran not only the clergy awaits the procession but also people from different groups in society, some of them arriving in lavish coaches. In seventeenth-century Rome the coach played an essential role in the public performance of social status; to watch the ceremony from a coach was not primarily a matter of comfort, but rather a display of status and wealth.

In the upper right-hand corner of the engraving, the procession passes the impressive ancient ruin of the Colosseum. A closer look reveals that people have gathered in the arcades as well as at the top of the ruin. This manner of using the Colosseum as a stand for spectators of the procession is mentioned for the first time in a published account of the *Possesso* of Innocence X in 1644, and in the second half of the century it is emphasized in

---

[15] L. Rouhier, 'La Cavalcata con le sue Cerimonie del Pontefice nuovo quando piglia il Possesso a Santo Giovanni Laterano', etching 363 x 495 mm, ed. G.G. de Rossi, Museo di Roma (inv. GS 100).

[16] From a contemporary account of the possesso, quoted in M. Fagiolo dell'Arco, *Corpus delle feste a Roma, 1: La festa barocca* (Roma, 1997), p. 373.

both engravings and written relations.[17] The ancient amphitheatre was thus turned inside out, the gazes of the people in the stands directed not towards the central arena but outwards, towards the city. According to the account of 1644, the Pope stopped in front of the Colosseum, where he was greeted with 'grand'applauso di voci, e d'allegrezza'.[18] An account of the *Possesso* of Clemens XI in 1700 describes a more elaborate exchange: passing the Colosseum, the Pope was presented with a memorial, which he immediately read before turning towards the people in the ruin and giving Benediction.[19] In this act of reciprocal attention – watching and being watched – there is an oscillation between actor and audience. In the context of the *Possesso*, the Colosseum is given the triple role of stage, auditorium and piece of scenery.

Both these engravings – and other seventeenth-century depictions of the *Possesso* as well – express an interaction between the people in the procession and the people alongside. The borders between actors and audience are blurred in a way that perhaps makes it more accurate to talk of everybody as participants in the rite. At the same time, the engravings indicate a gradual change, the papacy taking more and more control of the overall design of the rite, leaving less room for individual performances.

5. *Architectural space and moving bodies*

At its most fundamental level, a procession consists of two elements: the participants in the rite, and the space were it takes place. These two elements, space and moving bodies, are engaged in a constant interplay, having effects on, and transforming, each other. Space directs, or choreographs, movement. It imposes limits, offers possibilities, and encourages certain motions rather than others. The moving bodies, on the other hand, elevate the everyday streets and squares to a dignified, ceremonial space. They even bring about physical transformations of space: streets become straightened and broad-

---

[17] G.M. Bonelli de Rasori, *Copioso e compito racconto della cavalcata e cerimonie fatte nell'andare à prendere il possesso in S. Giovanni Laterano N. S. Innocentio X* (Roma, 1644), fol. 6 v.

[18] Bonelli 1644, fol. 6 v.

[19] '(...) vicino al Coliseo, gli fu presentado un Memoriale, che immediatamente si pose a leggere, e vedendo quantità di gente, che era su li finestrone, e ruvine del Coliseo, gli diede la benedizione' (Close to the Colosseum, a memorial was presented to him [the Pope], which he immediately stopped to read, and looking at the quantity of people, who were in the windows and in the ruins of the Colosseo, he gave them Benediction). From a printed account of the Possesso of Clemens XI, republished in Cancellieri 1802, p. 340.

ened, and squares architecturally articulated. Town planning in early modern Rome was to a great extent motivated by ceremonial demands.

Architectural space is also always political space, charged with questions of power, authority and status. The Pope claims authority over Rome
by means of physically intersecting the city, while citizens manifest their
presence and status by means of lavish decorations in front of their houses
and palaces. The *Possesso* processions could be described as a continuous
series of negotiations of authority; negotiations taking place in the interface
between bodily motion and architectural space, and leaving traces not only
in the shape of ephemeral decorations but also as permanent marks. Along
the best-preserved stretch of Via Papale, from Ponte S. Angelo to Piazza
Navona, many facades still carry sculptural decorations, paintings or inscriptions from the sixteenth, seventeenth and eighteenth centuries, clearly
directed at the processional route – when walking in the other direction one
hardly notices them. Some of them explicitly refer to the Pope; others are
emblematic or heraldic manifestations of the owner of the building in question, and still others have more general religious themes (fig. 4).

A comparison of the representation of space in *Possesso* engravings
from the late sixteenth century onwards reveals some general tendencies.
One is that the procession takes place in what appears more and more as a
coherent three-dimensional space. The first known print, depicting the *Possesso* of Sixtus V in 1585, shows the procession in nine straight lines, from
the lower right to the upper left corner.[20] No effort is made by the engraver
to indicate three-dimensional space. No spectators are included in the picture, and no buildings, except a very rudimentary depiction of the Lateran in
the upper left corner. All focus is on the procession itself and the order of its
participants. Twenty years later, in the depiction of the *Possesso* of Leo XI
in 1605, the procession winds into the imaginary pictorial space, interacting
with ephemeral monuments as well as permanent buildings (see fig. 2).[21]
Later in the century, in engravings of the *Possessi* of Clemens X in 1670, or
of Innocence XI in 1676, the procession is clearly situated in a topographi-
cal space, the spectator surveying the whole event from a bird's-eye view
(fig. 5).[22]

---

[20] The etching is published in Fagiolo dell'Arco 1997, p 171, without any information of collection, inv. no etc. It is not in the Museo di Roma.
[21] 'La solenniss.ma Cavalcata fatta in Roma per l'andata di N.S. Papa Leone XI. Al
Possesso D.S. Gio. Laterano', etching 243 x 378 mm, ed. G.A. de Paoli, Museo di
Roma (inv. GS 48).
[22] G.B. Falda, 'Nuovo disegno dell'ordine tenuto nella solenne cavalcata dal Pallazzo Vaticano alla Basilica Lateranense per il Possesso preso da Nostro Signore Papa
Clemente Decimo il di VIII giugno MDCLXX', etching 340 x 483 mm, ed. G.G. de

Closely linked to this tendency is the increasing visual importance given to buildings and monuments in Rome. From rudimentary indications of the Lateran as the goal for the procession, the engravings from the latter part of the seventeenth century include more and more precise representations of a number of buildings along the route: S. Peter's Church, from the 1660's with the new colonnades; Castel S. Angelo with recently fired cannons still smoking; the Capitol with spectators standing at the stairs and on the roofs of the buildings; the Colosseum with spectators in the arches; and finally the Lateran with the Clergy waiting outside to receive the Pope (figs. 3 and 5).

The engravings thus indicate a shift of focus in the staging of the *Possesso*, ephemeral triumphal arches and other decorative elements losing their importance while an increasing emphasis is put on permanent buildings and monuments, or certain significant stations along the route: the new Piazza San Pietro – the embracing arms of the Mother Church – as a permanent stage design for the start of the procession; Castel S. Angelo as a backdrop signalling papal military power; the Capitol as the stage on which the city's subjection to the Pope is performed; the Colosseum, transmitting the authority of Antiquity at the same time as it reminds of the early history of Christianity when martyrs died at the arena; and finally the Lateran, the processional goal, and symbol of the Roman episcopate. The moving bodies of the procession – or the procession as a moving body – thus reorganize the space of the city, creating meaningful links between these diverse, topographically scattered buildings, incorporating them in a spatial narrative about papal authority.

6. *Antiquity: model and contrasting picture*

The *paragone*, or comparison, with Antiquity was a commonplace in the discourse on art and architecture in seventeenth-century Rome. Ancient sculpture, on display in papal and private collections, formed a model for the visual representation of the human body, and a cornerstone in the definition of beauty; ruins of amphitheatres, temples and triumphal arches were an inexhaustible source of inspiration for new architectural enterprises at the same time as they were objects of restoration, reinterpretation and recoding.

Rossi, Museo di Roma (inv. GS 128); Giovanni Battista Falda, 'Nuovo disegno dell'ordine tenuto nella solenne cavalcata dal Palazzo Vaticano alla Basilica Lateranense per il Possesso preso da N. S. Papa Innocentio XI. il di VIII novembre MDCLXXVI', etching 323 x 466 mm, ed. G.G. de Rossi, Museo di Roma (inv. GS 136).

Artists, architects and theorists were engaged in an intense dialogue with Antiquity, imitating, emulating, and striving to surpass the ancient examples. Likewise, the *Possesso* took shape in a continuous dialogue with Antiquity. Its overall structure – the procession through the city – was explicitly derived from the ancient triumph, a link illustrated by the use of triumphal arches: ephemeral arches, erected for the occasion, as well as ancient arches adapted to the new situation with the help of temporary inscriptions and emblems. On at least one occasion, an ephemeral arch was decorated with genuine ancient sculpture.[23] Antiquity, its images and symbols, were in this manner intertwined everywhere in the contemporary, Christian context of the *Possesso*.

Antiquity thus played a central role in the staging of papal authority. In his performance of secular and sacred power, the Pope reused and emulated the imagery and gestures of the Roman Caesars and generals. But, as a close reading of the printed relations of the *Possesso* reveals, the role that Antiquity played was characterised by complexity and ambiguities. An account of the *Possesso* of Clemens X in 1670 begins by stating that of all the ceremonies in Rome the *Possesso* is the one that most resembles the ancient triumph. However, the account continues, this is just a matter of external resemblance. Essentially, the modern rite by far surpasses the ancient because it is about true religion as opposed to superstition and vanity.[24] Two decades later, in 1692, an account of the *Possesso* of Innocence XII opens with a brief historical retrospect: ancient Rome had seen its Caesars and its brave soldiers in triumphal processions, and eventually other kingdoms and realms saw their princes perform their power in similar ways. But none of these events, so the account claims, are comparable to the magnificence by which the new Pope takes possession of the pontificate. And this is just how it should be: the papal dignity is superior to all other powers.[25]

---

[23] Ingersoll 1985, p. 206.

[24] 'Tra le funtioni, che ne'giorni d'oggi sogliono celebrarsi in Roma, quella, che maggiormente assomiglia i Trionfi degli Antichi, é senza fallo la Cavalcata, che si fà da i nuovi Pontefici, quando portendosi dalla Basilica di S. Pietro in Vaticano, si conducono, trà gli applausi e le pompe della Città à prendere il possesso di S. Giovanni in Laterano. Mà vaglia il vero, la similitudine non è fuor, che nell'apparenza, rimanendo questa nella sostanza, tanto superiore à quelli, quanto si avanzano sù la superstitiosa superbia del secolo, i fasti della vera religione.' *Vera, e compita relatione della solenne cavalcata, e cerimonie fatte il di VIII Giugno MDCLXX dal Palazzo Vaticano alla Basilica di S. Gio Laterano per il possesso preso da N. S. Papa Clemente X* (Roma, 1670), fol.1 v.

[25] 'Gia' védde Roma i solenni Trionfi de' suoi Cesari, e de' suoi più valorosi soldati; dipoì tutti gl'Imperi, tutti' Regni, e tutte le Signorie hanno veduti, e veggono fin' al presente giorno tutti superbi festeggiamenti, che si fanno allora, quando i loro Sou-

In an unusually thorough and erudite account, describing the Possesso of Innocence XIII in 1721, the author already in the title signals the link to the ancient triumph: *Roma trionfante*.[26] The account begins by claiming Rome's unbroken tradition of dignity and decorum, from Antiquity onwards. But now its glory is greater than ever because it is dedicated to the cult of true religion.[27] The long introduction plays at length with comparisons between Antiquity and contemporary Rome, on the one hand founding the glory of the modern city upon its ancient past and, on the other, claiming the superiority of Christian, papal Rome over the pagan Rome of the Caesars. Halfway through the description of the procession, the author pauses to explain – particularly to foreigners – the tradition of erecting triumphal arches for a solemn occasion like this.[28] Interestingly, he does not derive this practice from the ancient triumphal entry, but from early Christian use. After referring to passages in 'gli Antichi libri Cerimoniali della Chiesa Romana' (the ancient ceremony books of the Roman Church), the author goes on to describe the early Christian basilica, in which the nave is separated from the choir by an arch, decorated with the image of the Saviour together with other images and inscriptions that demonstrate the victory of the Catholic faith over infidels and heretics.[29] This omission of the ancient origin of the triumphal arch is hardly the result of ignorance from the side of

---

rani pigliano'l possesso de'loro dominij. Ma non vi è paragone alcuno trà sudetti, e quei Trofei, che s' apprestan'al Vicario dell'Umanato IDDIO, mentre con solennissima pompa va alla Chiesa, ch'è Madre delle Chiese di Roma, e del Mondo, a prendervi 'Possesso del Ponteficato, a cui s'è compiaciuto l'Eterno Signore d'inalzarlo. E giustamente così debbe essere; poiche essendo la Dignità Ponteficia la maggiore, che possa conferirsi a un'uomo (per divenir egli Vice Cristo in terra) così superior' ad ogn'altra debbe esser la solennità, con cui egli va a pigliarne l'Possesso.' *Il trionfal Possesso preso dalla Santità di N. S. Papa Innocenzo XII. Il dì 13 Aprile 1692 Nella Basilica di S. Gio: in Laterano (...) Colla relatione esatta della solenne Cavalcata* (Roma, 1692), fol. 1 r.

[26] Luca Antonio Chracas, *Roma trionfante Nel glorioso Possesso preso il giorno di Domenica 16. Novembre 1721. Dalla Santità di Nostro Signore Papa Innocenzo XIII. Romano della nobilissima fameglia Conti.* (Roma, 1721).

[27] 'Roma non mai degenere dalla sua antica dignità, in ogni tempo sà fare buon' uso del proprio decoro; ma più volontieri, e più giustamente spiegalo intero agli occhi de'Cittadini, e de'Forastieri, quando la occasione di mostrarlo è diretta ad ossequie, e a culto di Religione.' *Roma trionfante* 1721, p. 5.

[28] *Roma trionfante* 1721, pp. 16-17.

[29] 'Pratticarono li Papi da che Costantino permise il pubblico culto di nostra Religione, e fondò le prime Basiliche, nell'Arco principale delle medesime, (che perciò fu detto Trionfale) collocare il trofeo della Croce, e l'immagine del Salvatore (...) e con varie altre inscrizzioni, e figure, che dimostrassero le vittorie ottenute dalla Fede Cattolica sopra gli errori della Infedeltà, e delle Ereice.', *Roma trionfante* 1721, p. 17.

the author, educated as he obviously is. Rather it must be regarded as a rhetorical device, intended to emphasize the truly Christian significance of the arch. The ancient symbol was indispensable for the staging of papal authority, but, for the symbol to work efficiently in the Christian context, its pagan roots had to be downplayed.

Nowhere was the intense but complex relation to Antiquity more strongly felt than at the Colosseum, the most venerable of ancient ruins and at the same time venue for the most brutal persecutions of early Christians. Since the fourteenth century, the ancient amphitheatre had served as a stage for mystery plays and other religious events.[30] In 1519 a small chapel, S. Maria della Pietà, was built in the ruin, and later in the same century Sixtus V presented ideas for the transformation of the whole ruin into a church. In the middle of the seventeenth century, the amphitheatre became the object of intensified attention and debate (it is no coincidence that it was incorporated into the staging of the *Possesso* at exactly this point). How was it to be interpreted? As a monument of ancient grandeur, or as a sanctuary, consecrated by the blood of the martyrs? And, depending on the answer, how should it be treated? Respectfully restored or innovatively transformed?

The great interest in the Colosseum at this particular time might be understood in relation to the new plans for Piazza San Pietro. From the very beginning in the late 1650s, Bernini's oval design for the Piazza was conceived in terms of *paragone*, or comparison, with ancient architecture in general and the amphitheatre in particular. In his magisterial treatise on S. Peter's, *Il Tempio Vaticano*, Bernini's pupil and follower Carlo Fontana summarizes and elaborates the *paragone*.[31] The Piazza was designed, he states, to surpass every ancient counterpart. On direct comparison with its most worthy rival, that is the Colosseum, the new Piazza appears superior in all essentials: size, quality, building material, and so on. Of even greater importance than the formal superiority, however, is the different aim and use of the two oval buildings: while the Colosseum was devoted to plays and festivities according to pagan custom, Piazza San Pietro was meant for piety and worship of the true God.[32]

---

[30] On the understanding and use of the Colosseum in the early modern period, see M. di Macco, *Il Colosseo. Funzione simbolica, storica, urbana* (Roma, 1971); H. Hager, 'Carlo Fontana's project for a church in honour of the 'Ecclesia Triumphans' in the Colosseum, Rome', *Journal of the Warburg and Courtauld Institutes*, Vol. 36, 1973, pp. 319-337.

[31] C. Fontana, *Il Tempio Vaticano e sua origine con gl'Edifitii più cospicui anitchi, e moderni fatti dentro, e fuori di Esso* (Roma, 1694).

[32] Fontana 1694, p. 179.

The *paragone* between Piazza San Pietro and the Colosseum was visually developed in the *Possesso* engravings. Beginning with the *Possesso* of Clemens IX in 1667, the first after the construction of the new Piazza, virtually all engravings include the two great ovals, mirroring each other in size and shape, and catenated by the procession (see e.g. fig. 5). It is as if the presence of one of the buildings called forth the other; as if they needed each other in order to be fully understandable and meaningful. The Colosseum seems to have played the role of the Other for Piazza San Pietro, a pagan counterpart making the glory of the Christian piazza stand out. And perhaps this could be said of Ancient Rome in general: it was the Other – at the same time attractive and repellent – against which the modern Christian city, and the papacy, shaped and established its own identity.

*

The procession thus proved to be a dynamic and variable commonplace in the performance of papal authority. In the shape of the *Possesso*, it was not a matter of repeating or imitating a fixed pattern. Neither was it a manifestation of an already existing power. It was, in all senses of the word, a performative act, performing and producing the authority that it appeared to express or manifest.[33] As a performative act, it also involved risk-taking, and awareness that the effect was not always in accordance with the intention. Lastly: if we think of the *Possesso* in terms of communicating, then the mode of communication was not mainly intellectual and verbal, but rather emotional and bodily. It could be described in terms of space and movement: on one hand a kinetic, bodily display of magnificence, that is, structure, on the other hand a spatial sense of togetherness, or *communitas*.

---

[33] On the concept of the performative, see J. L. Austin, *How To Do Things with Words* (London, 1962); J. Derrida, 'Signature, Event, Context', *Margins of Philosophy* (*Marges de la philosophie*, 1972) (Chicago, 1982); J. Butler, *Gender Trouble: Feminism and the Subversion of Identity* (New York/London, 1990).

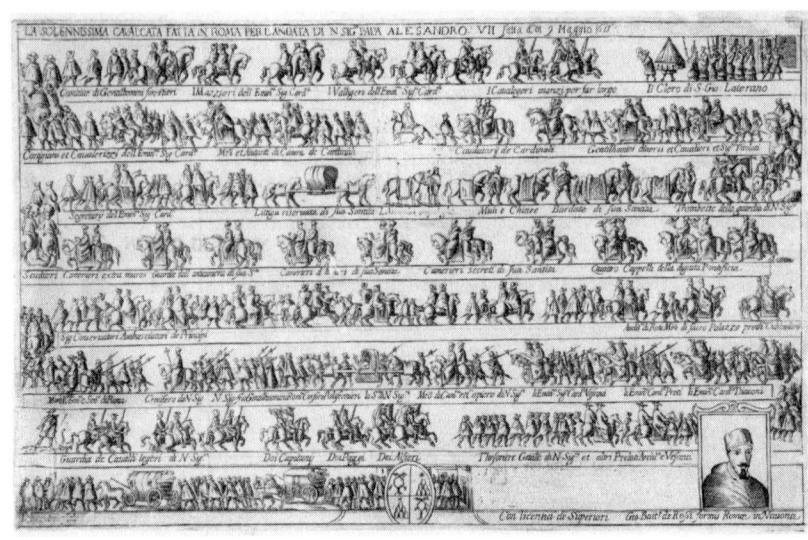

1. *La solennissima Cavalcata fatta in Roma per l'andata di n. Sig.re Papa Alessandro VII*, etching 242 x365 mm, ed. Giovanni Battista de Rossi, Museo di Roma (inv. GS 99). Photo: Museo di Roma.

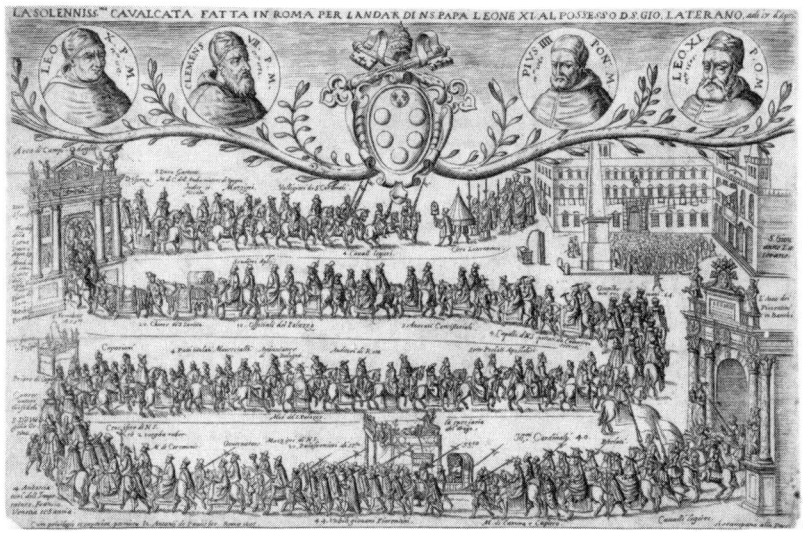

2. *La solenniss.ma cavalcata fatta in Roma per landata di n.s. Papa Leone XI al Possesso d. S. Gio. Laterano*, etching 243 x 378 mm, ed. Giovanni Antonio de Paoli, Museo di Roma (inv. GS 48). Photo: Museo di Roma.

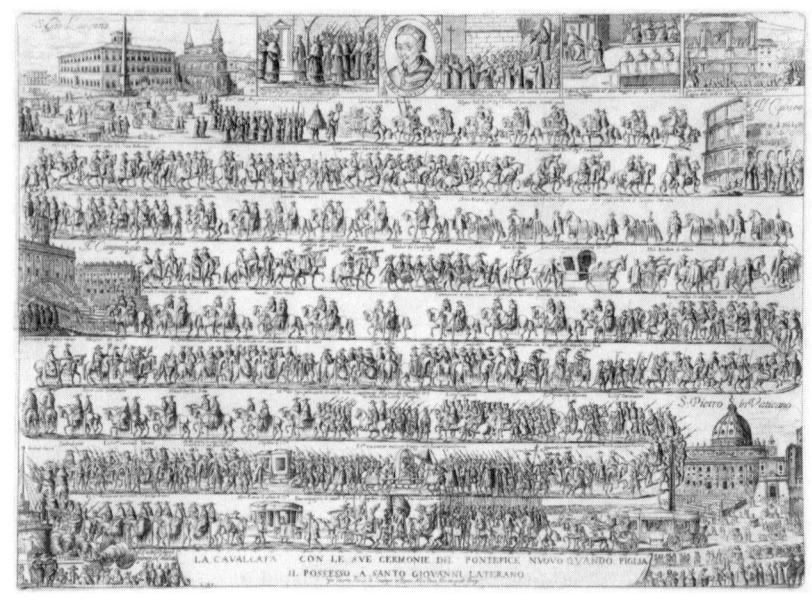

3. Louis Rouhier, *La Cavalcata con le sue Cerimonie del Pontefice nuovo quando piglia il Possesso a Santo Giovanni Laterano*, etching 363 x 495 mm, ed. Giovanni Giacomo de Rossi, Museo di Roma (inv. GS 100). Photo: Museo di Roma.

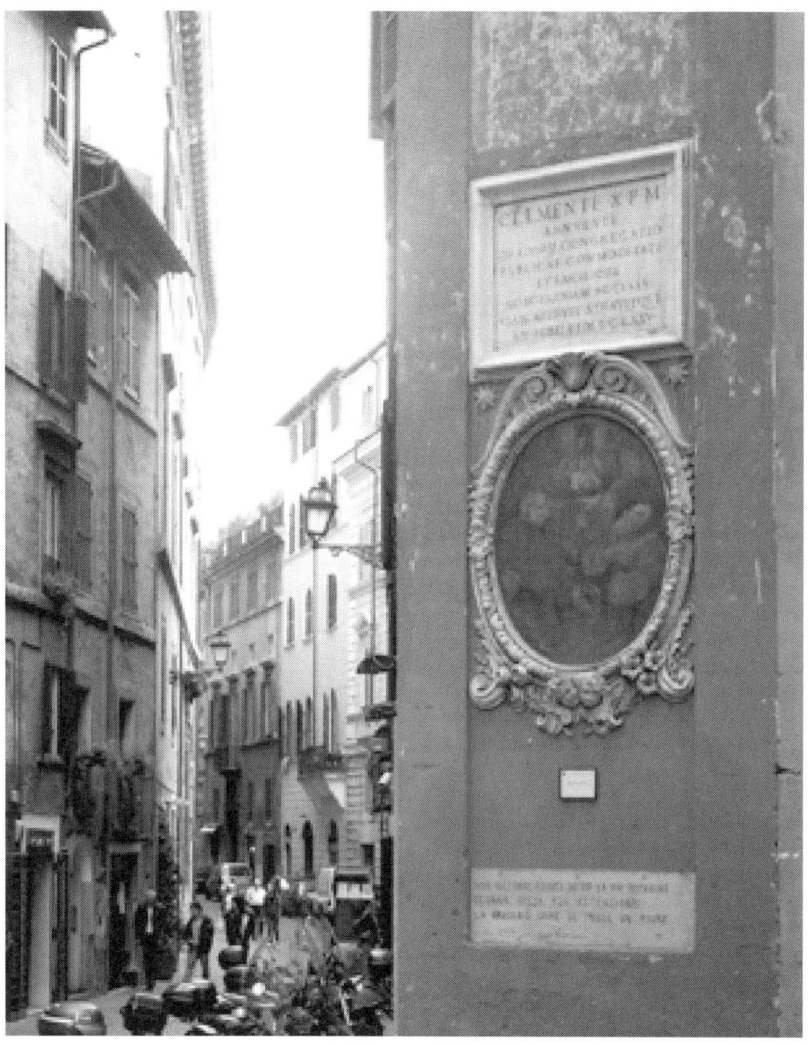

4. South-eastern corner of the crossing of Via d. Governo Vecchio and Via d. Corallo, with an inscription plate from 1675, honouring the Pope, and a framed painting of the Madonna with two saints, added in 1716. Photo: Mårten Snickare.

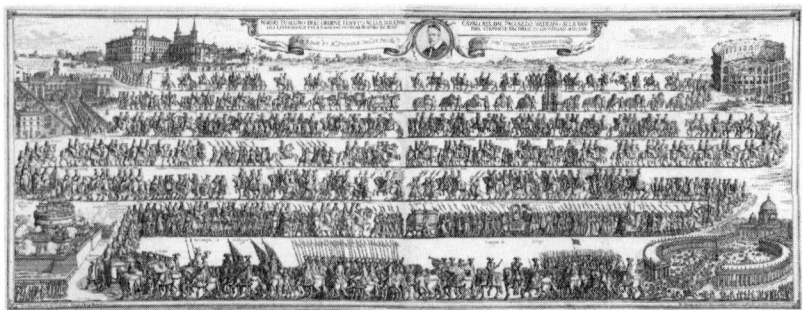

5. Giovanni Battista Falda, *Nuovo disegno dell'ordine tenuto nella solenne caval-cata dal Palazzo Vaticano alla Basilica Lateranense per il Possesso preso da Nostro Signore Papa Clemente Decimo il di VIII giugno MDCLXX*, etching 340 x 483 mm, ed. Giovanni Giacomo de Rossi, Museo di Roma (inv. GS 128). Photo: Museo di Roma.

MARVELS OF THE HOLY CITY

ON THE USE OF ROMAN CHURCH MUSIC AT LUTHERAN COURTS IN THE MID-SEVENTEENTH CENTURY

Lars Berglund

Enterprises of art and culture patronised by regimes and authorities during the early modern period were to a large extent articulations of political culture. They were directed both towards subjects and towards neighbouring or competing states and rulers, and to some extent at posterity. Such enterprises typically involved a variety of different means of communication: material, visual, verbal, written or acoustic, including both what in modern terminology would be termed 'the fine arts' and other practices which would have been considered art at the time, such as cooking or pyrotechnics, or the making of hats or wagons. Moreover, they incorporated a large repertoire of communicative means and patterns, which were universally used and understood, and which correspond to the notion of commonplaces, both in a narrow and in a more general sense.

The extensive use of Roman Catholic Church music at Protestant courts during the mid-seventeenth century provides us with a very specific and rather intriguing case of the exchange and dissemination of such cultural material between regions and states. Let us begin by looking at the example of *Salve Regina* becoming *Salve rex Christe*. The reproduction below shows a musical manuscript from the large Düben Collection at Uppsala University Library. It was copied by musicians at the Royal Swedish Court in the 1650s.[1]

The manuscript contains a composition by the Roman composer Giacomo Carissimi (1605–74), who was *maestro di cappella* at the Roman Jesuit seminary *Collegium Germanicum* and its adjacent church, S. Apollinare. In the original version, this is a polyphonic setting of the Marian antiphon *Salve Regina*. In Rome it could be performed at a church service or devotion dedicated to the Virgin Mary, either at Vespers, or at a specific so-called

---

[1] Uppsala University Library, Vmhs 53:10. The entire source and a bibliographic description is found in *The Düben Collection Database Catalogue*, ed. E. Kjellberg and K. J. Snyder, <http://www.musik.uu.se/duben/Duben.php>.

Salve service.[2] The original version of Carissimi's composition is preserved in several copies in Paris libraries.[3] The Uppsala manuscript, however, differs from the original version in slight, but crucial, ways. The text has been changed, so that the piece addresses not the Virgin Mary but her son:

Original hymn:	Uppsala manuscript version (modifications in italics):
Salve, Regina, Mater misericordiae, vita, dulcedo, et spes nostra, salve. Ad te clamamus, exsules filii Hevae, ad te suspiramus, gementes et flentes in hac lacrimarum valle.	Salve, *Rex Christe, Pater* misericordiae, vita, dulcedo, et spes nostra, salve. Ad te clamamus exulis filii Evae ad te suspiramus, gementes et flentes in hac lacrimarum valle.
Eia, ergo, advocata nostra, illos tuos misericordes oculos ad nos converte; et Jesum, benedictum fructum ventris tui, nobis post hoc exilium ostende. O clemens, O pia, O dulcis Virgo Maria	Eia, ergo *miserator noster*, illos tuos misericordes oculos ad nos converte; et *Patrem reconciliatum morte tua,* nobis post hoc exilium ostende, *ò dulcis Jesu, Rex Christe, ò clemens, ò pie, ò dulcis mundi salvator.*
Hail, holy Queen, Mother of Mercy, our life, our sweetness and our hope. To thee do we cry, poor banished children of Eve; to thee do we send up our sighs, mourning and weeping in this valley of tears. Turn then, most gracious advocate, thine eyes of mercy toward us; and after this our exile, show unto us the blessed fruit of thy womb, Jesus. O clement, O loving, O sweet Virgin Mary.	Hail, *Christ, our King, Father of Mercy,* our life, our sweetness and our hope. To thee do we cry, poor banished children of Eve; to thee do we send up our sighs, mourning and weeping in this valley of tears. Turn then, *most gracious commiserator,* thine eyes of mercy toward us; and after this our exile, show unto us *our Father, reconciled with us through your death. O sweet Jesus, Christ, our King, O clement, O loving, O sweet Saviour of the world.*

---

[2] J.S. Ingram and Keith Falconer, 'Salve regina', *Grove Music Online*, ed. L. Macy (Accessed February 2008), <http://www.grovemusic.com>.
[3] A. V. Jones, *The Motets of Carissimi*, vol. 2 (Ann Arbor, 1982), p. 99. A complete transcription of the original motet is found at pp. 455–463.

The reasons behind these changes are obvious: in order to be appropriate for performance during the Lutheran church services at the Swedish royal court, Carissimi's piece had to be cleansed of all 'papist' references to Virgin Mary. At the same time, the changes appear to be rather cosmetic. It must have been obvious to any informed listener that the piece they heard was actually a *Salve Regina*, with just minor modifications of the text. Much of the original text was still there, and Carissimi's composition begins with the original melody of the *Salve Regina* hymn.

The piece by Carissimi was not an isolated case. In the Düben Collection, there are several instances of Italian pieces with their texts altered in similar ways. There are, for instance, two original *Salve Regina* settings by Giovanni Rovetta and Didaco Philetari respectively, with their text likewise changed to *Salve Rex Christe*. In the Österreich-Bokemeyer Collection at Staatsbibliothek zu Berlin, a collection of musical manuscripts originally connected with the ducal court at Gottorp, we find similar cases, such as settings by Giovanni Battista Bassani of *Alma redemptoris* switched into *Alma Rex caelorum* and a *Salve Regina* modified into *Salve Rex Jesu*. Moreover, in the several printed collections of Italian church music published in Leipzig by the Breslau musician and editor Ambrosius Profe, there are Italian, Catholic works with their text modified in similar ways, in order to be acceptable in the Lutheran confession.[4]

The fact that these modified versions of the compositions by Carissimi and his contemporary Italian colleagues were part of the repertory of the Swedish *Hofkapelle* raises some interesting questions related to the dissemination, function and import of music at European institutions during the seventeenth century. Some of these questions shall be addressed in the following, focussing on the liturgical use of Roman sacred music in the Protestant areas of Germany and Scandinavia.

It must be stressed that the tradition of court music discussed here does not represent typical examples of the kind of overtly panegyric, allegorical cultural artefacts that have so often been used in studies on early modern political culture, not least in connection with absolutist regimes. The present discussion is meant rather as an example of how commonplaces of religious worship and of musical genre traditions could be taken into new contexts and new uses, and given new meanings. Furthermore, I will show how symbolic means of communicating the power and grandeur of ruling sovereigns was universal and exchangeable, even in the competition between

---

[4] G. Webber, *A Study of Italian Influence on North German Church and Organ Music in the Second Half of the Seventeenth Century, with Special Reference to the Collection of Gustav Düben* (Oxford, 1988, diss.), vol. 1, pp. 194–197

competing courts, realms or confessions, and in that respect represented cultural material with a commonplace character, in a general sense of the word.

Let us begin with a brief overview of the organisation and function of on the one hand, musical establishments at Lutheran princely courts and, on the other, the tradition of Roman church music.

The court music ensemble was an important, not to say indispensable part of a princely court during the early modern era. At many courts the music ensemble made up a considerable part of the principal household budget. The royal court chapel in Stockholm at this time counted some 20 ordinary musicians and singers. The royal music ensemble in Copenhagen had a similar size, and so did the court chapels at Halle and Weissenfels. Smaller institutions such as the Mecklenburg ducal courts in Güstrow and Schwerin still employed ensembles of around 10 musicians, whereas the Electoral court in Dresden during the 1660s salaried some 40–50 musicians.[5]

During the fifteenth and sixteenth centuries, such court chapels consisted of so called *Vokalkantoreien*, purely vocal ensembles, whose main task was to sing mass or polyphonic motets at the court services. From the late sixteenth century onwards, instrumentalists were added to this vocal chapel and the repertory was made broader. The music ensemble would perform at occasions of different kinds at court: *Tafelmusik* during the princely dinners, music during ballets and other court entertainments, as well as for birthdays and other annual festivals. Moreover, the court ensemble, possibly reinforced with a number of externally recruited musicians and singers, performed solemn music for large ceremonies of state, such as coronations, princely weddings or funerals.

For similar solemn ceremonies, both in the Swedish realm and in France, large scale musical settings of the Psalms of David, such as *Domine salvum fac regem* (Ps. 19:10) or *Domine in virtute tua lætabitur rex* (Ps. 20) were composed and performed.[6] These Psalm compositions were part of a tradition of connecting the ruling king with Kings of the Old Testament, such as David, Salomon and Hezekiah.[7] The tradition of associating the local king with biblical, mythical or historical rulers to lend him legitimacy and authority was common all over Europe.[8] These compositions were

---

[5] E. Kjellberg, *Kungliga musiker i Sverige under stormaktstiden* (Uppsala, 1979, diss.).

[6] L. Berglund, *Studier i Christian Geists vokalmusik* (Uppsala, 2002), pp. 221–231; J. R. Anthony, *French Baroque Music from Beaujoyeulx to Rameau* (London, 1974), pp. 170 and 401.

[7] N.Ekedahl, *Det svenska Israel* (Uppsala, 1999), pp. 18–21 and 68–86.

[8] P. Burke, *The fabrication of Louis XIV* (New Haven/London, 1992).

works with large scorings of voices and instruments, often including trumpets and drums, composed in a musical language which aimed to display an acoustic representation of power and magnificence. The musical language was highly conventional and straightforward, without any refinement of detail, replicating standard schemes and figures used and re-used at the different courts of Western Europe – a kind of flourish-and-drum-roll music, which had its closest equivalent in the much cherished contemporary fireworks. Music of this kind was of a more circumstantial character, serving to frame and shape a festival. Its recipients were arguably all members of the society, high or low, but it was directed not least towards the subjects of lower rank, aiming to overwhelm and to infuse subservience and obedience – in that sense it served a political function.[9]

However, the most important task of the musical ensembles at court, and the reason why such ensembles were commonly designated 'the court chapel', 'cappella' or 'Hofkapelle', was to perform liturgical music at the religious services at court, on a weekly or even daily basis. The importance of these religious services at court during the early modern era must not be underestimated. The frequent celebration of church services at a Lutheran court, such as the royal court of Sweden, was considered of outmost significance by court officials and subjects. We must understand this from the perspective of the sacred character which was still so strongly connected with kingship at this time. The anointed King was in the ideology of Lutheran Orthodoxy viewed as God's deputy. In this sense he performed a vicarious act during the court services, bringing redemption to the entire realm. Among the most important rituals, accordingly, were the services during which the King partook of the Communion.[10] The music adorned these ceremonies and added to their significance. The performance of advanced polyphonic music at the church services was therefore almost always connected with the presence of the regent, or some other member of the royal family.

These more or less regular court service ceremonies did not have the same large-scale, public character as the state ceremonies and festivals. For practical, perhaps also ideological reasons, they were restricted to a narrower circle of court officials, noblemen, pages, important members of the clergy and, not least, diplomatic envoys and other foreign guests or visitors

---

[9] W. Braun, *Die Musik des 17. Jahrhundert* (=Neues Handbuch der Musikwissenschaft; 4), (Wiesbaden, 1981), pp. 44–48.

[10] See L. Berglund, 'The Aria, the Stylus Melismaticus and the Holy Communion. Devotional Music from Northern Courts in the Late Seventeenth Century', in: *The Cultural Heritage of Medieval Rituals: Genre and Ritual*, ed. E. Østrem and M.Birkedal Bruun, N.H.Petersen and J. Fleischer (Copenhagen, 2005), pp. 251–270.

at court. It is clear that these ceremonies and the music performed there also served a political function, but the musical means were of a very different kind. Instead of the majestic but somewhat stereotyped musical representation of splendour and power, it was marked by refinement and artistry, directing itself to an audience with a sophisticated musical understanding and discrimination of taste. 'Until 1660, church music at courts as a rule also meant the art with the highest quality', Werner Braun states in his handbook of seventeenth-century music,[11] and this judgement is adequate not only within the huge repertoire of church music produced at the time, but for contemporary music in general.

The sovereign was accordingly judged not only for the outer splendour of his court, but also for the qualitative level of his court music, not least the liturgical music performed at his court services. This meant that the *Hofkapellmeister* had a very important function. His role was to guarantee the quality of the music at court, by keeping performance standards at a high level, by supplying his own compositions for the court services, and by evaluating and choosing among the music of his colleagues. More or less all Lutheran courts were organised in this way.

During the first half of the seventeenth century, the main stock of repertoire for such court church services was either music produced at court, by the local *Kapellmeister*, or music from widely disseminated collections of church pieces by German Protestant composers such as for instance Samuel Scheidt, Henrich Schütz or Andreas Hammerschmidt, many of which had German texts, presented elaborated versions of Lutheran hymns, or were in other ways distinctly connected with the Lutheran confession. But after the peace of Westphalia, from the 1650s and onwards, the repertory performed at Lutheran court services underwent important changes, marked by an extensive introduction of Italian, and especially Roman sacred music. At the Swedish court, this development can be said to start with the recruitment of an Italian ensemble of singers and instrumentalists in 1652, during Queen Christina's regency. A similar development can be seen at related courts such as Copenhagen and Dresden.[12] Thus, during the 1650s and especially 1660s, a large stock of Italian and Roman sacred motets were acquired by the Swedish *Hofkapellmeister* and his musicians. They were copied from printed collections or manuscripts brought to Stockholm by musicians, dip-

---

[11] 'Bis 1660 bedeutet höfische Kirchenmusik in der Regel auch die qualitativ beste Kunst'. Braun, *Die Musik des 17. Jahrhundert*, p. 59.
[12] L. Berglund, 'The Roman Connection. Dissemination and Reception of Roman Music in the North', *The dissemination of music in 17th-century Europe. Celebrating the Düben Collection*, proceedings from the conference in Uppsala 7–9 September 2006, ed. E. Kjellberg (forthcoming).

lomats and other travellers. The copy of Carissimi's *Salve Regina/Salve Rex Christe* is one of several hundred such manuscripts in the Düben Collection. They contain pieces by the leading musicians in Rome at this time, such as Giacomo Carissimi, Francesco Foggia and Bonifazio Graziani, as well as music by the Roman composers Vincenzo Albrici and Giuseppe Peranda, who during the 1660s and 1670s were employed at the court chapel in Dresden.

The extensive dissemination of Italian, Catholic motets at Lutheran courts and churches have been acknowledged for a long time, though there has been a certain tendency to dismiss them as a custom of lesser confessional or political import. Friedrich Blume, in his monumental study of Protestant church music from 1965, *Geschichte der evangelischen Kirchenmusik*,[13] touched briefly upon the problem, and suggested two explanations:

> The spreading of Italian music on Latin texts (and not only on liturgical texts in the strictest sense) within the contemporary Lutheran church was connected with traditional irenics whereby a far greater tolerance was extended toward Roman Catholicism than toward the reformed of Calvinist denominations. It may also have been connected with the Jesuit mission, which seems to have been very active musically in Germany. This development has yet to be recognized, let alone studied as a historical process.[14]

More recently, Geoffrey Webber disputed Blume's suggestion concerning the influence of the Jesuits in this context:

> (…) there is little evidence which might suggest that the music performed at the Jesuit missions in the North German region during the seventeenth century, was ever of a scale to match that of the main courts and town churches in the region, since they did not employ permanent professional musicians. (…) For the most part is seems likely that the presence of the Jesuits in the North German region during the seventeenth century had only an indirect influence on the spread of Italian music on Latin texts.[15]

As regards the importance and influence of the Jesuit missions and colleges in Germany and the Baltic area, Webber has an important point. But as I

---

[13] F. Blume, *Geschichte der evangelischen Kirchenmusik* (Kassel et al, [2]1965), p. 157.
[14] Quoted from the English translation: F. Blume, *Protestant Church Music: A History* (London, 1975), p. 234.
[15] Webber, *A Study of Italian Influence*, vol. 1, pp. 196–197.

shall argue, both he and Blume underestimated the effects and importance of the mission and propaganda apparatus of the Roman-Catholic church from a wider European perspective – a process in which the Jesuit Society doubtless played an important role.

Thus, all of the Italian composers mentioned above, exemplifying the large impact of Italian music on the Northern court establishments, were active in Rome during all or at least a part of their career, and in addition had a close connection with the Jesuit Society. Both Giacomo Carissmi and Bonifazio Graziani were in the service of the Jesuits – the former as already mentioned at the German College and its church S. Apollinare, the latter at the main Jesuit basilica, *Chiesa del Gesù* and its connected seminary, *Seminario Romano*. Francesco Foggia held some of the more prestigious posts at Roman churches, such as *Santa Maria in Trastevere, San Giovanni in Laterano* (during more than 30 years, 1637–1661) and *San Lorenzo in Damaso*. At the same time he was trained at the German College. Vincenzo Albrici and Gioseppe Peranda were trained at the same college by Carissimi, and both seem to have served at *Chiesa del Gesù* under Graziani before they left for Dresden.[16] Thus, the careers and compositions of these musicians reflect much of the agenda lying behind the musical activities of the Jesuit Society. This, in its turn, was part of a missionary and educational program, where the confidence in the rhetorical and emotional power of music in awakening the proper religious sentiments, bringing about piety, repentance and even conversion, was very strong.[17]

The aim in these circles was for a music that 1) lent the highest possible prestige to their institutions, in this case first and foremost the particular church and seminary in question, but also more generally the Catholic church and the city of Rome, and 2) was capable of moving the souls attending service in the most effective way possible, thereby bending their hearts towards the divine. This resulted in a rather pragmatic view of ecclesiastical music: a willingness to allow the modern innovations of the *musica moderna*, a music focussing primarily on the strong appeal to the listener's senses and affections, into the service of a religious rhetoric. It meant that the music produced and performed at the Jesuit churches and institutions in Rome was often innovative and boldly expressive, and did not hesitate to make use of the means explored in secular genres in a search for the most effective and moving musical setting of secular erotic texts. The texts set to music were not primarily biblical or liturgical, but consisted in affectionate

---

[16] Berglund, 'Dissemination'.

[17] See S. Parker Shimp, *The Art of Persuasion: Domenico Mazzocchi and the Counterreformation* (Ann Arbor, 2000 diss. Yale University).

love poems directed to Christ or to the Virgin Mary, expressed in a language borrowed from the Song of Songs, or from medieval mystical poems inspired by it.

The recipients of this music were in the first place Roman inhabitants. However, an important target audience for the Roman patrons was, to quote a father of one of the Jesuit seminarians, the 'people who spend time willingly in Rome' (*[la] Gente che passa volentieri il tempo in Roma*),[18] that is, pilgrims, travellers, foreigners. Not the least important for the patrons were travellers from the North, the constant stream of young noblemen from Protestant countries visiting Rome during their peregrination or grand tour. They spent several weeks or even months in the city, studying buildings, ruins and monuments, visiting art collections and wonder-rooms, and listening to musical performances at the palaces and, not the least, in the churches. They made records of their observations in their travelling diaries, and reported home in letters as well as at their homecoming about the marvels they had seen in the papal city. They were generally utterly impressed – a few of them even to the extent of converting and staying in the south. But even though every convert of course represented a triumph for the church, the primary aim was arguably a more general and long-term missionary and propagandist program, aiming at implanting impressions of the grandeur and supremacy of the Catholic Church and the city of Rome in northern minds. Precisely this particular tradition of Roman ecclesiastical music, then, was to gain a dominant position at European Protestant courts, from around 1650 until the 1680s.

Evonne Levy has recently argued that the art and architecture produced and ordered by the Jesuit Society at this time could and should reasonably be termed propaganda.[19] Such a claim in fact finds historical support from the etymology of the word propaganda, being originally derived from the *Congregatio de propaganda fide*, the pontifical Congregation for propagating the faith, established in Rome in the early seventeenth century, and 'charged with the spread of Catholicism and with the regulation of ecclesiastical affairs in non-Catholic countries'.[20]

Without trying to invoke the notion of any kind of conspiracy, it is clear that this process of spreading Roman church music to the north was

---

[18] Th. D. Culley, *Jesuits and music: I. A Study of the Musicians connected with the German College in Rome during the 17th Century and of their Activities in Northern Europe* (Rome, 1970), p. 199.

[19] E.Levy, *Propaganda and the Jesuit Baroque* (Berkeley/Los Angeles/London, 2004).

[20] Quoted from art. 'Sacred Congregation of Propaganda', *Catholic Encyclopedia* (accessed February 2008) <http://www.newadvent.org/cathen/12456a.htm>.

not just a coincidence. The music was to a large degree introduced through widely circulated collections printed in Rome, not least the 22 anthologies of Roman music edited by the Roman priest and singer Florido de Silvestris.[21] Moreover, individual collections of music, especially those by Graziani and Foggia, were printed in Rome and spread all over Europe. Another work of immense importance for the propagation of Roman ecclesiastical music was *Musurgia universalis* (Rome, 1650), a monumental theoretical treatise on music written by the German Jesuit Athanasius Kircher, who was a professor of mathematics at the Jesuit college *Collegio Romano*. The work was known all over Protestant Europe, and a German translation was published in 1662. One of Kircher's points was the supremacy of contemporary Roman music, especially the works composed and performed at the major Roman churches and congregations, and above all the works by Giacomo Carissimi.

The introduction of Roman church music at Lutheran courts and churches was not without resistance. Especially in the clerical community the confessional and moral implications of this kind of sacred music were questioned. In Stockholm, for instance, the rector of the German School, J. Herbinus, did not mince his words when he complained in a petition from 1667 about the music performed in church by the Royal court musicians:[22]

> (…) it is very much to regret, that they have abolished the old, holy, highly profound musical church motets, and instead of them brought in crookedly and confusedly twisted concertos from Italy and France (from which springs the sounds of Antichrist with a lot of fashionable additions, and of vulgar and profane vainness), that are truly very artful, but little edifying (…)

> (…) hoch ist es zu beklagen, dass man die alte, heilige, sehr gestreiche Musikalische Kirchen-Moteten abgeschafft, und an statt deren die in Italien und Frankreiche (auss welchen des Anti Christi lauden läuter complementen alla moden (…)) krum und bund gedrähte concerten auffgebracht, die zwar sehr künstlich, aber wenig erbawlich sind.

---

[21] J. Whenham, 'Silvestris, Florido de', *Grove Music Online*, ed. L. Macy (accessed February 2008), <http://www.grovemusic.com>
[22] The document is in Stockholm's City Archive, Tyska församlingen, KIIIc2:2. It is published in E. Kjellberg, *Kungliga musiker i Sverige under stormaktstiden* (diss. Uppsala, 1979), p. 228 f.

Similarly in Rostock in 1661, the priest and theologian Theophil Grossbauer attacked the use of Italian music in worship with sarcastic words:[23]

> And just as the world is not earnest / but thoughtless / and the old, peaceful devotion has been lost: likewise songs are sent to us from Italy and Germany / in which the biblical texts have been torn apart / and cut into small pieces through the gargle of quick roulades.

> Und gleich wie die Welt nun nicht ernsthafftig ist / sondern leichtsinnig / und alte stille Devotion verlohren hat: Also sind uns Gesänge auss Welschland und Teutschland zugeschickt / worinnen die Biblischen Texte zurissen / und durch der Gurgel geschwindte Läuffte in kleine Stücken zerhacket werden.

In his critique Grossbauer focuses on musical aspects and also on the audibility of the text and on qualities of expressivity and decorum. Still, both texts make very clear – Grossbauer's more implicitly, and Herbinus's with its reference to the Antichrist more explicitly – that the resistance to Italian church concertos was certainly not just a matter of musical taste.

The introduction of this foreign musical culture could also awaken concern on more general confessional grounds. At the electoral court in Dresden, the eager interest in Italian music displayed by Prince Johann Georg II, resulting in the engagement of a large group of Italian musicians (including, as we have seen, the Romans Vincenzo Albrici and Gioseppe Peranda), seems to have been an important reason behind the recurring allegations of papist leanings, and the constant rumours circulating about his approaching conversion.[24] And in fact there were previous examples that could arouse such suspicions: in 1652, just two years before her abdication and ensuing conversion to the Catholic faith, Queen Christina of Sweden had engaged a similar Italian ensemble of singers and instrumentalists at her court, with a young Vincenzo Albrici as its most prominent member.

What did this music represent, looked at from a Roman Catholic and a North European Lutheran perspective respectively? And how did the new repertory function in its new context? Here we may discern two related but nonetheless different aspects: the confessional ones and the political ones.

The strictly confessional or even liturgical obstacles to using this 'Catholic' music at Protestant courts were probably, as indicated in the quo-

---

[23] Quoted from C. Bunners, *Kirchenmusik und Seelenmusik* (Göttingen, 1966), p. 94.
[24] M.E. Frandsen, *Crossing confessional boundaries: the patronage of Italian sacred music in seventeenth-century Dresden* (New York, 2006), pp. 76–100.

tation from Friedrich Blume above, less severe than one would perhaps imagine at first. The Latin language was admittedly normally replaced by the vernacular at Lutheran services, but it was not at all prohibited. Moreover, the differences between Lutheran and Catholic liturgy were not so drastic. One important exception was texts dedicated to Virgin Mary: as exemplified by Carissimi's composition at the beginning of this essay, they had to be adopted before they could be used in Protestant worship. Texts attributing a sacrificial character to the sacrament of the Eucharist were also problematic.

The Roman motets which were imported to the North were not primarily musical settings of strictly liturgical texts, but presented a freer repertoire of devotional prayers and poems. These texts responded to pious trends and currents common to different confessions at this time. The large repertory of mystical and strongly sentimental devotional texts typical of the Italian motets, which reflect the strong trend of devotionalism characteristic of the Catholic spiritual revival of the Counter-reformation, thus responded to related currents of mystical devotionalism in Lutheran Orthodoxy. In Italy, settings of such Christological texts were connected with Eucharist devotion. This strong emphasis on the exposure and devotion of the Eucharistic host was typical of the Counter-reformation, not only in the music and liturgy, but also in the shaping of the ritual space, with altarpieces that accentuated the sacrificial status of the Eucharist, and thus stressed one of the main points of dispute between Catholic and Lutheran faith.[25]

It is also important to note that the reception of Roman culture in the North was not restricted to music. Thus, in Sweden there was also a strong influence from Roman art and architecture during the last decades of the seventeenth century. This is particularly well reflected in the royal castle at Drottningholm, not least in the main staircase, which was designed by Nicodemus Tessin and his father (during the 1660s–80s), taking Roman church and palace architecture by Gianlorenzo Bernini and Pietro da Cortona as models.[26] Similarly remarkable is the roof, which was an emulation of Giovanni Battista Gaulli's design of the roof at the main church of the Jesuit Society, *Chiesa del Gesù* ('Triumph of the Name of Jesus', 1678–9), in its combination of frescos, stucco and sculpture.

---

[25] K. Downes, 'Baroque', *Grove Art Online*, Oxford University Press, (accessed February 2008), <http://www.groveart.com>.
[26] M. Snickare, 'Trapphuset och Övre galleriet – gestaltning och funktion', *Drottningholms slott. Från Hedvig Eleonora till Lovisa Ulrika*, vol 1, ed. Göran Alm and Rebecka Millhagen (Stockholm, 2004), pp. 174–199.

The interest and admiration for Roman art and culture in general was a result of its particularly high artistic standards, which in its turn was the result of a large venture of building and decoration in the city during the seventeenth century, as part of a most deliberate propagandist program from the authorities of the Roman church. From this broad perspective, there can be no doubt that the rapid dissemination of Roman church music in northern Europe from 1650 onwards, even in Lutheran strongholds such as Saxony, Denmark and Sweden, was part of such a large scale agenda, and must have represented a triumph for the Catholic church and for the organisation with the strongest involvement in the propagation of the Catholic faith at this time, the Jesuit Society.

At the same time I would like to stress that there are important differences between church and palace architecture on the one hand, and liturgical church music on the other. The sacred musical works imported from Italy brought into Lutheran worship a very specific religious culture, with a strong emphasis on themes and ingredients precisely at the heart of the agenda of Counter-reformation, and not least the Jesuit Society: in particular, the strong focus on the Eucharist and Eucharistic devotion, and texts devoted to Virgin Mary with only scant and superficial modifications.

Regarding the intentions and considerations behind introducing this Roman, Catholic repertory at the Lutheran courts, the interpretations must necessarily be somewhat tentative. To begin with, it is clear that the music at a princely court can be understood as part of what Jürgen Habermas termed the 'representative publicity' characteristic of early modern society.[27] Following the Danish historian Sebastian Olden-Jørgensen, we may define this as a kind of publicity which is utterly aware of status (*umådelig status-bevidst*), and aims at expressing the fundamental norms and structures of the society in a public and symbolic form, at the same time functioning as a kind of 'aura of power'.[28]

In the case of the ceremonial church music discussed here, it is clear that much of the content or import of the text are common for much of western Christianity, and in that sense the pieces in a broad sense represent commonplaces of Christianity. But we have also seen that certain themes typical of the Counter-reformation movement were strongly accentuated,

---

[27] J. Habermas, *Strukturwandel der Öffentlichkeit : Untersuchungen zu einer Kategorie der bürgerlichen Gesellschaft* (Frankfurt am Main 1990).
[28] S. Olden-Jørgensen, 'Statsceremoniel, hofkultur og politisk magt i overgangen fra adelsvaelde til enevaelde – 1536 til 1746', *Fortid og nutid* (1996), pp. 3–20.

and that the use of such music in a Lutheran context was strongly criticised, not least by the clergy.

For the agents and recipients in the Northern court environments, probably not much of the significance of these artefacts lay in the confessional implications, but rather in the musical design. But it was not so much the musical structures or signifiers per se – generic conventions, compositional schemes, and so on – that acted as carriers of meaning. The import instead lay in the potential value judgments, and in what could, anachronistically, be called the aesthetic appreciation of the music. The prestige of the prince was in this sense, to put it drastically, partially dependent on the quality of the music performed at his court. During the decades immediately after the Peace of Westphalia, the Roman sacred music as represented by composers in Jesuit service such as Giacomo Carissimi and Bonifazio Graziani represented the highest possible prestige in this sense. It was associated with the highest degree of artistry and the finest discrimination of taste. Therefore the acquisition of such music and of musicians skilled to perform it was more or less a necessity, even for a Lutheran ruler. Products of local composers could admittedly work as a substitute – a good example is the already mentioned Kaspar Förster, *Hofkapellmeister* in Copenhagen, who was trained in Rome, and was able to compose music which can barely be distinguished from the Roman originals. Still, what he presented was precisely very skilled imitations of the Roman idiom. Moreover, Förster was himself a professed Catholic.

This representative prestige was directed at several target groups at the same time. One such group consisted of the subjects, and especially the nobility and aristocracy. To them, this kind of court culture was clearly supposed to work as a means of social demarcation, symbolically articulating the hierarchy, being founded simultaneously on a capacity for expenditure (a quantitative means, one could say) and a concept of taste (a qualitative criteria). Another target group was made up by rival rulers and states, represented by ambassadors and other foreign visitors at court. Here, the primary goal was rather to fulfil an appropriate level of decorum; where the ambitions of court music extended far beyond this level, it can usually be explained by a specific interest in musical culture on behalf of the ruler, as in the cases of Queen Christina of Sweden and Johann Georg II of Saxony, or an extraordinary propagandist program, as in the case of Louis XIV of France.

The prestige connected with particular musical genres, styles and artefacts, performance practices and general musical evaluations could, as we have seen, simply be taken from one context to another. In the case of the use of Roman Catholic church music at Lutheran courts this process appears particularly intriguing, since the imported musical culture in this case in several ways appear to represent the opposite of what the Lutheran rulers and regimes stood for in the time after the Peace of Westphalia, both politically and regarding confessional questions. But even though this potential conflict was pointed out and criticized by contemporary observers, the prestige borrowed by performing this exquisite Roman music at court was obviously given primacy.

Arguably, this story about the use of Roman church music at Lutheran courts also tells us something about the still relatively weak national identity in a realm such as Sweden during the mid seventeenth century: it was regarded as a European kingdom among others, rather than as an individual nation. Idiomatic and specific expressions were not a priority. The notion of the state was still closely tied to the ruling dynasty, and the symbolic means used for communicating and upholding it were by preference precisely commonplaces of power and sovereignty, that is, universal signs easily codified for any contemporary European observer. This was in fact something that would gradually change during the last decades of the century: from the 1680s and on, we can see traces of an increasing ambition to find distinctive and independent symbols to represent the Swedish King and his realm. Thus, for instance, from the 1680s the Sun was dropped as a symbol representing King Charles XI of Sweden and his reign, obviously by then being too strongly associated with Louis XIV of France. It was instead replaced by the Pole star. The allegory was explained by an emblem with the motto *Nescit occasum* – 'it knows not of setting' – thus demonstrating Charles's constancy and steadfastness, and at the same time cunningly intimating that Louis was instead rather fickle and that the day of his decline was near.[29]

Paradoxically, it was precisely at this time, from the 1680s onwards, that the reception of French baroque opera began at the Swedish court, at the same time as at several other courts in Northern Europe – a process which in Sweden finally led to the recruitment of a French opera company at court in 1699. This is paradoxical because of the dissemination and reception of the operas by Jean-Baptiste Lully, who was Louis XIV's *surintendant de la musique*. These operas were produced as unequivocal allegorical apotheosises of the grandeur of Louis and his accomplishments and victories. The musical scores were printed in magnificent editions – something very unusual for operas at this time – and disseminated all over Europe in a way reminiscent of the dissemination of Roman motets. This must be considered a propaganda triumph of a similar kind: at North Ger-

---

[29] K.Johanneson, *I polstjärnans tecken. Studier i svensk barock* (Stockholm, 1968), pp. 103–107 and 123–125.

man and Scandinavian courts, the splendour and quality of the rulers and
their court establishments were demonstrated by means of the borrowed
plumes of one of their major competitors, *Le Roi-Soleil*.

In this way, even in realms and regimes which were rivals for political
and/or confessional reasons, the means and symbols by which authority and
prestige were upheld were to a large extent of a commonplace character,
both in a more narrow sense of the word, as *loci communes* in speech or
writing, and in a more general sense, as widely spread and universally recognized patterns of cultural material of any kind. Such material was con-
stantly borrowed 'from the enemy', so to speak, even in cases where the
borrowings must have been well recognized, and even problematic on ideological or confessional grounds. The priority was to present the latest and
most fashionable expressions of culture and the highest acquirable degree of
artistry, irrespective of its actual provenance and original meaning.

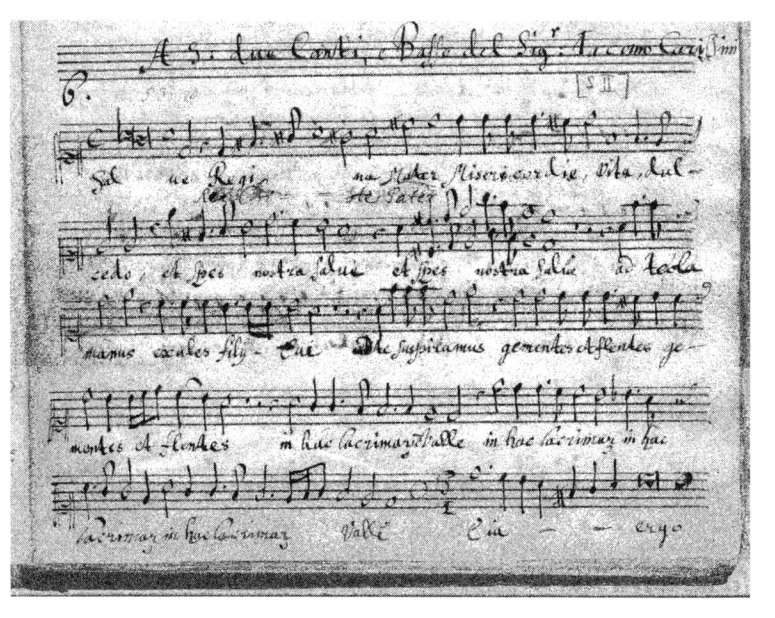

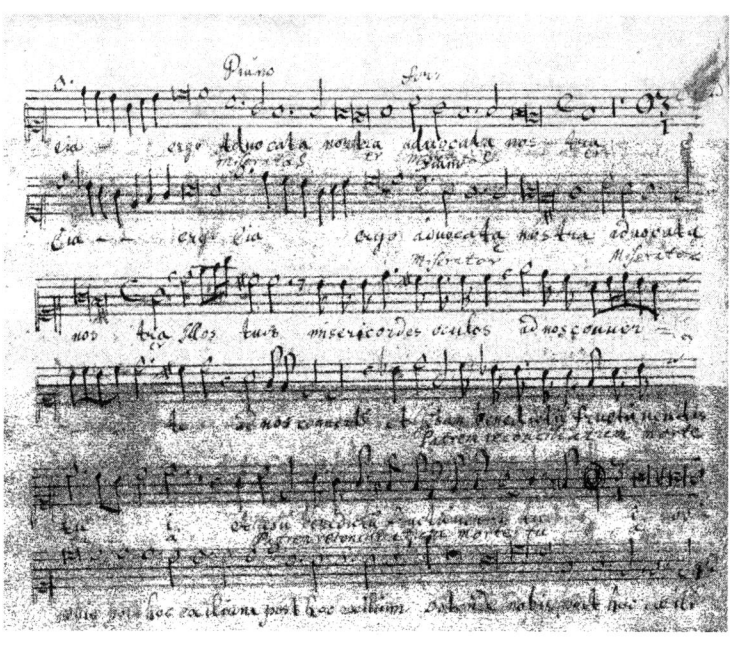

1. Giacomo Carissimi, *Salve Rex Christe*, copied by Gustav Düben the Elder. Uppsala University Library, Vmhs 53:10.

HEALTH AND ILLNESS OF THE *LEVIATHAN*

HOBBES'S USE OF THE COMMONPLACE METAPHOR
OF THE BODY POLITIC

Andreas Musolff

1. *Metaphor as Commonplace in 'Leviathan'*

Thomas Hobbes's use of the metaphor of the state as a body, or, in its lexicalised form, the *body politic,* in *Leviathan* (1651) has been described variously as marking the final phase of the classical commonplace metaphor of the state as a human body or as the start of a new tradition in the history of thought, reflecting the change from the ancient humoral model of disease to a more 'modern' one.[1] Such periodisations, based as they are on presupposed 'grand narratives' of historical progression, tend to gloss over the textual and pragmatic details of the metaphor use in question. This paper will instead concentrate on the way Hobbes employed the argumentative potential of the *body politic* metaphor to advance a new perspective on politics. In focusing on this discursive function of what was by Hobbes's time an already established metaphor, I hope to elucidate some of the mechanisms of subverting a commonplace's traditional mainstream meaning. As Moss highlights, the method of compiling and using commonplaces as developed over the course of the 16th century appealed to and often claimed for itself traditional authority.[2] Although the initial 'conservative' bias of commonplace-based argumentation had been thoroughly eroded in the moral and political disputes during the Reformation,[3] the technique of arguing *against* established authorities by way of commonplace still required the existence

---

[1] For the former view cf. e.g., D. Hale, *Body Politic: A Political Metaphor in Renaissance English Literature* (The Hague, 1971), pp. 128-130; S. Sontag, *Illness as Metaphor* (New York, 1978), pp. 77-78; for the latter, J. G. Harris, *Foreign Bodies and the Body Politic. Discourses of Social Pathology in Early Modern England* (Cambridge, 1998), pp. 141-143.

[2] A. Moss, 'Power and Persuasion: Commonplace Culture in Early Modern Europe', in: *Commonplace Culture in Western Europe in the Early Modern Period*, vol. I: *Reformation, Counter-reformation and Revolt*, eds David Cowling and Mette B. Bruun (Leuven, 2010), pp. 1-17 (pp. 5-6).

[3] Moss, 'Power and Persuasion', pp. 7-13.

of a 'common' frame of reference and established knowledge so that its more or less radical modification could be identified and understood.

Before we can begin to analyse Hobbes's use of the *body politic* metaphor, we need to clarify his attitude to metaphor in general. Such an explication is necessary as Hobbes is considered by some modern metaphor-theorists as one of the chief 'empiricist' detractors of metaphor and of figurative language use in general.[4] The reason for this notoriety lies in the metaphor-critical pronouncements in *Leviathan* that appear to demonstrate Hobbes's opposition to metaphor as an '*abuse* of speech', for instance when he compares it, together with 'senslesse and ambiguous words', to *ignes fatui* that distract from proper reasoning and mislead their victims into 'wandering amongst innumerable absurdities', so that the end is 'contention, and sedition, or contempt'.[5]

However, against this seemingly absolute condemnation of metaphor has to be set Hobbes's equally emphatic acknowledgement that in 'Demonstration, in Councell, and all rigourous search of Truth ...sometimes the understanding have need to be opened by some apt similitude'.[6] *Similitudes*, i.e. in modern terminology *similes*, are not disqualified by Hobbes at all; on the contrary, he endorses their use for showing good *Wit* and 'rarity of (…) invention'.[7] Such praise of 'similitude' as a rhetorical strategy was in line with the humanist tradition of using similes as argumentative commonplaces.[8] In his English paraphrase of Aristotle's *The Art of Rhetoric*, published anonymously in 1637,[9] Hobbes had defined a similitude as 'a *Meta-*

---

[4] M. Johnson, 'Introduction: Metaphor in the Philosophical Tradition', in: Johnson, M., ed., *Philosophical Perspectives on Metaphor* (Minnesota, 1981), pp. 3-47 (pp. 11-12); similarly, G. Lakoff and M. Johnson, *Metaphors we live by* (Chicago, 1980), pp. 11-2; D. E. Cooper, *Metaphor* (Oxford, 1986), pp. 17-8; M. Leezenberg, *Contexts of Metaphor* (Amsterdam, 2001), p. 1; A. Goatly, *Washing the Brain. Metaphor and Hidden Ideology* (Amsterdam and New York, 2007), p. 28.

[5] T. Hobbes, *Leviathan*, ed. Richard Tuck, revised ed. (Cambridge, 1996), p. 36; for similar condemnations of *misleading* 'metaphors' cf. *ibid.*, pp. 25-26, 31, 35-36. Page references to *Leviathan* in all the notes refer to the 1996 edition.

[6] Hobbes, *Leviathan*, p. 52.

[7] Hobbes, *Leviathan*, p. 50-51. For the status of the category of *Wit* in Hobbes's 'reconsideration of eloquence' cf. Q. Skinner, *Reason and Rhetoric in the Philosophy of Hobbes* (Cambridge, 1996), pp. 369-375; for Hobbes's vindication of perspicuous 'similitude' against deceptive 'metaphor' cf. A. Musolff, '*Ignes fatui* or apt similitude? — the apparent denunciation of metaphor by Thomas Hobbes', *Hobbes Studies* 18 (2005), pp. 96-113 (pp. 105-113).

[8] Moss, 'Power and Persuasion', p. 11.

[9] Cf. Hobbes, 'A Briefe of the Art of Rhetorique', in: Harwood, J. T., ed., *The Rhetorics of Thomas Hobbes and Bernard Lamy* (Carbondale and Edwardsville, 1986), pp. 33-128. For discussions of the impact of Aristotle's *Rhetoric* on Hobbes's later work, especially on *Leviathan*, cf. L. Strauss, *The Political Philosophy of Hobbes:*

phor dilated', and metaphor itself as characteristic of perspicuous 'oration', for 'in a *Metaphor* alone there is *perspicuity, Novity,* and *Sweetnesse*'.[10] By the time of writing *Leviathan,* however, Hobbes had, as his above-quoted verdict on metaphors as *ignes fatui* shows, developed a more critical view of 'metaphor'. It now stands in opposition to the concept of 'similitude', as the latter still is regarded by Hobbes a means of achieving the ideal of argumentative perspicuity. It is therefore plausible to interpret 'similitude' as covering the non-deceptive uses of figurative language, including what is today called 'metaphor'. The accusation against Hobbes that he was an opponent of 'metaphor' in the modern sense thus appears to rest on a double-confusion between his changing specialised uses of the term 'metaphor' (i.e. in the Aristotle paraphrase as positively valued part of oratory, in *Leviathan* as a rhetorical trick of deception) and the more general, modern meaning of 'metaphor' as the 'mapping' or 'blending' of concepts from different 'domains' of knowledge and experience.[11]

Hobbes's alleged hostility to metaphor and figurative language is (or rather, would be, were it true) also in blatant conflict with his massive use of rhetorical tropes in most of his writings but particularly in *Leviathan,* where figures such as metaphor, metonymy, simile, analogy and allegory, to mention only the most prominent ones, abound. The very title of his *opus magnum* is derived from the name of the allegorical sea monster mentioned in the Biblical book *Job* (40-41) as the 'King of all the children of pride', who still has to obey God's commands.[12] The frontispiece[13] and the first part of the introductory chapter present the state ('Common-wealth') as a giant model of a human body that comprises in it the smaller bodies of subjects/citizens. But why did Hobbes give such prominence to a metaphor that lacked at least one of the central features of metaphor praised in Aristotle's *The Art of Rhetoric*, i.e. 'Novity'? For the metaphor of the state as a body was anything but novel even in Hobbes's time. Its history[14] can be traced

---

its Basis and its Genesis, transl. Sinclair, E.M. (repr. Chicago, Ill., 1952), pp. 35-36; J. T. Harwood, 'Introduction: Thomas Hobbes's *Briefe of the Art of Rhetorique*', in: Harwood, J. T., ed., *The Rhetorics of Thomas Hobbes and Bernard Lamy* (Carbondale and Edwardsville, 1986), pp. 1-32 (pp. 13-32); Skinner, *Reason and Rhetoric in the Philosophy of Hobbes*, pp. 239-242.

[10] Hobbes, 'A Briefe of the Art of Rhetorique', pp. 109-110.

[11] For classic cognitive accounts of metaphor as conceptual mapping/blending cf. Lakoff and Johnson, *Metaphors we live by* and G. Fauconnier and M. Turner, *The Way we think: Conceptual Blending and the Mind's Hidden Complexities* (New York, 2002).

[12] Cf. Hobbes's reference to *Job* in *Leviathan*, pp. 9, 221.

[13] Cf. Figure 1 (p. 191).

[14] For overviews of the metaphor's conceptual development up to the seventeenth century cf. Hale, *The Body Politic,* pp. 18-107; G. Dhorn van Rossum and E.-W.,

back to pre-Socratic thinkers in Ancient Greece, then to Plato and Aris-
totle's writings and to the Aesopian 'fable of the belly', which was retold by
Hellenistic and Roman historians, and was passed on, via the Stoics and
medieval philosophers, to Renaissance authors, including Shakespeare (cf.
Coriolanus I, 1: 101-169). In another tradition that originated in St. Paul's
Epistles to the Romans and Corinthians and was carried further by the
Church Fathers and later theologians, the Church was defined as the mystical 'body of Christ', and this definition was transferred by jurists onto
socio-political entities.[15]

Based on these traditions, the *body-state* metaphor was established as a
commonplace to advocate discipline, co-operation and solidarity among the
body's members. Most accounts of the *body politic's anatomy* written during the Middle Ages and the Renaissance, from John of Salisbury's (*c.*
1115-1180) treatise *Policraticus* to the *Dialogue Between Reginald Pole
and Thomas Lupset* by Henry VIII's chaplain, Thomas Starkey (1495-
1537), stressed the necessity of the *head* caring for all, even the lowest
members of the body, i.e. the *feet*/peasants.[16] Up to the sixteenth century, the
body politic was mainly attributed to the ruler as his/her mystical quality in
addition to having a *body natural*.[17] By the seventeenth century, the concept
came to mean the state itself: this was the basis of Hobbes's theory of
'*Pacts* and *Covenants*, by which the parts of this Body Politique were at
first made'.[18]

Böckenförde, 'Organ, Organismus, Organisation, politischer Körper', in: Brunner,
O., Conze, W. and Koselleck, R., eds., *Geschichtliche Grundbegriffe. Historisches
Wörterbuch zur politisch-sozialen Sprache in Deutschland*, vol. 4, (Stuttgart, 1978),
pp. 519-622 (pp. 519-554); R. Guldin, *Körpermetaphern: Zum Verhältnis von Politik und Medizin* (Würzburg, 2000), pp. 1-79; A. Koschorke, S. Lüdemann, T. Frank,
and E. Matala de Mazza, *Der fiktive Staat. Konstruktionen des politischen Körpers
in der Geschichte Europas* (Frankfurt am Main, 2007), pp. 15-102.

[15] Cf. Q. Skinner, *The Foundations of Modern Political Thought*, 2 vols (Cambridge,
1978), vol. 1, pp. 3-62; C. Nederman and K. L. Forhan, eds., *Readings in Medieval
Political Theory 1100-1400* (Indianapolis, 1993).

[16] John Of Salisbury, *Policraticus. Of the Frivolities of Courtiers and the Footprints
of Philosophers*, ed. and transl. Nederman, C. J. (Cambridge, 1990), pp. 66-67, 69,
125-126; T. Starkey, *A Dialogue between Pole and Lupset*, ed. Mayer, T.F. (repr.
London, 1989).p. 123.

[17] Cf. E. H. Kantorowicz, *The King's Two Bodies: A Study in Mediaeval Political
Theology* (repr. Princeton, N.J., 1997), pp. 7-23; S. Bertelli, *The King's Body: Sa-
cred Rituals of Power in Medieval and Early Modern Europe*, transl. Litchfield, R.
B. (University Park, Pennsylvania, 2001), passim.

[18] Hobbes, *Leviathan*, p. 9.

2. The anatomy and functioning of the body politic in Leviathan

Leviathan contains two major passages that depict the 'Common-wealth, or State, (in latine Civitas)' as an 'Artificiall Man; though of greater stature and strength than the Naturall':[19] one at the start of the introductory chapter and a further one in Chapter 23, which treats '*Of the* publique ministers *of Soveraign Power*'. A few further references to organs and functions of the *body politic* are scattered throughout the book. Tables 1 and 2 give an overview over these conceptual mappings (see Tables 1 and 2 in the Appendix, p. 189). Some salient *body parts,* such as the *head, heart* and *feet,* which had been regularly included in traditional versions of the *body-state* analogy, are missing and there is one minor discrepancy: the source concept of *nerves* is used to depict both a political function (reward, punishment) and the state functionaries themselves (*Publique ministers*). Furthermore, the second list contains as many psychological and social functions as physical ones. It is thus evident that there is no a systematic anatomical account in *Leviathan* – a fact that motivated David Hale in particular to list Hobbes among those who put 'an end to sustained or serious use of organic imagery in political discussion'.[20] But then Hobbes nowhere claimed comprehensiveness or competence in this respect: his considerable interest in (natural) sciences centred on mathematics and physics, not biology or medicine.[21] To decide, for instance, in what sense nerves can be considered bodily functions or 'parts organicall' was not his concern: all that he needed for his argumentation in *Leviathan* were source concepts that fitted the target concepts of state institutions he wanted to analyse.

Even if some *body parts* appear to be underspecified or absent, the *body politic* depicted in the text of *Leviathan* is just as complex as that on the frontispiece, which shows (against varying emblematic backgrounds, depending on the year of the imprint) the crowned figure of a man from the waist upwards, holding a sword and a crosier in his hands, with arms and the trunk consisting of a multitude of miniature figures symbolising the people.[22] If we assume that the *head* of this figure is the 'seat' of the *soul* that is mentioned in the introductory chapter, we may perceive a rough

---

[19] Hobbes, *Leviathan*, p. 9.
[20] Hale, *The Body Politic,* p. 130.
[21] Cf. Q. Skinner *Visions of Politics,* three vols, vol. 3: *Hobbes and Civil Science* (Cambridge, 2002), pp. 5-37.
[22] Cf. Figure 1 (p. 191) for the title page of the first edition. For detailed analyses of the frontispiece cf. R. Brandt, 'Das Titelblatt des Leviathan', *Zeitschrift für Sozialwissenschaft* 15 (1987), pp. 164-186; N. Malcolm, 'The Title Page of *Leviathan,* Seen in a Curious Perspective', in: Malcolm, N., *Aspects of Hobbes* (Oxford, 2002), pp. 200-233.

equivalence of the pictorial and textual allegories, despite the missing *head* in the text. The 'headlessness' of the *body politic* in the textual presentation in *Leviathan* could also be motivated by the fact that since the decapitation of Charles I in 1649, two years before the publication of Hobbes's treatise, the contemporary English *body politic's* dynastic sovereign was literally without his (natural) head. However, as Ernst H. Kantorowicz has pointed out, even during the civil war, the head of the 'King body politic' was retained by Parliament as a state symbol on the great seal and coins: 'the king body natural in Oxford had become a nuisance to Parliament; but the King body politic was (...) still present in Parliament, though only in his seal image'.[23] What mattered was the sovereign's political 'will', i.e., the *soul* of the 'Artificiall Man', and as the symbolic seat of that soul, the *head* of the *body politic* was not necessarily a problematic concept even after the 'King body natural' had lost his.

In any case, the *body politic* that Hobbes presents is an artificial one in both the frontispiece and the text. The picture of a man consisting of many little figures is evidently an allegorical representation, and the textual exposition of the analogy similarly stresses the 'constructedness' of the correspondence between the two bodies:

> NATURE (the Art whereby God hath made and governes the World) is by the *Art* of man, as in many other things, so in this also imitated, that it can make an Artificial Animal. For seeing life is but a motion of Limbs, the beginning whereof is in some principall part within; why may we not say, that all *Automata* (Engines that move themselves by springs and wheeles as doth a watch) have an artificiall life?[24]

The 'Artificial Animal' of the state is a machine construed by Man, by means of which he tries to imitate 'that *Fiat*, or the *Let us make man*, pronounced by God in the Creation'.[25] Where God simply uttered a command in order to create human beings, Man is forced to put together laboriously a socio-political construction. Much has been made of Hobbes's acknowledgement of the contemporary mechanistic conception of the body, as promoted by René Descartes (1596-1650), and of Hobbes's acquaintance with and admiration for William Harvey's (1578-1657) theory of blood circulation.[26] But surely the most important point for Hobbes in using the *body-*

---

[23] Kantorowicz, *The King's Two Bodies,* pp. 20-23.
[24] Hobbes, *Leviathan,* p. 9.
[25] Hobbes, *Leviathan,* p. 10.
[26] Cf. Hale, *The Body Politic,* pp. 109, 129-130; D. Johnston, *The Rhetoric of Leviathan* (Princeton, NJ, 1986), p. 124; Guldin, *Körpermetaphern,* pp. 80-89; Goatly, *Washing the Brain,* pp. 362-363.

state metaphor was not an application of the latest anatomic insights (if indeed these were as recognizable for contemporaries as for later historians of thought who had the benefit of hindsight).[27] Rather, what recommended the mechanistic model as a source concept to Hobbes was the fact that it suited perfectly the target focus of his political argument, i.e. the notion of the 'Common-Wealth' based on an artificial covenant that was not derived from the 'state of nature', where life was 'solitary, poore, nasty, brutish, and short'.[28] The artificial body of the state based on the covenant was meant to relieve Man from that very condition of unchecked nature, i.e. constant warfare. Hobbes's emphasis on the artificiality and the mechanical principle of the 'Common-wealth' does not contradict the organic aspects of the *body politic* metaphor – it just implies that he saw both the physical and the political body as a product of 'Art' – with God and humanity as the respective 'artificers'.

The correspondences between anatomic and functional aspects of the human body and the state that we have sketched so far are neither systematic nor particularly innovative as regards the source concepts employed: Hobbes picks and chooses from the commonplace tradition what is suitable for his analysis of the state as a hierarchical and functional whole. However, his *body-state* analogies are not exhausted by these general references; *Leviathan* also includes a vivid account of the *body politic's illnesses*, which we need to take into consideration in order to assess the overall argumentative import of the metaphor.

3. The pathology of the Leviathan

Hobbes devotes a whole chapter of *Leviathan* to *'things that Weaken, or tend to the Dissolution of a Common-wealth'*,[29] which is not surprising in view of his own experience of the English Civil War that forced him into

---

[27] The assumption of a unitary modernization of medicine in the early 17th century that underlies this motivation of Hobbes's insistence on the mechanical nature of bodies is by no means unproblematic. A. Cunningham ('William Harvey: The Discovery of the Circulation of Blood', in: Elmer, P. and Grell, P.E., eds., *Health, disease and society in Europe 1500-1800: A source book* (Manchester and New York, 2004), pp. 173-178 (pp. 176-7)) has pointed out that Harvey, far from accepting Descartes' mechanistic views, saw his discovery of blood circulation as a reformulation and essentially, reaffirmation, of Aristotle's views regarding the functions of the heart. The subsequent mechanistic reinterpretation of Harvey's theory should not be projected retrospectively onto his discovery, let alone attributed to Hobbes's knowledge of it. Its transfer onto political imagery seems even more speculative.

[28] Hobbes, *Leviathan*, p. 89.

[29] Chapter 29 of *Leviathan*, pp. 221-230.

exile and, after his return to England in 1652, led to a precarious existence first under Cromwell's, then Charles II's rule.[30] He begins his political *diagnosis* by discussing *Defectuous Procreation,* i.e. 'Imperfect Institution' of states, which he equates with the lack of power and resources of the sovereign.[31] Secondly, he considers '*Diseases* of a Common-wealth, that proceed from the poison of seditious doctrines'.[32] He refutes six doctrines that question the moral and political authority of the sovereign and then goes on to discuss the underlying causes of sedition. Here, *illness* imagery plays a significant role. The first cause that Hobbes highlights is the 'Example of different Government' in other nations,[33] which is so seductive that people cannot leave it be, 'though they be grieved with the continuance of disorder; like hot blouds, that having gotten the itch, tear themselves with their own nayles, till they can endure the smart no longer.'[34] The reference to *hot blouds* appears to be an oblique allusion to the theory of the *humours*, which surfaces in *Leviathan* on a few further occasions, e.g. when unlawful 'systemes' or assemblies are described as 'Wens, Biles, and Apostemes, engendered by the unnaturall conflux of evill humours'.[35] However, the '*hot blouds'* passage itself derives its vividness less from humoral theory than from the graphic account of scratching an open wound.

This focus on graphic symptoms is also prominent in Hobbes's discussion of the second cause of *poisoning* by seditious doctrines, i.e. 'the Reading of the books of Policy, and Histories of the antient Greeks, and Romans', which incite 'young men and all others that are unprovided of the Antidote of solid Reason' to emulate their rebellions without considering the resultant 'frequent Seditions, and Civill warres'.[36] Ancient republicanism appears *poisonous* to Hobbes, because it justifies regicide or, as its supporters euphemistically (from Hobbes's viewpoint) call it, 'Tyrannicide':

---

[30] Cf. A. P. Martinich, *Thomas Hobbes* (Basingstoke, 1997), p. 13-23; also Hobbes's own commemoration of one of its victims, Sydney Godolphin (1610-1643), 'who hating no man, nor hated of any', was 'slain in the beginning of the late Civil warre, in the Publique quarrell, by an undiscerned, and an undiscerning hand' (*Leviathan,* p. 484).

[31] Hobbes, *Leviathan,* p. 222. In a earlier chapter Hobbes used *Procreation* as a synonym for the 'Children of a Common-wealth', i.e., at the target level, '*Plantations, or Colonies*' (*Leviathan,* p. 175).

[32] Hobbes, *Leviathan,* p. 223.

[33] Hobbes provides historical and contemporary examples (e.g. the Low Countries as a model for English revolutionaries (*Leviathan,* pp. 225-226)).

[34] Hobbes, *Leviathan,* p. 225.

[35] Hobbes, *Leviathan,* p. 165; cf. also Hobbes's reference to the link between different kinds of 'Madnesse', including 'melancholy', as one of the four classical humors, and an 'evill constitution of the organs of the Body' (*Leviathan,* p. 54).

[36] Hobbes, *Leviathan,* pp. 225-226.

this 'Venime' he 'will not doubt to compare to the biting of a mad Dogge, which is a disease the Physicians call *Hydrophobia*, or *fear of Water*'.[37] Hobbes parallelizes the symptoms in a strictly analogical way:

> For as he that is so bitten, has a continuall torment of thirst, and yet abhorreth water; and is in such an estate, as if the poison endeavoureth to convert him into a Dogge: So when a Monarchy is once bitten to the quick, by those Democraticall writers, that continually snarle at that estate; it wanteth nothing more than a strong Monarch, which neverthelesse out of a certain *Tyrannophobia*, or fear of being strongly governed, when they have him, they abhorre.[38]

Hobbes's extended horror scenario of the 'Democraticall writers' biting a state 'to the quick' calls into question not only Hale's assertion that in *Leviathan* the *body-state* 'comparisons are not insisted upon',[39] but also Sontag's inclusion of Hobbes in a list of pre-modern thinkers who employed illness metaphors benignly to encourage 'rulers to pursue a more rational policy'.[40] Rather, in the comparison of his ideological adversaries with *mad dogs,* whose *venom* can *kill* the state, Hobbes seems to come close to suggesting that such dangerous *beasts must be put down,* lest they ruin the *body politic.* The *poisoning* scenario seems to have been as potent an image to justify the elimination of a category of groups of people in the 17th century as it was in the 20th century, when the Nazis spoke of 'the Jew' as entering and poisoning the bloodstream of the supposed 'Aryan' race (and endeavoured to stop this *disease* by eliminating its supposed *carriers*).[41]

However, whilst the vividness as well as the conclusiveness of an infection of *Tyrannophobia* as the political equivalent of physical *Hydrophobia* may come close to that of modern 'master illness' metaphors,[42] Hobbes still adheres to the humanistic tradition of introducing the metaphor didactically with the assertion that he 'will not doubt to compare'. He thus highlights the fact that his analogy is based on a comparison, *not* a literal description. Its purpose is that of a warning, rather than, as Sontag saw in the

---

[37] Hobbes, *Leviathan*, p. 226.
[38] Hobbes, *Leviathan*, p. 174.
[39] Hale, *The Body Politic*, p. 128.
[40] Sontag, *Illness as Metaphor*, pp. 75-76.
[41] For analyses of the *blood poisoning* myth in Nazi-ideology cf. C. Schmitz-Berning, *Vokabular des Nationalsozialismus* (Berlin and New York, 2000), pp. 460-464; F. Rash, *The Language of Violence: Adolf Hitler's Mein Kampf* (New York, 2006), pp. 125-156; A. Musolff, 'Which role do metaphors play in racial prejudice? The function of anti-Semitic imagery in Hitler's 'Mein Kampf'', *Patterns of Prejudice* 41/1 (2007), pp. 21-44 (pp. 36-40).
[42] Sontag, *Illness as Metaphor*, pp. 71-72.

20th century uses of illness as a metaphor, the desire to 'impute guilt, to prescribe punishment'.[43] Hobbes employs the analogy to drive home his warning as forcefully as possible but the readers are invited to consider it critically for themselves.

Hobbes's discussion of the third type of serious political *diseases* starts out from medical speculation: as there 'have been Doctors, that hold there be three Soules in a man: so there be also that think there may be more Soules (...) than one'.[44] The import of this comparison is a polemic against the Church's claims to '*Supremacy* against the *Soveraignty*', which he sees as the chief cause of fanaticism that leads to civil war.[45] In Hobbes's view, 'this is a Disease which not unfitly may be compared to the Epilepsie, or Falling-sicknesse', because in both cases 'an unnaturall spirit' causes 'violent, and irregular motions' of the *members*, thus putting the victim (the person or the state) in danger of falling (e.g. into fire/water or into 'the Fire of Civill warre').[46] The implication is that the sovereign must remain the sole *soul* of the state; any other rival authority is seen as a mortal danger to the *health* of the *body politic*. The last major challenge to the sovereignty as the political *soul* of the state that Hobbes considers is the idea of dividing government between two or three powers. These are likened to life-functions, i.e. the powers of 'levying mony, (which is the Nutritive faculty,)', 'of conduct and command, (which is the Motive faculty,)' and 'of making Lawes, (which is the Rationall Faculty,)'.[47] As with the 'State vs. Church' rivalry for the *soul*, Hobbes dismisses any such arrangement as a dangerous 'irregularity of Common-wealth'.[48]

After having discussed defective *procreation*, *poisoning* and rivalry of several *souls* in one *body politic* as the *diseases* 'of the greatest and most present danger', Hobbes goes on to describe less dangerous but still important conditions, which 'are not unfit to be observed'.[49] Of these he notes seven: i) 'difficulty of raising Mony' ('Ague caused by congested arteries obstructing the 'passage for the Bloud'), ii) monopolies that hoard 'the treasure of the Common-wealth' ('pleurisie', i.e. intrusion of blood in the lungs), iii) 'Popularity of a potent Subject' that tempts him to become leader of a rebellion ('the effects of Witchcraft'), iv) immoderate growth of towns, corporations and concomitant 'liberty of Disputing' ('wormes in the entryles'), v) expansionist policies ('Bulimia'), which in their consequence, lead

---

[43] Sontag, *Illness as Metaphor*, p. 80.
[44] Hobbes, *Leviathan*, p. 226.
[45] Hobbes, *Leviathan*, pp. 226-228.
[46] Hobbes, *Leviathan*, p. 227.
[47] Hobbes, *Leviathan*, p. 228.
[48] Hobbes, *Leviathan*, p. 228.
[49] Hobbes, *Leviathan*, p. 228.

to '*Wounds* (…) received from the enemy; and the *Wens*, of (...) conquests', vi) excessive 'Ease' ('Lethargy') and vii) 'Riot and Vain Expense' ('Consumption').[50] Hobbes rounds off the discussion of detrimental and destructive developments in the political *body* with a description of a defeat in war as its *dissolution,* when the sovereign, as its *soul*, loses all command of its *members* and only leaves the 'carcase' of the state.[51]

To gain an overview, we can again draw up a list of matching pairs of source and target concepts. (See Table 3 in the Appendix, p. 190). It is evident from the overlaps between various categories and the mix of concepts from various medical theories (humours, blood circulation, witchcraft, bulimia etc.), that, as in the case of anatomical and functional aspects, Hobbes makes no attempt to provide a systematic medical account. Writing more than a century before Hobbes, Thomas Starkey had still made systematic use of Galenic humoral principles in the distinction of eight principal diseases of the *body politic, consumption, dropsy, palsy, pestilence, disproportion, weakness, frenzy* and *gout*, as causing 'temperamental' imbalances in the state.[52] By contrast, Hobbes, even though he occasionally includes references to the 'humours', is not interested in their system or in the analysis of illness as an upset humoral equilibrium. Only diseases relating to blood circulation are coherently and, again, graphically, depicted,[53] but this aspect does not structure his general account of political *illnesses* (which, as we have seen, is organized chiefly according to the relative danger of *body politic defects* at the level of the target domain).

Hobbes's lack of commitment to a systematic medical theory has left some critics unimpressed. Hale found his account of the state's *diseases* so 'heterogeneous' and unspecific that it leaves open 'the details which make his comparisons appropriate'.[54] Harris contends that Hobbes, for lack of a 'live humoral vocabulary' failed to find the equivalent of the defect of 'mixed government', i.e. the case of a threefold division of constitutional powers (cf. above): 'To what Disease of the Naturall Body of man I may exactly compare this irregularity of a Common-wealth, I know not'.[55] Harris

---

[50] Hobbes, *Leviathan*, pp. 228-230.

[51] Hobbes, *Leviathan*, p. 230.

[52] Cf. Starkey, *A Dialogue between Pole and Lupset*, pp. 39-58.

[53] Cf. Hobbes's discussion of the impediments to the 'free passage' of blood (*Ague* and *Pleurisy*) in Chapter 29 (pp. 228-229), which is prefigured in the definition of the state's *Strength* as 'Wealth and Riches' in the introductory chapter, the depiction of money circulation as the 'Sanguification of the Common-wealth' in Chapter 24, and the reference to the 'Nutritive faculty' in Chapter 29.

[54] Hale, *The Body Politic*, p. 128.

[55] Harris, *Foreign Bodies and the Body Politic*, p. 143; the reference is to *Leviathan*, p. 228. Harris' remark is part of an argument that reads Hobbes's political pathology

omits, however, Hobbes's following explanation, which does in fact provide an approximate source equivalent to the target issue:

> 'But I have seen a man, that had another man growing out of his side, with an head, armes, breast, and stomach, of his own. If he had had another man growing out of his other side, the comparison might then have been exact.'[56]

Hobbes compares here what he saw as an unworkable political organisation, i.e. a three-way division of powers, to a condition that would be met by *conjoined triplets*: only they apparently did not exist in his experience. The next best (or, for the sufferers, worst) thing was the condition of *conjoined twins* – and this image is duly mentioned. As source concept for the comparison, it is sufficient to convey what mattered to Hobbes, i.e. the evaluation of divided sovereignty as an unworkable (and 'unlivable') monstrous body. Hobbes does not lack a source concept here at all but only mentions that he has not known any case of conjoined triplets from experience. Instead of 'failing' to fit his target issue into the source account, Hobbes achieves his argumentative aim by flexibly fitting the source concept to the target notion even though the numbers of powers in a state and conjoined siblings do not match exactly.

The image of the state as a *monstrous body* that Hobbes invokes here should therefore not be viewed as an indication of a theoretical deficit but rather as a metaphor that serves to support an emphatic political statement. The *monstrous body politic* marks the borderline between what is considered 'normal' and what is 'beyond' the known universe of physical/political entities. Less than two decades after the publication of *Leviathan*, in 1667, Samuel von Pufendorf described the 'Holy Roman Empire of German Nation' in its disastrous state after the Thirty Years War as a *body* that resembled a *monster* ('*irregulare aliquod corpus et monstro simile*'), on account of the conflicting powers of emperor, electors and estates, which made central government impossible.[57] Like Hobbes's supposed 'failure' to describe a mixed government in terms of the corporeal/medical metaphor, Pufendorf's

---

as indicative of the 'breakdown not only of the logic of correspondence, but also to the endogenous pathological discourses which modelled disease as an internal bodily state rather than as a determinate foreign body' (*Foreign Bodies and the Body Politic*, p. 143). Harris himself notes the exception of epilepsy (p. 175, note 4); in fact, as Table 3 shows (see Appendix, p. 190), the alleged 'exceptions' of internal diseases in Hobbes's account at least match, if not outnumber the exogenous diseases.

[56] Hobbes, *Leviathan*, p. 228.

[57] S. von Pufendorf, *Die Verfassung des deutschen Reiches.* (Latin and German), ed. Horst Denzer. (Frankfurt am Main 1994), p. 198.

characterisation of the 'irregular' Empire was not motivated by any insufficiency of his source domain vocabulary but rather by the fact that the target referent's condition transcended the limits of classical political theory: it was *so* 'irregular' that it could only be viewed as an abnormal phenomenon and as the opposite of rational political order. Monstrosity as a feature of the *body politic* is not a shortcoming of the 'source input' into the body-state metaphor but rather a 'borderline' concept that conveys an emphatic negative characterisation of a state that, from the perspective of the respective political theory, suffers from a fundamental pathological condition.

4. *Conclusion*

Hobbes's use of physiological and medical source concepts in the political theory put forward in *Leviathan*, was, as has been noted by Hale and Harris, not systematically based on the humoral theory of medicine, nor on any other framework of medical knowledge. Nonetheless, Hobbes did provide a coherent and, in its own terms, comprehensive account of the *body politic* as regards the main target concept aspects that he wanted to clarify. He explained the unitary character of the state as a body in which every action by any member is or should be controlled by the *soul*, and he accounted for the main dangers that threatened this unity in terms of *illnesses of the body politic*. Hobbes was indeed not interested in exploring equivalences between physical and socio-political levels or links of the *Great Chain of Being*;[58] his use of the *body politic* metaphor in *Leviathan* marks a break with a conceptual tradition that had its beginning in antiquity and lasted into the age of humanism and Reformation. Instead, his focus was on exploiting the established *body politic* metaphor for the purpose of elucidating the conditions and functions of political entities, with a certain bias towards exploring their problematic, pathological aspects. The commonplace 'similitude' between body and state was not relevant for him as an ontological statement but served as a well-considered method to 'open the understanding' for the complexities of how political rule works (and ceases to work in the case of civil war). Hobbes could rely on this classical *topos* of political theory being part of the shared knowledge of his readers, especially against the back-

---

[58] For the connections between the *body politic* metaphor and the conceptual complex of the *Great Chain of Being* cf. E. M. W. Tillyard, *The Elizabethan World Picture* (repr. Harmondsworth, 1982), pp. 101-106; K. Banks, 'Interpretations of the Body Politic and of Natural Bodies in Late Sixteenth Century France' in: Musolff, A. and Zinken, J., eds., *Metaphor and Discourse*. Basingstoke, 2009), pp. 205-218 (pp. 210-216); J. Zavadil, 'Bodies Politic and Bodies Cosmic: the Roman Stoic Theory of the 'Two Cites'', in: Musolff, A. and Zinken, J. (eds.), *Metaphor and Discourse* (Basingstoke, 2009), pp. 219-232 (pp. 221-226).

ground of its revival in Tudor politics over the course of the 16th century. He uses this knowledge as a 'platform' to highlight those aspects which he wanted to impart as *new* insights to his readers, i.e., the need to combat immediately and without any complacency any dangerous political influences, especially those that undermine the sovereign's power.

It is for this chief purpose of alerting the readers to the dangers of political complacency and/or naivety that Hobbes describes political *illnesses* in the most alarming and gory details. In doing so, he transcends the limits of the commonplace tradition of the *body-state* metaphor as a conservative-harmonising argument in favour of the status quo. He also transcends, as we have seen in detail, the limits of his own lay medical knowledge; in fact, there is no consistent physiological or pathological account of the *body politic* to be found in *Leviathan*. However, medical or physiological consistency was irrelevant for this political argument, and Hobbes's supposedly 'failed' definition of a chaotic state in terms of *conjoined siblings* was, like Pufendorf's view of the post-Thirty Years War German Empire as a *monstrosity,* a desperate warning of political *diseases* for which there was no *cure*. Unlike traditional political thinkers, both Hobbes and Pufendorf dared to speak about a fundamentally *ill* state, not just as a 'worst-case but still repairable' scenario but as the nightmarish possibility of an irrationally organised, hence doomed state. The implied moral appeal was still linked to that of the commonplace implication of the metaphor – i.e., that the members of the *body politic* must strive to avoid such a condition of political chaos and disintegration – but the concept of the state developing into a *monstrous body* appears to have taken on a new realistic appearance for them. In 'failing' to apply the traditionally salutary *body politic* metaphor to their respective target concepts (the state in general and the German Empire, respectively), Hobbes, and later Pufendorf, became pioneers of analysing its pathology.

Table 1.

Source concepts	Target concepts
Body	Common-Wealth
Soul	Soveraignty
Joynts	Magistrates
Nerves	reward, punishment
	Publique Ministers: Protectors, Vice-Roys, and Governors
Hands	Publique Ministers: executioners etc.
Eyes	Publique Ministers: govt. Spies
Eare	Publique Ministers: govt. receivers of petitions
Blood	mony, gold and silver
Muscles	lawful Systemes, and Assemblyes of People

Mappings: Body parts/fluids – Political institutions.

Table 2.

Source concepts	Target concepts
Strength	wealth, riches
Safety	Businesse
memory	Counsellors
reason and will	equity and laws
Health	Concord
Death	civill war
God´s Fiat (Genesis)	pacts, covenants
Voice	Judges
nutritive faculty	Power of levying mony
motive faculty	Power of conduct and command
rationall faculty	Power of making Lawes
procreation, children	Colonies

Mappings: Life functions – Political functions.

Table 3.

Source concepts	Target concepts
Disease, infirmities	Things that weaken the Common-wealth
Sicknesse	Sedition
unlawfull conflux of evill humours	unlawful assemblies in common-wealth
hot blouds	desire of novelty
Defectuous Procreation	Imperfect Institution
Biting of Mad Dogge, Hydrophobia	Tyrannophobia
Epilepsie, or Falling-sicknesse	Belief in Ghostly Kingdome
Conjoined twins	mixt government
Ague (obstructed Heart arteries)	difficulty of raising Mony
Pleurisie	Monopolies
Witchcraft	Rebellion by charismatic army leaders
wormes in entryles	liberties of great towns, corporations, liberty to Dispute
bulimia	appetite of enlarging Dominion
wens	conquests
	unlawfull systemes in the Common-wealth
biles	unlawfull systemes in the Common-wealth
apostemes	unlawfull systemes in the Common-wealth
lethargy	Ease
consumption	Riot and Vain Expense
dissolution	Warre
poison, venime	seditious doctrines
- contagion	Greek dæmonology
- antidote	Reason

Mappings: Illnesses/diseases – Threats to the State.

Figure 1.

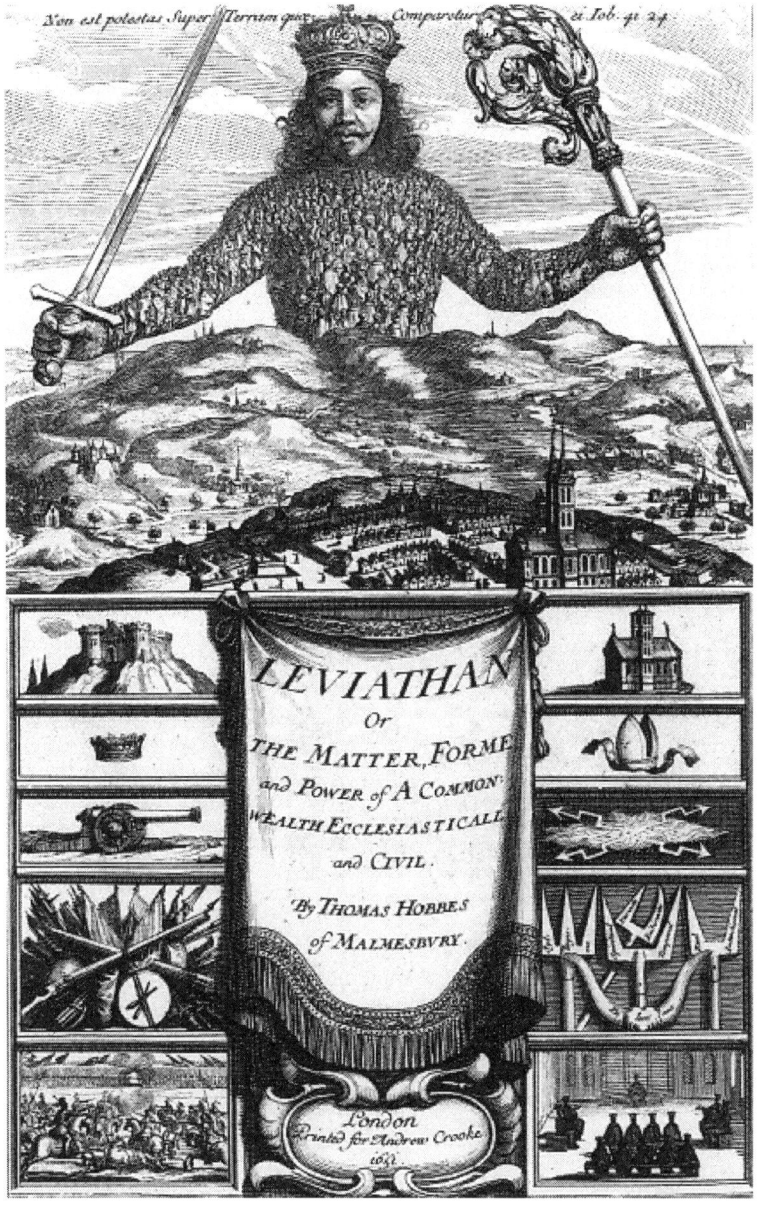

Title page. Source: Hobbes (1651). Leviathan. Or The Matter, Forme and Power of A Common-Wealth Ecclesiasticall and Civil. (Picture is in the Public Domain).

BIBLIOGRAPHY

Abrams, M.H., and G.G. Harpham, *A Glossary of Literary Terms* (Boston, 2005⁸).

Alföldi, A., 'Die Geburt der kaiserlichen Bildsymbolik. Kleine Beiträge zu ihrer Enstehungsgescihte. 3 *Parens patriae.*' In: *Museum Helveticum* 7 (1950), pp. 1-13; 9 (1952), pp. 204-243; 10 (1953), pp. 103-124; 11 (1954), pp. 133-169. (repr. *Idem, Der Vater des Vaterlandes im römischen Denken* (Darmstadt, 1978).

Ames, G.J., 'Colbert's Indian Ocean Strategy of 1664-74: a Reappraisal', *French Historical Studies* 16 (1990), pp. 536-559.

Andrup, O., 'Hoffet og dets Fester' in Clausen, J., and Krogh, ed.s, *Danmark I Fest og Glæde* I (Copenhagen, 1935).

Anthony, J. R., *French Baroque Music from Beaujoyeulx to Rameau* (London, 1974).

Arblaster, P., '"Dat de boecken vrij sullen wesen": Private Profit, Public Utility and Secrets of State in the Seventeenth-Century Habsburg Netherlands', in: Koopmans, J.W., ed., *News and Politics in Early Modern Europe (1500-1800)*, Groningen Studies in Cultural Change, XIII (Leuven, Paris, Dudley Ma., 2005), pp. 79-95.

Arellano, I., *Historia del teatro español del siglo XVII* (Madrid, 1995).

Armstrong, K., *The End of Silence: Women and the Priesthood* (London, 1993).

Austin, J. L., *How To Do Things with Words* (London, 1962).

Bal, M., *Death and Dissymmetry: The Politics of Coherence in the Book of Judges* (Chicago/London, 1988).

Banks, K., 'Interpretations of the Body Politic and of Natural Bodies in Late Sixteenth Century France', in: Musolff, A. and Zinken, J., eds., *Metaphor and Discourse* (Basingstoke, 2009), pp. 205-218.

Berglund, L.,*Studier i Christian Geists vokalmusik* (Uppsala, 2002).

———, 'The Aria, the Stylus Melismaticus and the Holy Communion. Devotional Music from Northern Courts in the Late Seventeenth Century', in: *The Cultural Heritage of Medieval Rituals: Genre and Ritual*, ed. Eyolf Østrem, Mette Birkedal Bruun, Nils Holger Petersen, och Jens Fleischer (Copenhagen, 2005).

———, 'The Roman Connection. Dissemination and Reception of Roman Music in the North', *The dissemination of music in 17th-century Europe. Celebrating the Düben Collection*, proceedings from the conference in Uppsala 7-9 September 2006, ed. Erik Kjellberg (forthcoming)

Bertelli, S., *The King's Body: Sacred Rituals of Power in Medieval and Early Modern Europe,* transl. Litchfield, R. B. (University Park, Pennsylvania, 2001).

Blair, A., *The Theater of Nature: Jean Bodin and Renaissance Science* (Princeton, NJ, 1997).

Bloemendal, J., 'Rond de Vader des Vaderlands. Oranje, Heinsius en Leiden.' In: Karl Enenkel, Sjaak Onderdelinden and Paul J. Smith (eds), *"Typisch*

Nederlands". De Nederlandse identiteit in de letterkunde (Voorthuizen, 1999), pp. 11-25.

Bloemendal, J., and P. Smith, 'Inleiding', in: *idem* (eds.), *De Muze en de Mythe. Over de literaire verwerking van het verleden* (Amersfoort, 2007), pp. 7-8.

Blume, F., *Geschichte der evangelischen Kirchenmusik* (Kassel et al, [2]1965).

————, *Protestant Church Music: A History* (London, 1975).

Boesen, G., *Danmarks Riges Regalier / The Danish Coronarion Regalia* (Copenhagen, 1986).

Bonelli de Rasori, G. M., *Copioso e compito racconto della cavalcata e cerimonie fatte nell'andare à prendere il possesso in S. Giovanni Laterano N. S. Innocentio X* (Roma, 1644).

Bouchard, L. *Tragic Method and Tragic Theology: Evil in Contemporary Drama and Religious Thought* (University Park, 1989).

Bouhours, D. (ed.), *Recueil de vers choisis, nouvelle edition* (Paris, 1701).

Boyer, C., *La Fête de Vénus* (Paris, 1669).

Bøgh Rasmussen, M., "Portrætter af Christian 4." in Heiberg, S., ed., *Christian 4. og Frederiksborg* (Copenhagen, 2006).

Brandt, R., 'Das Titelblatt des Leviathan', *Zeitschrift für Sozialwissenschaft* 15 (1987), pp. 164-186.

Braun, W., *Die Musik des 17. Jahrhundert* (=Neues Handbuch der Musikwissenschaft; 4), (Wiesbaden, 1981), pp. 44-48.

Brevis narratio Triumphi quo a Senatu populogue Traiectensi... Robertus DudlAEus Comes LeicESTRIVS... (Utrecht, 1586) (Knuttel no. 763).

Briels, J. G. C. A., *De Zuidnederlandse boekdrukkers en boekverkopers in de Republiek der Verenigde Nederlanden omstreeks 1570-1630. Een bijdrage tot de kennis van de geschiedenis van het boek* (Nieuwkoop, 1974).

Briels, J., 'De Zuidnederlandse immigratie 1572-1630', in: *Tijdschrift voor geschiedenis* 100 (1987), pp. 331-355.

Bvlle Oft Mandaet des Paus van Roomen/ aen de Gheestelicheydt al om bevolen/ om haer advijs te vernemen opt stuck vanden Vrede-handel met de Hollantsche Ketters. Met oock de beschryvinghe des Conciliums, by de Gheestelickheyt daer ouer ghehouden. Elcx Ordens bysonderen Raedt ende Antwoorde (s.l., s.d.) (Knuttel no. 1444).

Bunners, C., *Kirchenmusik und Sehlenmusik* (Göttingen, 1966).

Burke, P., *The Fabrication of Louis XIV* (New Haven/London, 1992).

Butler, J., *Gender Trouble: Feminism and the Subversion of Identity* (New York/-London, 1990).

Buyr-praetjen: Ofte Tsamensprekinge ende Discours, opden Brief vanden Agent Aerssens uyt Vranckrijck, aende Edele Moghende Heeren Staten Generael geschreven. Dienende tot ontdeckinge van der Spaengiaerden ende hare adherenten listicheyt/ trouweloosheyt/ ende wreede wraeckgiericheydt (s.l., s.d.) (Knuttel no. 1526).

Calderón de la Barca, Pedro, *El alcalde de Zalamea*, ed. A. Cortina (Madrid, 1971).

Cancellieri, F., *Storia de' solenni possessi de' sommi pontefici* (Roma, 1802).

Castro, A., *De la edad conflictiva* (Madrid, 1961).

Catechismvs. Dialogvs oft Tzamensprekinge ghemaect op den Vrede-handel. Ghestelt by Vraghe ende Antwoordt. Overghezet wt de Fransoysche in onse Neder-duytsche tale (s.l., 1608) (Knuttel no. 1415).

Catholic Encyclopedia, <http://www.newadvent.org/cathen/>.

Chappuzeau, S., *Le Théâtre français* (Lyon, 1674) (repr. Plan de la Tour (Var), 1985).

Chracas, L. A., *Roma trionfante Nel glorioso Possesso preso il giorno di Domenica 16. Novembre 1721. Dalla Santità di Nostro Signore Papa Innocenzo XIII. Romano della nobilissima fameglia Conti*. (Roma, 1721).

Christout, M.-F., *Le Ballet de cour de Louis XIV (1643-1672)* (Paris, 1967).

Clarke, J., 'The Expulsion of the Italians from the Hôtel de Bourgogne in 1697', *Seventeenth-Century French Studies* 14 (1992), pp. 97-117.

————, *The Guénégaud Theatre in Paris (1673-1680). Volume One: Founding, Design, Production* (Lewiston-Queenston-Lampeter, 1998).

————, *The Guénégaud Theatre in Paris (1673-1680. Volume Three: the Demise of the Machine Play* (Lewiston-Queenston-Lampeter, 2007).

Consideratien vande Vrede in Nederlandt gheconcipieert (s.l., 1608) (Knuttel no.1448a).

Cooper, D. E., *Metaphor* (Oxford, 1986).

Copye van een Discours tusschen een Hollander ende een Zeeuw (s.l., s.d.) (Knuttel no. 1454).

Corneille, P., *La Conquête de la Toison d'or*, ed. M.-F. Wagner (Paris, 1998).

Corneille, T., *Bellérophon* (Paris, 1679).

————, *Circé*, ed. Jan Clarke (Exeter, 1989).

————, *Psyché* (Paris, 1678).

Covarrubias, Sebastián de, *Tesoro de la lengua castellana o española*, ed. M. de Riquer (Barcelona, 1993).

Cox, R. L. *Between Earth and Heaven: Shakespeare, Dostoevsky, and the Meaning of Christian Tragedy* (New York, 1969).

Cunningham, A., 'William Harvey: The Discovery of the Circulation of Blood', in: Elmer, P. and Grell, P.E., eds., *Health, disease and society in Europe 1500-1800: A source book* (Manchester and New York, 2004), pp. 173-178.

Culley, T. D., *Jesuits and music: I. A Study of the Musicians connected with the German College in Rome during the 17th Century and of their Activities in Northern Europe* (Rome, 1970).

[David, J.], *Kettersche Spinnecoppe, VVaer inne (deur de natuere der Spinnecoppe) claerlick bevvesen vvort, hoe deghelick en orborlick een saecke een ketter is, en kettersche voere. Gemaeckt by M. Jason Petronius/ Doctoor in de vermaerde vrije consten van Leyden* (Brussels, 1595) (Wulp, Catalogus, no. 812).

De Artijckelen ende besluyten der Inquisitie van Spaegnien/ om die vande Nederlanden te overvallen ende verhinderen. Dat overheylige Officie der Inquisitie/ dat soo menichmael in syne Majesteyts Nederlanden verachtert is/ sal op dese seer expediente wijse inghestelt ende ghevordert worden (s.l., 1568) (Knuttel no. 156).

De Benserade, I., *Ballets pour Louis XIV*, ed. Marie-Claude Canova-Green, 2 vols (Paris, 1997).

————, *Les Oeuvres de Monsieur de Bensserade*, 2 vols (Paris, 1698).

————, *Les Oeuvres de Monsieur de Bensserade*, 2 vols ([Amsterdam?], Suivant la Copie à Paris, 1698).

Dees wonder-Maer end' Prophetsije wis/ Door's Geests gesicht/ gebooren is/ Eens Patriots, out end' bedaecht/ Diwyl (zo't schijnt) hy zeer vertsaecht/ Geworden was doort overdencken/ Des vredes die wel mochte krencken/ Dees landen zoo der spaenschen raet/ Na haren wil end' wensch voort gaet (s.l., s.d.) (Knuttel no. 1465).

Delmas, C., *Mythologie et mythe dans le théâtre français (1650-1676)* (Geneva, 1985).

Derrida, J., "Signature, Event, Context", *Margins of Philosophy* (*Marges de la philosophie*, 1972) (Chicago, 1982).

Den Nederlandschen Bye-korf: Waer in Ghy lieden beschreven vindt/ al tghene dat nu wtghegaen is/ op den Stilstant ofte Vrede/ zeer nootzakelijc om te lesen van alle Liefhebbers des Vaderlandts... (s.l., 1608) (Catalogue Knuttel no.1474).

De Schepper, M., 'Quem patriae patrem voluit (Deus). Georgius Benedicti Wertelo over Willem van Oranje.' In: *Hermeneus* 56 (1984), pp. 244-50.

Dhorn-van Rossum, G. and Böckenförde, E.-W., 'Organ, Organismus, Organisation, politischer Körper', in: Brunner, O., Conze, W. and Koselleck, R., eds., *Geschichtliche Grundbegriffe. Historisches Wörterbuch zur politisch-sozialen Sprache in Deutschland*, vol. 4, (Stuttgart, 1978), pp. 519-622.

Dictionnaire de l'Académie-Française (Paris, 1694).

Di Macco, M., *Il Colosseo. Funzione simbolica, storica, urbana* (Roma, 1971).

Discovrs by Forme van Remonstrantie: Vervatende De noodsaeckelickheyd vande Oos-Indische navigatie, by middel vande vvelcke, de vrye Neder-landsche Provintien, apparent zijn te gheraecken totte hooghste Prosperiteyt, int stuck vande alder-rijck ende costelijckste vvaren vande gheheele vverelt (s.l., 1608) (Knuttel no.1428).

Discovrs Van Pieter en Pauwels/ Op de Handelinghe vanden Vreede (s.l., 1608) (Knuttel no. 1456).

Downes, K., "Baroque", *Grove Art Online*, Oxford University Press, <http://www.-groveart.com>.

Dresden, S., 'Thomas Mann and Marcel Proust. On Myth and Antimyth.' In: Joseph P. Strelka (red.), *Literary Criticism and Myth* (Pennsylvania, 1980), pp. 25-50.

DROOM-GESICHT eenes metter Herten tot GODT op-getrockenen mensches: In hem veroorzaeckt (zoo't schijnt) door voor-gaende over-denckinge van GODES Goetheyt (bijzonder nu/ door d'aenmerckinghe der goeder hope tot den lang gewenschten Vrede vernieut zijnde) Ende der menchen Quaetheyt: Tot stichtinghe ende waerschouwinghe aller Menschen. BLY-EYND-SPELS-WYZE in Druck uyt-ghegeven (s.l., 1607) (Knuttel no. 1408).

Düben Collection Database Catalogue, The, ed. Erik Kjellberg and Kerala J. Snyder, <http://www.musik.uu.se/duben/Duben.php>

Dunn, K., *Pretexts of Authority: The Rhetoric of Authorship in the Renaissance Preface* (Stanford, Cal., 1994).

Duke, A., 'The Elusive Netherlands: The Question of National Identity in the Early Modern Low Countries on the Eve of the Revolt', *Bijdragen en Mededelingen betreffende de Geschiedenis der Nederlanden* 119 (2004), pp. 10-38.

Duym, J., *Het Moordadich Stvck van Balthasar Gerards, begaen aen den Doorluchtighen Prince van Oraignen, 1584 van Jonkheer Jaboc Duym (1606), vergeleken met Auriacus sive Libertas Saucia (1602) van Daniël Heinsius*. Ed. L.F.A. Serrarens en N.C.H. Wijngaards (Zutphen, [1977]). Klassiek Letterkundig Pantheon 218.

Eemeren, F. van and R. Grootendorst, *Speech Acts in Argumentative Discussions: A Theoretical Model for the Analysis of Discussions Directed Towards Solving Conflicts of Opinion* (Dordrecht, 1984).

Ekedahl, N., *Det svenska Israel* (Uppsala, 1999).

Elaut, L., 'Nicolaus Mulerius uit Brugge, de eerste medische hoogleraar te Groningen (1564-1630)', *Scientiarium historia. Driemaandelijks tijdschrift voor de geschiedenis van de geneeskunde, wiskunde en natuurwetenschappen* 1 (1959), pp. 3-13.

Eller, P., *Salvingerne på Frederiksborg*, (Copenhagen, 1976).

Enenkel, K. A. E., *Imagines agentes: geheugenboeken en de organisatie van kennis in de Neolatijnse literatuur* (Leiden, 2005).

Erlanger, P., *Monsieur, frère de Louis XIV* (Paris, 1981).

Fagiolo dell'Arco, M. *Corpus delle feste a Roma, 1: La festa barocca* (Roma, 1997).

Fauconnier, G. and Turner, M., *The Way We Think: Conceptual Blending and the Mind's Hidden Complexities* (New York, 2002).

Fernández-Canadas de Greenwood, P., *Pastoral Poetics: The Uses of Conventions in Renaissance Pastoral Romances* (Ph.D.thesis, Ann Arbor, Mich., 1981).

Fontana, C., *Il Tempio Vaticano e sua origine con gl'Edifitii più cospicui anitchi, e moderni fatti dentro, e fuori di Esso* (Roma, 1694).

Frandsen, M. E., *Crossing confessional boundaries. The patronage of Italian sacred music in seventeenth-century Dresden* (New York, 2006).

Foucault, Michel, *The Order of Things: An Archaeology of the Human Sciences* (New York, 1973)
———, *The History of Sexuality, Volume 1* (New York, 1980).

Fraser, A., *Love and Louis XIV: the Women in the Life of the Sun King* (London, 2006).

Geck, M., *Die Vokalmusik Dietrich Buxtehudes und der frühe Pietismus* (Kassel, 1965).

Gelderen, M. van, 'Aristotelians, Monarchomachs and Republicans: Sovereignty and *Respublica mixta* in Dutch and German Political Thought, 1580-1650', in: Gelderen, M. van & Skinner, Q., eds, *Republicanism: A Shared European Heritage, Vol. I: Republicanism and Constitutionalism in Early Modern Europe* (Cambridge, 2002), pp. 195-217.

Gerhardt, M. I., *Essai d'analyse littéraire de la pastorale dans les littératures italienne, espagnole et française* (Assen, 1950).

Ghelyck als die Joden brvyt worden door Coningin Hester/ Alsoo gonne ons Godt oock te gheschieden door Milorde-lester. So ick dese Tracteringhe verghelijcke als eenen landt-dach der Bloemmen/ Sal elcke Bloeme by eene particuliere Provincie verstaen zijn/ Ende hoe oock ghetrouwicheyt vraecht naer haer Suster gherechticheyt. De Godt gunne dat sy allthans ghevonden werde (Utrecht, 1586) (Petit catalogue no. 443).

Gilbert, G., *Les Peines et les plaisirs de l'amour* (Amsterdam, 1705).

Goatly, A., *Washing the Brain. Metaphor and Hidden Ideology* (Amsterdam and New York, 2007).

Goyet, F., *Le sublime du 'lieu commun': L'invention rhétorique dans l'Antiquité et à la Renaissance* (Paris, 1996).

Grævius, J.-G., *A Funeral Oration (. . .) upon the Death of Mary II* (London, 1695).

————, *In obitum Guilielmi III (. . .) oratio* (Utrecht, 1702).

————, *Oratio de auspicatissima Expeditione Britannica: cum Guilielmus, Arausionensis Princeps, Angliæ, Galliæ et Hiberniæ Rex inauguraretur* (London, 1689).

Groenhuis, G., *De Predikanten. De sociale positie van de gereformeerde predikanten in de Republiek der verenigde Nederlanden voor +/- 1700* (Groningen, 1977).

Groenveld, S., '"Natie" en "patria" bij zestiende-eeuwse Nederlanders', in: van Sas, N.C.F., ed., *Vaderland. Een geschiedenis vanaf de vijftiende eeuw tot 1940*, Reeks Nederlandse Begripsgeschiedenis I, (Amsterdam, 1999) pp. 55-81.

Guevara, A. de, *Menosprecio de corte y alabanza de aldea*, ed. A. Rallo Gruss (Madrid, 1984).

Guldin, R., *Körpermetaphern: Zum Verhältnis von Politik und Medizin* (Würzburg, 2000).

Haan, M., *Vaderlandsch trots'. De negentiende eeuw* (Warnsveld, 2005).

Hager, H., 'Carlo Fontana's project for a church in honour of the "Ecclesia Triumphans" in the Colosseum, Rome', *Journal of the Warburg and Courtauld Institutes*, Vol. 36, 1973, pp. 319-337.

Hale, D., *The Body Politic: A Political Metaphor in Renaissance English Literature* (The Hague, 1971).

Harline, C. E., *Pamphlets, Printing, and Political Culture in the Early Dutch Republic* (Dordrecht, 1987).

Harris, J. G., *Foreign Bodies and the Body Politic. Discourses of Social Pathology in Early Modern England* (Cambridge, 1998).

Hart, M. C. 't, *The Making of a Bourgeois State: War, Politics and Finance during the Dutch Revolt* (Manchester/New York, 1993).

Harwood, J. T., 'Introduction: Thomas Hobbes's *Briefe of the Art of Rhetorique*', in: Harwood, J. T., ed., *The Rhetorics of Thomas Hobbes and Bernard Lamy* (Carbondale and Edwardsville, 1986), pp. 1-32.

Heiberg, S., *Christian IV – en europæisk statsmand* (Copenhagen, 2006).

Heinsius, D., *Auriacus, sive Libertas saucia (1601)*. Ed. Jan Bloemendal (Voorthuizen, 1997).

Henkel, A. and A. Schöne, *Emblemata, Handbuch zur Sinnbildkunst des XVI.-XVII. Jahrhunderts* (Stuttgart-Weimar, 1996).

Hermenegildo, A., *Juegos dramáticos de la locura festiva: pastores, simples, bobos y graciosos del teatro clásico español* (Palma de Mallorca, 1995).

Het alghemeyn eynde ende voornemen des Spaengiaerts, twelc is d'oprechtinghe van een voorghenomene vijfde Monarchie (Delft, 1586) (Knuttel, no. 765).

Het Testament vande Oorloghe. Het Testament vande Oorloghe vvort hier vertelt, Deur Selden tijt, zonder strijdt, In Baladen ghestelt (s.l., 1607) (Knuttel no. 1409).

Hobbes, T., 'A Briefe of the Art of Rhetorique', in: Harwood, J. T., ed., *The Rhetorics of Thomas Hobbes and Bernard Lamy* (Carbondale and Edwardsville, 1986), pp. 33-128.

——, *Leviathan. Or The Matter, Forme and Power of A Common-Wealth Ecclesiasticall and Civil* (London, 1651).

——, *Leviathan*, ed. Richard Tuck, revised ed. (Cambridge, 1996).

Holm, B., *Solkonge og månekejser. Ikonografiske studier i Francois Fossards Cabinet* (Copenhagen, 1991).

——, "Tyrken og tæven" in *Kritik* 179 (Copenhagen, 2006).

Hooft, P.C.., *Theseus en Ariadne*. Ed. A.J.J. Wille (Zutphen, [1972]). Klassiek Letterkundig Pantheon, 191.

Hovt en beleght. Een oudt Schipper van Monickendam (s.l., 1608) (Knuttel no. 1472).

Huet, P.-D., letter to Gilles Ménage, dated 8 August 1689: BNF, Paris, MS n.a.f. 1341.

Hunt, B. J., *The Paradox of Christian Tragedy* (New York, 1985).

Il trionfal Possesso preso dalla Santità di N. S. Papa Innocenzo XII. Il dì 13 Aprile 1692 Nella Basilica di S. Gio: in Laterano (...) Colla relatione esatta della solenne Cavalcata (Roma, 1692).

Ingersoll, R. J., *The Ritual Use of Public Space in Renaissance Rome*, (unpublished diss. University of California, 1985).

Ingram, J. S. and Falconer, K., "Salve regina", *Grove Music Online* ed. L. Macy <http://www.grovemusic.com>.

Intermèdes pour une comédie (Paris, 1673).

Isherwood, R., *Music in the Service of the King: France in the Seventeenth Century* (Ithaca, 1973).

Israel, J. I., *The Dutch Republic: Its Rise, Greatness, and Fall, 1477-1806* (Oxford, 1995).

——, *Radical Enlightenment: Philosophy and the Making of Modernity, 1650-1750* (Oxford, 2001)

Jameson, J. F., *Willem Usselinx: Founder of the Dutch and Swedish West India Companies*, Papers of the American Historical Association, II, no.3 (New York, London, 1887).

Jardine, L., *The Awful End of Prince William the Silent. The first assassination of a head of state with a hand-gun* (London, 2005).

Jensen, L., *De verheerlijking van het verleden. Helden, literatuur en natievorming in de negentiende eeuw* (Nijmegen, 2008).

Johannesson, K., *I polstjärnans tecken* (Stockholm 1968).

Johannsen, H., "Den ydmyge konge" in Johannsen, H., ed., *Kirkens bygning og brug* (Copenhagen, 1983).

John of Salisbury, *Policraticus. Of the Frivolities of Courtiers and the Footprints of Philosophers,* ed. and transl. Nederman, C. J. (Cambridge, 1990).

Johnson, M., 'Introduction: Metaphor in the Philosophical Tradition', in: Johnson, M., ed., *Philosophical Perspectives on Metaphor* (Minnesota, 1981), pp. 3-47.

Johnston, D., *The Rhetoric of Leviathan* (Princeton, NJ, 1986).

Jones, A. J., *The Motets of Carissimi*, vol. 2 (Ann Arbor, Mich., 1982).

Kantorowicz, E. H. *The King's Two Bodies: A Study in Mediaeval Political Theology* (repr. Princeton, N.J., 1997).

Kjellberg, E., *Kungliga musiker i Sverige under stormaktstiden* (diss. Uppsala, 1979).

Knuttel, W. P. C., ed., *Catalogus van de pamfletten-verzameling, berustende in de Koninklijke Bibliotheek,* Vol. I (1486-1620) (The Hague, 1899).

Konst, J., 'De motivatie van het offer van Ifis: en reactie op de Jeptha-interpretatie van F.-W. Korsten', *Tijdschrift voor Nederlandse Taal- en Letterkunde* 116 (2000), pp. 153-167.

Korsten, F.-W., *The Wisdom Brokers: Narrative's Interaction with Arguments in Cultural Critical Texts* (Amsterdam, 1998)

——, 'Waartoe hij zijn dochter slachtte: *enargeia* in een modern retorische benadering van Vondels *Jeptha*', *Tijdschrift voor Nederlandse Taal- en Letterkunde* 115 (1999), pp. 315-333.

——, 'Een reactie op "De motivatie van het offer van Ifis" van Jan Konst', *Tijdschrift voor Nederlandse Taal- en Letterkunde* 116 (2000), pp. 168-171.

——, 'Sovereignty and Inviolability: God as a Commonplace in the Work of Joost van den Vondel', in this book.

Koschorke, A., Lüdemann, S. Frank, T. and Matala de Mazza. E., *Der fiktive Staat. Konstruktionen des politischen Körpers in der Geschichte Europas* (Frankfurt am Main, 2007).

Kossmann, E. H., *Political Thought in the Dutch Republic: Three Studies* (Amsterdam, 2000)

Küng, H., *Die Frau im Christentum* (Munich, 2001).

La Bruyère, J. de, *Les Caractères*, in: *Œuvres complètes*, ed. J. Benda (Paris, 1951).

——, *The Characters, or the Manners of the Age. By Monsieur De La Bruyere, of the French Academy. Made English by several hands* (London, 1699).

La Gorce, J. de, *Carlo Vigarani* (Paris, 2005).

——, *L'Opéra à Paris au temps de Louis XIV: histoire d'un théâtre* (Paris, 1992).

Lakoff, G. and Johnson, M., *Metaphors we live by* (Chicago, 1980).

Leezenberg, M., *Contexts of Metaphor* (Amsterdam, 2001).

Le Moyne, P., *De l'art de regner* (Paris, 1665).

——, *Le Ministre sans reproche* (Paris, 1645).

——, *Les Œuvres poetiques du P. Le Moyne* (Paris, 1671).

——, *Les Triomphes de Louys le Juste en la reduction des Rochelois et des autres rebelles de son royaume* (Reims, 1629).

León, Fray Luis de, *De los nombres de Cristo*, ed. C. Cuevas (Madrid, 1977).

Levy, E., *Propaganda and the Jesuit Baroque* (Berkeley/Los Angeles/London, 2004).

Ligtenberg, C., *Willem Usselinx* (Utrecht, 1914).

López Estrada, F., 'La comedia pastoril en España', in: M. Chiabò and F. Doglio, eds., *Origini del dramma pastorale in Europa* (Viterbo, 1985), pp. 235-256.

Lough, J., *Paris Theatre Audiences in the Seventeenth and Eighteenth Centuries* (London, 1957).

Luther, Martin, English version of treaty on Turks Skovgaard-Petersen, K., "Danske konger og romersk herskersymbolik" in Due, O.S. and Isager, J., eds., *Imperium Romanum* II (Aarhus, 1993).

Lynn, J. A., *The Wars of Louis XIV 1667-1714* (Harlow, 1999).

Maber, R., 'Colbert and the scholars: Ménage, Huet, and the royal pensions of 1663', *Seventeenth-Century French Studies* 7 (1985), pp. 106-114.

Malcolm, N., 'The Title Page of *Leviathan*, Seen in a Curious Perspective', in: Malcolm, N., *Aspects of Hobbes* (Oxford, 2002), pp. 200-233.

Maravall, J. A., *Teatro y literatura en la sociedad barroca* (Madrid, 1972).

————, *La cultura del barroco* (Madrid, ^{2}1980).

Martin, H., *Histoire de France depuis les temps les plus reculés jusqu'en 1789*, 17 vols (Paris, 1855-60).

Martinich, A. P., *Thomas Hobbes* (Basingstoke, 1997).

McKinney, R. H., 'Coping with Postmodernism: Christian Comedy and Tragedy', *Philosophy Today* 41 (1997), pp. 520-529.

Ménage, G., *Juris Civilis amœnitates* (Paris, 1664).

————, *Laertii Diogenis de vitis, dogmatis et apophthegmatis eorum qui in philosophia claverunt libri X* (London, 1664).

————, letter to Pierre-Daniel Huet, dated 3 August 1689: Biblioteca Medicea Laurenziana, Florence, MS Ashburnham 1866. 1277.

————, *Lettres inédites à Pierre-Daniel Huet (1659-1692), publiées d'après le dossier Ashburnham 1866 de la Bibliothèque Laurentienne de Florence*, ed. L. Caminiti Pennarola (Naples, 1993).

————, *Ménagiana*, 4 vols (Paris, 1729).

Moine, M.-C., *Les Fêtes à la Cour du Roi Soleil* (Paris, 1984).

Moss, A., *Printed Commonplace Books and the Structuring of Renaissance Thought* (Oxford, 1996)

————, 'The *Politica* of Justus Lipsius and the Commonplace-Book', *Journal of the History of Ideas* 59 (s.l., 1998), pp. 421-436.

————, *Renaissance Truth and the Latin Language Turn* (Oxford, 2003).

————, Power and Persuasion: Commonplace Culture in Early Modern Europe', in: *Commonplace Culture in Western Europe in the Early Modern Period*, vol. I: *Reformation, Counter-reformation and Revolt*, eds David Cowling and Mette B. Bruun (Leuven, 2010), pp. 1-17.

Mulerius, N., *Waerachtich ende ghenoechlijck discours/ van D.D.Nicolaum Mulerium, van Brugge/ Doctor inde Medicynen/ van wegen der stadt Groeningen ende de omme-landen: Hoe dat wy door Godes ghenade/ aen de Nederlandtsche Vrede-handel zijn ghecomen Waerachtich ende ghenoechlijck discours* (s.l., 1608) (Knuttel, no.1411a).

Musolff, A. '*Ignes fatui* or *apt similitude?* — the apparent denunciation of metaphor by Thomas Hobbes', *Hobbes Studies* 18 (2005), pp. 96-113.

————, 'Which role do metaphors play in racial prejudice? - The function of anti-Semitic imagery in Hitler's "Mein Kampf"', *Patterns of Prejudice* 41/1 (2007), pp. 21-44.

————, 'Power and Persuasion. Commonplace Culture in Early Modern Europe.', http://ritualcenter.net/commonplaces/wp-content/uploads/2006/12/moss.doc (05-09-2007).

Nederman, C. and Forhan, K. L., eds., *Readings in Medieval Political Theory 1100-1400* (Indianapolis, 1993).

Néraudau, J.-P., *L'Olympe du Roi-Soleil, ou comment la mythologie et l'Antiquité furent mises au service de l'idéologie monarchique sous Louis XIV à travers la littérature, la peinture, la musique, les fêtes, la sculpture, l'architecture et les jardins, à Vaux-le-Vicomte, Meudon, St Cloud, Sceaux, Marly, St Germain et Versailles* (Paris, 1986).

Olden-Jørgensen, S., "Statsceremoniel, hofkultur og politisk magt i overgangen fra adelsvaelde til enevaelde – 1536 til 1746", *Fortid og nutid* (1996), pp. 3-20.

Ovid, *Metamorphoses*, ed. F. J. Miller, 2 vols (repr. London/Cambridge, Mass., 1968-1971).

Relazione del Viaggio fatto dall S. di N.S. P. Leone XI. nel pigliare il Possesso a S. Gio. Laterano con la descrittione degli Apparati, Archi, Trionfi, et Inscrittioni, ed. Guglielmo Facciotto (Roma, 1605).

Rudén, J.-O., "Vattenmärkning och musikforskning" (diss. Uppsala, 1968); accessible at <http://www.ordommusik.se/duben/index.htm>.

Petit, L. D., ed., *Bibliotheek van nederlandsche pamfletten. Verzamelingen van de bibliotheek van Joannes Thysius en de Bibliotheek der Rijks-universiteit te Leiden*, Vol. 1 (1500-1648) (The Hague, 1882).

Plett, H. F., 'Rhetorik der Renaissance-Renaissance der Retorik', in: Plett, H. F., ed., *Renaissance Rhetoric* (Berlin/New York, 1993a), pp. 1-20.

―――, '*Theatrum Rhetoricum*: Schauspiel-Dichtung-Politik.' in: Plett, H. F., ed., *Renaissance Rhetoric* (Berlin/New York, 1993b), pp. 328-368.

Pollmann, J., *Een andere weg naar God: De reformatie van Arnoldus Buchelius (1565-1641)* (Amsterdam, 2000).

Pollmann, J. and A. Spicer, eds, *Public Opinion and Changing Identities in the Early Modern Netherlands. Essays in Honour of Alastair Duke*, Studies in Medieval and Reformation Traditions 121 (Leiden, 2007).

Pranger, B., *De kunstmatigheid van het Christendom. Enkele opmerkingen over contemptus mundi* (Amsterdam, 1995). Inaugural oration.

―――, *The Artificiality of Christianity. Essays on the Poetics of Monasticism* (Stanford, Cal., 2003).

Price, J. L., *Holland and the Dutch Republic in the Seventeenth Century: The Politics of Particularism* (Oxford, 1994).

―――, *The Dutch Republic in the Seventeenth Century* (London, 1998).

Proeve Des nu onlangs uyt-ghegheven Drooms/ off t'samen spraack tusschen den Coning van Hispanien ende den Paus van Roomen (s.l., [1608]) (Knuttel no.1401).

Pufendorf, S. v., *Die Verfassung des deutschen Reiches.* (Latin and German), ed.. Horst Denzer (Frankfurt am Main, 1994).

Quinault, P., *Alceste* (Paris, 1674), in: *Livrets d'opéra*, ed. Buford Norman, 2 vols (Toulouse, 1999), vol. I, pp. 53-106.

―――, *Atys* (Paris, 1676), in: *Livrets d'opéra*, ed. Buford Norman, 2 vols (Toulouse, 1999), vol. I, pp. 171-227.

―――, *Cadmus et Hermione* (Paris, 1673), in: *Livrets d'opéra*, ed. B. Norman, 2 vols (Toulouse, 1999), vol. I, pp. 1-51.

————, *Isis* (Paris, 1677), in *Livrets d'opéra*, ed. by Buford Norman, 2 vols (Toulouse, 1999), I, 229-280.

————, *Proserpine* (Paris, 1680), in: *Livrets d'opéra*, ed. Buford Norman, 2 vols (Toulouse, 1999), vol. II, pp. 1-54.

————, *Thésée* (Paris, 1675), in: *Livrets d'opéra*, ed. Buford Norman, 2 vols (Toulouse, 1999), vol. I, pp. 107-169.

Raetsel. Discours of t'samensprekinghe tusschen den Coning van Spaengien ende Jan Neyen/ vanden Vrede-handel der Vereenichde Nederlanden (s.l., s.d.) (Knuttel no. 1418).

Rancière, J., *The Politics Of Aesthetics: The Distribution of the Sensible* (London/New York, 2004).

————, *Politique de la littérature* (Paris, 2007).

Rash, F., *The Language of Violence: Adolf Hitler's Mein Kampf.* (New York, 2006).

Recueil de plusieurs pieces d'eloquence et de poësie, presentées à l'Academie Françoise pour les prix de l'année 1673 (Paris, 1694).

Resoluties Staten van Holland (s.l., s.d.; copy University Library Leiden).

Resolutiën der Staten-Generaal van 1576 tot 1609, XIV (1607-1609), Rijks Geschiedkundige Publicatiën 131 (The Hague, 1970).

Rodríguez Puértolas, J., 'El campesino en la comedia del Siglo de Oro', in: *De la Edad Media a la edad conflictiva* (Madrid 1972), pp. 325-338.

Rojas Zorrilla, Francisco de, *Del rey abajo, ninguno,* , ed. B. Wittmann (Madrid, 1996).

Rozas, J. M., *Significado y doctrina del 'Arte Nuevo' de Lope de Vega* (Madrid, 1976).

Rummel, E., ed., *Biblical Humanism and Scholasticism in the Age of Erasmus* (Leiden, 2008).

Salomon, N., *La vida rural castellana en tiempos de Felipe II* (Barcelona, 1982).

————, *Lo villano en el teatro del Siglo de Oro* (Madrid, 1985).

Schmitz-Berning, C., *Vokabular des Nationalsozialismus* (Berlin and New York, 2000).

Schuyt-praetgens, Op de Vaert naer Amsterdam/ tusschen een Lantman, een Hovelinck, een Borger, ende Schipper (s.l., 1608) (Knuttel no. 1450).

Sendbrief. In forme van Supplicatie aen die Coninclicke Maiesteyt van Spaengien: Van wegen des Princen van Orangien/ der Staten van Hollandt ende Zeelandt. Mitsgaders alle andere syne ghetrouwe Ondersaten van dese Nederlanden/ die haer van des Hertoghen van Alva ende der Spaengiaerden tyrannie ende ghewelt teghen alle recht verdrucket ende vervolghet vinden (Dordrecht, 1572) (Knuttel no.213).

Shakespeare, W., *The Complete Works*, eds Wells, S., Taylor, G., Jowett, J., and Montgomery, W. (Oxford, 1986).

Shimp, S.. Parker, *The Art of Persuasion: Domenico Mazzocchi and the Counter-reformation* (diss. Yale Univ., Ann Arbor, 2000).

Skinner, Q., *The Foundations of Modern Political Thought*, 2 vols (Cambridge, 1978).

————, *Reason and Rhetoric in the Philosophy of Hobbes* (Cambridge, 1996).

————, *Visions of Politics*, 3 vols, vol. 3: *Hobbes and Civil Science* (Cambridge, 2002).

Smit, W. A. P., *Van Pascha tot Noah: Een verkenning van Vondels drama's naar continuiteit en ontwikkeling in hun grondmotief en structuur* (Zwolle, 1962).

Snickare, M., "Trapphuset och Övre galleriet – gestaltning och funktion", *Drottningholms slott, Från Hedvig Eleonora till Lovisa Ulrika*, vol 1, ed. Göran Alm and Rebecka Millhagen (Stockholm, 2004), pp. 174-199.

Sontag, S., *Illness as Metaphor* (New York, 1978).

Starkey, T., *A Dialogue between Pole and Lupset*, ed. Mayer, T.F. (repr. London, 1989).

Steele, M., *Christianity, Tragedy, and Holocaust Literature* (Westport, 1995).

Steiner, G., *The Death of Tragedy* (London, 1961).

Strauss, L., *The Political Philosophy of Hobbes: its Basis and its Genesis*, transl. Sinclair, E.M. (repr. Chicago, Ill., 1952).

Stucken gementioneerd in den Byenkorf die byde ... Staten Generael ... toeghestaen ende niet verboden worden ... (The Hague, 1608) (Knuttel no. 1477).

Tayler, W. E., 'Milton's *Samson*: The Form of Christian Tragedy', *English Literary Renaissance* 3 (1973), pp. 306-321.

Tillyard, E. M. W., *The Elizabethan World Picture* (repr. Harmondsworth, 1982).

Tirso de Molina, *La república al revés*, in: *Obras dramáticas completas*, I, ed. B. de los Ríos, (Madrid, 1946), pp. 375-428.

————, *La prudencia en la mujer*, in: *Obras dramáticas completas*, III, ed. B. de los Ríos (Madrid, 1958), pp. 893-951.

Toetststeen, Waer aen men waerlick beproeuen mach, hoe valsch ende ongefondeert, dat zijn de leugenachtighe calumnieuse Libellen, Pasquillen ende faemroouische schriften, die door eenige Spaensche oft jesuits gesinde in Brabant, Vlaenderen oft elders versiert, ende alhier in onse Landen gestroyt/ ende in Druck ouer ghesonden werden. Midtsgaders oock onlancx door haren schijnighen Domphoren, haer vergift ende bitterhyt teghen ons wtspouwen ende openbaren, Ende dese dienende, als voor generale verantwoordingh tegen der seluer ghestelt. (s.l., 1603) (Knuttel no. 1230).

Tozzi, S., *Incisioni barocche di feste e avvenimenti* (Museo di Roma, 2002).

Turner, V., *The Ritual Process. Structure and Anti-Structure* (London, 1969).

[Usselincx, W.,], *Memorie vande gewichtige redenen die de Heeren Staten generael behooren te beweghen om gheensins te wijcken vande handelinghe ende vaert van Indien* (s.l., s.d.) (Knuttel no.1431).

————, *Naerder Bedenckingen, Over de zee-vaerdt/ Coophandel ende neeringhe/ als mede de versekeringhe vanden Staet deser vereenichde Landen/ inde teghenwoordighe Vrede-handelinghe met den Coninck van Spangnien ende de Aerts-hertoghen. Door een lief-hebber eenes oprechten, ende bestandighen vredes voorghestelt* (s.l., 1608) (Knuttel no. 1441).

————, *Vertoogh, hoe nootwendich, nut ende profijtelick het sy voor de vereenighde Nederlanden te behouden de Vryheyt van te handelen op West-Indien, Inden vrede metten Coninck van Spaignen* (s.l., 1608) (Knuttel no. 1442).

Van Beysterveldt, A.A., *Répercussions du souci de la pureté de sang sur la conception de l'honneur dans la 'comedia nueva' espagnole* (Leiden, 1966).

Vanden Spinnenkop ende t'Bieken (s.l., s.d.) (Knuttel no. 1463a).

Van den Vondel, J., *De werken van Vondel: Volledige en geïllustreerde tekstuitgave in tien delen*, eds Sterck, J.F.M., Moller, H.W.E., de Vooys, C.G.N., Klerk, C.R. de (Amsterdam, 1927).

Van Dorsten, J.A., *Poets, Patrons and Professors. An Outline of some Literary Connexions between England and the University of Leiden 1575-1586* (Leiden, 1962).

Van der Wulp, J. K., ed., *Catalogus van de tractaten, pamfletten, enz. over de geschiedenis Nederland, aanwezig in de bibliotheek van Isaac Meulman*, vol. I (1500-1648) (Amsterdam 1866-1868).

Van Eysenga, W. J. M., *De wording van het Twaalfjarig Bestand van 9 april 1609*

Van Gennep, A., *Les rites de passage: étude systématique des rites* (Paris, 1909).

Van Heel, O. F. M., *De Goudse drukkers en hun uitgaven* IV (Gouda, 1952). (Amsterdam, 1959).

Van Zuilen, V. 'The Politics of Dividing the Nation? News Pamphlets as Vehicle of Ideology and National Consciousness in the Habsburg Netherlands (1585-1609)', in: J.W. Koopmans, ed., *News and Politics in Early Modern Europe (1500-1800)*, Groningen Studies in Cultural Change, vol. XIII (Leuven, Paris, Dudley Ma., 2005), pp. 61-79.

Vega y Carpio, Lope de, *Fuenteovejuna*, ed. F. López Estrada (Madrid, [2]1973).

―――, *Peribañez y el comendador de Ocaña*, ed. A. Zamora Vicente (Madrid, 1969).

―――, *El mejor alcalde, el rey*, ed. J. M. Díez Borque (Madrid, 1974).

―――, *El villano en su rincón*, ed. J.M. Marín (Madrid, 1987).

Vélez de Guevara, Luis, *La serrana de la Vera*, ed. E. Rodríguez Cepeda (Madrid, 1967).

Vera, e compita relatione della solenne cavalcata, e cerimonie fatte il di VIII Giugno MDCLXX dal Palazzo Vaticano alla Basilica di S. Gio Laterano per il possesso preso da N. S. Papa Clemente X (Roma, 1670).

Verhael Vande Occasie ende Oorsaeck waer door de Nederlanden gecomen zijn aenden Vreede handel (s.l., s.d.) (Knuttel no.1457).

Walthaus, R., 'The Sun and Aurora: Philip IV of Spain and his Queen-consort in royal festival and spectacle', in: M. Gosman, A. MacDonald and A.Vanderjagt, eds., *Princes and Princely Culture 1450-1650*, II (Leiden/Boston, 2005), pp. 277-308.

Webber, G., *A Study of Italian Influence on North German Church and Organ Music in the Second Half of the Seventeenth Century, with Special Reference to the Collection of Gustav Düben* (diss. Oxford, 1988).

Weekhout, I., *Boekencensuur in de Noordelijke Nederlanden. De vrijheid van drukpers in de zeventiende eeuw* (The Hague, 1998).

Whenham, J., "Silvestris, Florido de", *Grove Music Online* ed. L. Macy (Accessed February 2008), <http://www.grovemusic.com>.

Wijdeveld, J., 'Princeps Auriacus. De Prins van Oranje in het neolatijnse epos en drama.' In *Hermeneus* 56 (1984), pp. 234-42.

Yu, A. C., 'Review of Roger L. Cox 1969', *Modern Philology* 69 (1972), pp. 275-277.

Zavadil, J., 'Bodies Politic and Bodies Cosmic: the Roman Stoic Theory of the "Two Cites"', in: Musolff, A. and Zinken, J. (eds.): *Metaphor and Discourse* (Basingstoke, 2009), pp. 219-232.

Zverius, M., *Claeg-dicht Over de doot vanden ... Heere Philips Marnix van St. Aldegonde. By maniere van tsamensprekinghe* (Leiden, 1600) (Knuttel no.1156).

—

VISUAL SOURCES

Performing Papal Authority. Procession as a Commonplace in Seventeenth Century Rome, pp. 143-158.

Falda, Giovanni Battista, 'Nuovo disegno dell'ordine tenuto nella solenne cavalcata dal Pallazzo Vaticano alla Basilica Lateranense per il Possesso preso da Nostro Signore Papa Clemente Decimo il di VIII giugno MDCLXX', etching 340 x 483 mm, ed. Giovanni Giacomo de Rossi, Museo di Roma (inv. GS 128).

Falda, Giovanni Battista, 'Nuovo disegno dell'ordine tenuto nella solenne cavalcata dal Palazzo Vaticano alla Basilica Lateranense per il Possesso preso da N. S. Papa Innocentio XI. il di VIII novembre MDCLXXVI', etching 323 x 466 mm, ed. Giovanni Giacomo de Rossi, Museo di Roma (inv. GS 136).

'La solennissima Cavalcata fatta in Roma per l'andata di n. Sig.re Papa Alessandro VII', etching 242 x365 mm, ed. Giovanni Battista de Rossi, Museo di Roma (inv. GS 99).

'La solenniss.ma cavalcata fatta in Roma per landata di n.s. Papa Leone XI al Possesso d. S. Gio. Laterano', etching 243 x 378 mm, ed. Giovanni Antonio de Paoli, Museo di Roma (inv. GS 48).

Rouhier, Louis 'La Cavalcata con le sue Cermionie del Pontefice nuovo quando piglia il Possesso a Santo Giovanni Laterano', etching 363 x 495 mm, ed. Giovanni Giacomo de Rossi, Museo di Roma (inv. GS 100).

INDEX